HPB87RKS   In print   14 95
                                10 95

D0793878

The Baroque Arsenal

Also by Mary Kaldor

*The Arms Trade with the
Third World*
The Disintegrating West

THE
BAROQUE
ARSENAL

———

Mary Kaldor

ANDRE DEUTSCH

First published 1982 by
André Deutsch Limited
105 Great Russell Street London WC1

Printed and bound in Great Britain by
Blackwell Press Limited
London Worcester and Guildford

ISBN 0 233 97388 5

To my parents

Acknowledgments

Many people helped me while writing this book by discussing the subject or guiding me to new sources of information and I am grateful to all of them. I would like to offer especial thanks to Robert Neild, who suggested the term "baroque," and to the shop stewards at Vickers Elswick, particularly their convenor Jim Murray, who spent many hours explaining to me how arms are produced and whose experiences inspired many of the ideas in this book. I would also like to thank those people who read and commented extensively on the manuscript—Ulrich Albrecht, Piers Burnett, David Holloway, Robert Neild, Julian Perry Robinson, Judith Reppy, Emma Rothschild and Arthur Wang, as well as Keith Pavitt, Ed Sciberras, Anthony Sheil, and Dan Smith who also gave me helpful comments and advice.

I am very grateful also to the Joseph Rowntree Charitable Trust for providing financial support; to the UN Group of Governmental Experts on the Relationship between Disarmament and Development for allowing me to include large parts of my report *Military Technology and Industrial Development*, which I submitted to them in April 1980; to the Armament and Disarmament Information Unit at the University of Sussex, especially its Information Officer, Harry Dean, for invaluable assistance in gathering data; to Viv Johnson who helped me track down many obscure literature references; to Maureen Kelly, who typed and retyped the manuscript; and to Gillian Joyce, who typed the bibliography. Finally I would like to thank Julian Perry Robinson for moral support.

Contents

The Baroque Arsenal

Introduction

The 1980s have begun with a renewed demand for armaments. Western leaders seem to believe that increased military spending can restrain Soviet adventurism and remedy American impotence in the face of economic insecurity, Third World defiance, and crumbling alliances. The purchase of bigger and better weapons is seen as a kind of instant antidote to the troubles of the present epoch.

My purpose is to show that this line of thought is not only misguided, it is self-defeating. Modern military technology is not advanced; it is decadent. Over the years, more and more resources have been spent on perfecting the military technology of a previous era. As a consequence, modern armaments have become increasingly remote from military and economic reality. They are immensely sophisticated and elaborate; they are feats of tremendous ingenuity, talent, and organisation; and they can inflict unimaginable destruction. But they are incapable of achieving limited military objectives, and they have successively eroded the economy of the United States and the economies of those countries that have followed in her wake. Further spending can only make things worse.

Underlying my argument throughout is a conception of long waves in capitalist history. Thinkers like Joseph Schumpeter and Nikolai Kondratieff[1] have pointed out that capitalism has developed in waves, each wave associated with a different technology and a different location (although their concept of waves was more precise than historical evidence warrants). The era of engineering and shipbuilding was associated with Britain, the era of automobiles and aircraft with the United States, and the most recent era of electronics is associated with Japan. Military technology is rarely in phase with civilian developments. In some periods, armaments are very advanced, stimulating new civilian technology, even affecting the transition from one era to another. And in other periods, armaments are decadent, dragging the economy backwards towards some earlier golden age. Just as the warship contributed to Britain's economic decline after 1870, so, I shall argue, the tank and the aircraft played a similar role in the United States after World War II.

"Baroque" armaments* are the offspring of a marriage between private enterprise and the state, between the capitalist dynamic of the arms manufacturers and the conservatism that tends to characterise armed forces and defence departments in peacetime. On the one hand, soldiers and weapons designers have clung to particular notions about how wars should be fought and the kinds of weapons with which they should be fought. These notions are largely drawn from the experience of World War II; they justify certain military roles, the existence of military units to carry them out, and the maintenance of certain types of industrial capacity. On the other hand, competition to win contracts and stay in business allied to rivalry between the armed services and the various branches of government, has led to an ever-increasing technological effort. The consequence is what is sometimes called "trend innovation"—perpetual improvements to weapons that fall within the established traditions of the armed services and the armourers.

---

* The term "baroque" in relation to armament was first used by Herbert York, one of the nuclear physicists who developed the atom bomb, former Director of the Livermore Radiation Laboratories and top United States government official, when he wrote of "baroque, even rococo varieties of A bombs and H bombs."[2]

As it becomes more and more difficult to achieve "improvements," the hardware becomes more complex and sophisticated. This results in dramatic increases in the cost of individual weapons. But it does not increase military effectiveness. On the contrary, as I shall try to show, "improvements" become less and less relevant to modern warfare, while cost and complexity become military handicaps: sophisticated weapons are difficult to handle; they go wrong; they need thousands of spare parts; they absorb funds that could otherwise be used for training, practise, pay, ammunition, etc.; and they are prime targets.

Baroque military technology is not unique to America. Military fashions are set by the politically prominent. The Western way of arming has spread, as I shall show, to the Soviet Union, through competitive reaction, and to the Third World, through the direct import of hardware, training, advice, etc.

The industrial base of the modern armament sector was created in World War II. It consisted of the dominant companies of the period, mainly the manufacturers of automobiles and aircraft. By maintaining and even expanding this base, military spending has helped to preserve the industrial structure of the 1940s. In the first two postwar decades, this may have helped to mobilize resources for investment and innovation and to avoid the crises to which rapidly changing capitalist economies are prone. But this is no longer true, as I shall argue. Baroque military technology artificially expands industries that would otherwise have contracted. It absorbs resources that might otherwise have been used for investment and innovation in newer, more dynamic industries. And it distorts concepts of what constitutes technical advance, emphasising elaborate custom-built product improvements that are typical of industries on the decline instead of the simpler mass-market process improvements which tend to characterise industries in their prime. It has thus contributed to the slowdown of capital investment and productivity growth and to the gradual degeneration of the American economy.

In the Soviet Union, as I shall argue, the military competition
with the United States has provided a mechanism for introducing
technological change into the economy. In the 1940s and 1950s,
this may well have helped to raise the general technological level
of the Soviet Union. But as weapons have become baroque, this
form of technological change may have distorted the whole direction of Soviet development. Something similar may well have occurred in the Third World, where the import of arms and even
arms-manufacturing facilities seems to have been associated with
the spread of industries that are already on the decline in advanced industrial countries.

The consequences of baroque military technology are not merely
economic. The American and Soviet victory in 1945 provided the
basis for their postwar leadership. Weapons were the visible symbols of their power. As weapons and military alliances spread,
more and more countries were drawn into the technical legacy of
World War II and came to share a common set of criteria for
assessing military power. As the memory of World War II fades,
however, and as modern wars, in Southeast Asia or the Middle
East, challenge the utility of baroque armament, these criteria
are called into question and the political position of the superpowers is correspondingly undermined.

The characteristics of baroque military technology and its institutional environment are described in Chapter 1. The second
chapter looks at an earlier form of baroque technology—the late
nineteenth-century battleship—and at the lessons to be learned
from the British experience. Chapter 3 is about the development
of the modern military industrial complex in the United States
and its role in the American economy. The nature of armaments
and their role in the Soviet economy is contrasted and compared
in the fourth chapter. Chapter 5 describes the spread of armaments
to the Third World and its consequences for the so-called development process. The penultimate chapter is about the growing crisis
of baroque armaments—their increasing cost, their declining ef-

fectiveness, and what this means for soldiers and defence workers. And in the conclusion, I attempt to outline the implications of this crisis for wider world economic and military problems and to consider briefly the alternatives to baroque military technology.

Many people who read this book will miss a discussion of national security, of strategy and tactics. These important issues are not ignored; indeed, they arise from the discussion in this book. *The Baroque Arsenal* looks at the arms race from a new perspective. It is fundamentally about the way we arm, rather than why we arm. These two questions are not, of course, separable; indeed, as I shall argue, they are deeply interconnected. The way we arm has come to overshadow our whole thinking about power and international relationships so that many people have really forgotten why we arm.

There is a controversy, among students of arms control, about whether decisions on armaments are determined by international tension or by domestic influences. I believe that domestic influences tend to prevail in peacetime. This is because there are so many different ways of assessing and responding to the circumstances in which armaments might be used. Only battle, which Clausewitz compared to the act of exchange in the marketplace, can provide a decisive answer to the question: "How much is enough?"[3] In the absence of trial by battle, the quantity and nature of the armaments we acquire is determined as much by the environment in which we take decisions as it is by the posture of a potential adversary. This book starts with the domestic environment of decision-making and then goes on to discuss the way in which our decisions rebound on the international context of armaments—in the Third World no less than in the Soviet Union.

The ideas in this book are based on several years of research on arms production and trade. During the course of this research, I have interviewed government officials, defence industry executives and workers, and military personnel in both Europe and the United States, and I have discussed the subject with academics

and others who study the armament process. I have made use of a
wide range of published and unpublished primary sources, including official documents, commercial publications such as company
reports and business newsletters, various military reference books
and journals, newspapers and magazines, as well as secondary
sources. The data is of course very uneven. For example, there is
a mass of material available on methods of weapons acquisition in
the United States, if one is prepared to master the terminology,
which is itself baroque—for example, PERT (Program Evaluation
and Review Technique), DSARC (Defense System Acquisition
Review Council), or MENS (Mission Element Need Statement)—and which makes reports, etc., virtually incomprehensible
to the uninitiated. Yet information about the decision-making
process in the Soviet Union and in most Third World countries
is extremely hard to obtain. And there are other subjects, such as
the overlap between military and civil technology, which have
never been properly researched, although information is potentially available. For these reasons and because of the scope of the
book, many of the propositions are necessarily speculative. They
are offered as a contribution to the current debate.

It is a debate of some urgency. The 1980s may turn out to be
one of those rare moments in history when real change is possible.
Modern military technology is currently in crisis. This is manifested in the "unreadiness" of the armed forces, the financial
problems of the armourers, and, above all, the growing disaffection
of soldiers and defence workers in many countries.

And this crisis is of course part of a wider breakdown in the
international system, to which armaments have contributed—the
instability of the world economy; new rivalries within the West;
dissidence and repression in the Soviet Union; mass starvation,
revolution, and militarism in the Third World. There is a very
real danger of war. But there is also a possibility that the disintegration of the military-industrial consensus, the new fluidity of
international politics, and the tide of protest in favour of more

humane values could lead to a change in direction: to a rejection of baroque arms and the calculus of terror that goes with it and to the recognition that peace between nations, like peace within nations, and human development in the fullest sense can ultimately be achieved only through a process of disarmament.

1
The Weapons System

It has become commonplace to compare the command of an army with the management of a large corporation. But there is one essential difference. It is easier to persuade men to work than to kill or to risk getting killed. The basis of persuasion in the armed forces has varied according to time and place. It has involved such things as personal loyalty, the appeal to ideas like patriotism and democracy, and discipline. Yet is it probably true to say that in modern society the persuasive techniques used by military officers have more nearly come to resemble the techniques adopted in industry. Except during the Vietnam War, when, as we shall see, the inadequacies of military persuasion were acutely revealed, the output of the armed forces, the business of killing has become more remote, and the production of armed forces, the organisation of men and machines, has become more and more of an industrial undertaking.

Morris Janowitz, in his seminal book *The Professional Soldier*, which was published in 1960, described "the shift from authoritarian domination to greater reliance on manipulation, persuasion and group consensus."[1] And he ascribed this shift to modern technology:

> *The technology of warfare is so complex that the coordination of a complex group of specialists cannot be guaranteed simply by authoritarian discipline. Members of a military group recognize their greater mutual dependence on the technical proficiency of the team members, rather than on the formal authority structure.*[2]

In industry the embodiment of technology is the machine, and much has been written about the domination of man by machine in the twentieth century. The military equivalent of the machine is the weapons system. The weapons system combines a weapons platform: ship, aircraft or tank; a weapon: gun, missile, or torpedo; and the means of command and communication. The concept of the weapons system emerged in the late nineteenth century with the Anglo-German naval arms race and came to fruition in World War II as the aircraft and the tank came of age, although the term was not used until the 1950s. It was associated, as we shall see, with the entry of capitalist industry into the arms market; shipbuilding and heavy engineering in Britain in the 1880s, aircraft and automobiles in the 1940s.

As the term is used in this book, the "weapons system" is more than just a military classification of hardware. It is a classification of people as well. The weapons system implies the existence of an entire supporting cast—scientists to invent the weapons, workers to build them, soldiers to use them, and technicians to repair them. Indeed, the concept was developed by the U.S. Air Force in the 1950s as a tool of management, in order to organise this ever-growing cast. The institutions and language of "systems" however, served eventually to conceal the relationship between government and industry, which underlies the very concept of the weapons system.

In most Western countries, the procurement of armaments, what one might call the fixed capital of warfare, accounts for about half the military budget. Moreover, the procurement budget is dominated by a few major weapon systems. In the United States, for example, the Trident submarine and the new nuclear-powered aircraft carrier, together with their missiles and aircraft, account for about 60 percent of the naval procurement budget. The latest Air Force fighters, F–15 and F–16, account for more than 40 percent of the Air Force procurement budget, while the XM–1 battle tank accounts for a major share of the Army budget. The same is true in Western Europe. In Britain, the Multi Role

Combat Aircraft (MRCA) Tornado accounts for around 40 percent of the Royal Air Force budget; the three anti-submarine warfare cruisers, with their associated escort and support ships, probably account for a fifth to a quarter of the British naval procurement budget.

The major weapons system defines, by and large, the lines of command in modern armed forces. Navies, for example, are organised by ship, with groups of ships organised hierarchically into task forces. At the apex of the U.S. surface navy is the aircraft carrier, requiring destroyers and a submarine or two for protection, aircraft to fly from its deck, and supply ships of various kinds. The bomber and the battle tank have a similar role in the Air Force and Army. The Air Force is divided into bomber, fighter, and transport commands. The Army is made up of armour, artillery, parachute, and infantry units. But the armoured units are, to quote Colonel Vernon Pizer, "the mailed fist that strikes hard, fast and deep,"[3] the core of the combined arms team. The House Armed Services Committee of the U.S. Congress recently reasserted its belief that "the tank is—and will continue to be—the heart of land warfare."[4] The independence of individual services or military units is achieved through independent strategies associated with particular weapons systems. This would explain why strategic bombing is so central to the U.S. Air Force or why the British Navy remains committed to an oceangoing role associated with carriers, long after the abandonment of overseas commitments.

The growing capital intensity of warfare is also reflected in the composition of skills. The direct labour of war, which includes infantrymen, tank crews, artillerymen, fighter and bomber crewmen, fighting ships' personnel, who actually do the fighting, has declined dramatically as a proportion of total military manpower. It is known as the declining "teeth to tail" ratio.

In all the [U.S.] services fewer than one out of every six persons in uniform—360,000 out of 2,200,000—currently serve in a com-

bat specialty. *By way of historical comparison; better than nine
of every ten persons serving in the Union forces during the
American Civil War had combat specialties.*[5]

The lone fighter pilot, who was the heroic individual of World
War II, was in fact part of a team that serviced, operated, and
maintained his aeroplane; a team which today has grown to
seventy people. The tendency to substitute "the firepower and
mobility of improved war machines for manpower"[6] is also reflected in what is known as "grade creep," the increase in middle-
level officers—the white-collar military technicians—so that the
traditional pyramid shape of the military hierarchy has come to
look like a diamond.

The role of the individual is thus defined in relation to the
weapons system, and the lower his position in the hierarchy, the
more specialised is his job. At the base of any modern military
organisation is the small group of about ten to thirty enlisted men,
identified by occupation (e.g., a division of ship's cooks) or by
function (e.g., a gun crew). Modern military sociologists argue
that the individual thinks of himself as a member of a specific
skill group rather than of a social class and that his motivation is
based on technical pride in his work. There is a powerful ideology
of team spirit in the well-integrated, technically efficient military
unit, which, combined with modern awe for technology, is supposed to supplement, if not supplant, traditional techniques of
command and control. According to Morris Janowitz, this is
symbolised in the uniform of the soldier. In the past, smart uni-
forms were an expression of the military idea of honour. Today,
the occupational uniform of both the U.S. Army and U.S. Air
Force is the fatigue suit.

*The uniform which obscures the differences between ranks
similarly obliterates the difference between the military and the
industrial. It is a persistent expression of the thought that military men are not only representative men, but representative of*

the technical contemporary society rather than of a previous historical period.[7]

The link between the military and the industrial is not only an idea, it is materialised in the weapons system. Like the machine, the weapons system is both an object of use and an object of production. The military capabilities of a particular weapons system, which define its role in a particular military unit, reflect the manufacturing capabilities of a particular defence company. Thus, there are parallels, which have become closer over time, between military organization and industrial structure.

The design, development, and production of weapons systems is, by and large, undertaken by a handful of companies known as prime contractors. With a few significant exceptions, to be discussed in a later chapter, the prime contractors are generally the manufacturers of weapons platforms—aircraft, shipbuilding, automobile, or engineering companies.* They assemble the complete weapons system, subcontracting subsystems, like gun or missile, the engine and the electronics and components, and so create an interdependent network of big and small companies. The prime contractors are generally among the largest industrial companies. Since World War II, between forty and fifty companies have regularly appeared both on *Fortune*'s list of the top one hundred United States companies and on the Pentagon's list of the one hundred companies receiving the highest prime contract awards. The stability of the primes has been widely noted. Since the war, firms have disappeared through merger or, in Europe, through nationalisation, but there have been virtually no closures and virtually no new entrants.

Each of the primes specialises in types of weapons systems. Boeing, General Dynamics, and Rockwell are bomber enterprises. Grumman and Vought make fighters for the Navy; McDonnell

---

* In Europe tanks are made by engineering companies rather than by automobile companies.

Douglas and General Dynamics make fighters for the Air Force:
Lockheed makes heavy air transports as well as submarine-based
missiles. Chrysler and General Motors are the prime contractors
for battle tanks. Dassault in France, MBB in Germany and British
Aerospace in Britain make combat aircraft. Fokker in Holland
makes transport aircraft. Westland, in Britain, like Sikorsky (now
a division of United Technologies), Bell, or Boeing Vertol in
America, or Sud Aviation (now Aerospatiale) in France, are the
manufacturers of helicopters. Electric Boat, now owned by General Dynamics, has made submarines since the 1890s, when it
was purchased by the British company Vickers. Today Electric
Boat is building the Trident submarine, the projected system for
the American underwater nuclear forces in the 1980s. Newport
News makes aircraft carriers. And so on.

Each of these companies represents a manufacturing experience,
a particular combination of plant, equipment, and people, a specific mix of skills and techniques, an hierarchical organisation of
people, of relationships with customers (the military units) and
suppliers (the subcontractors). The president of Newport News,
when justifying financial claims on the government to a congressional committee, explained:

> What we have built at Newport News is a unique ship-manufac-
> turing complex—the only one in the United States that has the
> facilities, equipment and human resources to build, repair, over-
> haul and refuel the full range of Navy vessels and the only one
> now building nuclear-powered surface ships. Newport News is
> truly a national asset.[8]

Literally thousands of subcontractors are dependent on the
primes. Some are very large and are prime contractors themselves.
These would include the engine companies like Rolls Royce, Pratt
and Whitney (now United Technologies), and General Electric,
or the electronic companies like Texas Instruments, Raytheon,
Westinghouse in the United States, or Ferranti and Marconi-
Elliot in Britain. There are also many small suppliers; some are

established by the primes to produce a particular component. The small subcontractors are not at all stable. Their composition varies along with technology, and in the lean years it is they who go bankrupt.

Very often, prime contractors and their families of subcontractors dominate a region, so that the economic impact of producing a weapons system may be very great. Boeing is the biggest company in the state of Washington. Several aircraft companies—Lockheed, Rockwell, Douglas, for example—are located in Southern California. McDonnell dominates manufacturing in St. Louis, while Bath Ironworks, which makes destroyers, is the most important employer in Maine. Hundreds and thousands of people may work on a single contract. At Electric Boat in Groton, Connecticut, 31,000 people are estimated to work on the Trident submarine. And this does not include the people employed by subcontractors or the ripple effect on the producers of consumer goods purchased by the people employed or the capital goods acquired by the contractors. At Rockwell, 13,000 people were working on the B–1 bomber project when it was cancelled in 1977, and about 40,000 people were said to have been employed by Rockwell's subcontractors throughout the nation. Had the B–1 bomber gone into production, many thousands more would have been employed. In the 1960s, it was estimated that, although military contracts account directly for only 8 percent of California's employment, the total impact including indirect employment by subcontractors and indirect employment among producers of consumer and capital goods was 40 percent.[9] And if we also take into account the fact that many small firms which produce both military and civil goods are dependent on the military market to ensure their survival, then it is evident that the defence industry is deeply embedded in the economy as a whole.

The weapons system is subject to a technological dynamic characteristic of its industrial environment. As the social structure of industry and the armed forces converge, the competition which epitomizes private industrial enterprise pervades the various insti-

tutions which make up the organisation of defence. The National
Security Industrial Association, an organisation of American defence contractors, reports:

> Within DoD [the U.S. Department of Defense] itself, compe-
> tition is a very active force. This is reflected in DoD's drive to
> stay ahead of our potential enemies by fielding weapons which
> incorporate the latest possible technology; in DoD's relation-
> ships with other governmental departments; in the efforts of the
> military services to protect and expand their respective roles and
> missions and to obtain a larger share of the defense budget; in
> the relationship between the military services and the Office of
> the Secretary of Defense; and in the competition among the
> branches, commands, arsenals, yards, centers, and laboratories
> of the military services.
>
> For industry, competition is keen because the overall total of
> defense business is seldom adequate to support the available
> capacity of even the hard-core defense contractors, thus forcing
> the companies into a continuous life-and-death struggle to ob-
> tain defense contracts. Defense programs often are of gigantic
> magnitude, which results in competition more intensely con-
> centrated than is typically encountered in the commercial mar-
> ketplace.[10]

The consequence of this competition is rapid technical change,
in which every component part of successive weapons systems is
pushed up to and beyond the "state of the art." It is the fantastic
space-age dimensions of much modern weaponry which so awes
the soldier and the civilian observer. And yet the direction of
technical change, it can be argued, is confined within limits that
are defined by the persistence of military and industrial institutions. The stability of prime contractors and their customers has
helped to preserve traditions about the kind of military equipment
that is considered appropriate. Indeed, the very sophistication and
complexity of hardware may be a sign of conservatism and narrow
perspective. In peacetime, in the absence of external necessity

imposed by war, decisions about what constitutes technical advance are necessarily subjective. They tend to be taken by people who make and use the weapons systems, whose ideas are necessarily shaped by institutional experience and interest in survival. "We have," writes John Downey, an eminent British soldier,

> a situation in which the nature of present strategy (deterrence) precludes the acid test of war, while complexity invalidates the rough and ready evaluations of public opinion.[11]

The consequence is that

> the system is almost completely introverted, concentrating on the perpetual perfection of itself against some future day of judgement. The dynamic tensions, commonly regarded as necessary in all systems, must also be generated internally and can only come from debate between vigorous minds. But although the system strives hard to recruit able people, it chooses and trains them in its own image.[12]

Morris Janowitz makes much the same point when he emphasises the routinisation of innovation in the military establishment, with the consequence that

> traditional thinking has more often than not led to trend thinking, to a concern with gradually perfecting technical instruments, rather than strategic re-evaluation of weapons systems. This orientation in itself is a form, though a modified one, of technological conservatism whether the problem is missiles or manpower, planning toward the future tends to be a perfection of trends rather than an imaginative emphasis on revolutionary development.[13]

This is what we mean by baroque technology. "Baroque" technical change consists largely of improvements to a given set of "performance characteristics." Submarines are faster, quieter, bigger, and have longer ranges. Aircraft have greater speed, more powerful thrust, and bigger payloads. All weapons systems have more destructive weapons, particularly missiles, and greatly improved capabilities for communication, navigation, detection, identification, and weapon guidance. Even the development of nuclear weapons can be regarded as an extension of strategic bombing. While the basic technology of the delivery system has not changed much, such marginal improvements have often entailed the use of very advanced technology; e.g., radical electronics innovations such as microprocessors or nuclear power for submarines, and this has greatly increased the complexity of the weapons system as a whole.

Any "improvement" to a particular performance characteristic tends to beget others, and any "improvement" to a particular weapons system as a whole tends to infect whole families of weapons systems. Witness this description of the carrier:

> To achieve greater air capability . . . the individual naval aircraft and the ships' complement have grown in size and complexity . . .
>
> These trends have caused growth in the carrier itself, because of the need for more aviation fuel, more hangar-deck space, greater strength and size of the landing deck to support the heavier aircraft with higher landing speeds and so forth. As all parts of the design move together, the carrier, its power plant, its auxiliary services, and its crew have all grown. . . .[14]

Baroque technical change may also lead to versatility, the development of multipurpose weapons systems. Competition tends to promote institutional expansion. Military branches, services, and commands poach the roles of others; corporations imitate the capabilities of competitors. The Army emphasises the development of amphibious and airborne missions. The Navy clings to the ability to fly aircraft and land Marines. The Air Force, in order to retain its organisational autonomy through its bombing role, insists that fighter aircraft be able to strike deep into enemy territory. Prime contractors tend to diversify into a wider range of defence products. Lockheed, Litton, and General Dynamics, aerospace companies, have purchased shipyards. North American Aviation merged with Rockwell, the company which makes axles for army trucks. The Ford Motor Company has acquired an aerospace subsidiary. At the same time, the growing cost of individual weapons systems has tended to result in a decline in their number and variety so that military units have had to share the same systems and contractors have learned to collaborate in development and production.

The consequence is the all-rounded weapons system: the number of "performance characteristics" specified for a weapons system is increased. The different characteristics that were formerly specified for several individual systems are now combined into one. The F–111, which was to have been the main combat aircraft of the American Air Force and Navy during the 1970s, was expected by Tactical Air Command to have to take off from short and rough landing strips and to fly the Atlantic non-stop,

> to travel extremely long distances, carrying a load of nuclear weapons and fly at treetop level . . . engage in aerial combat at high altitudes and at speeds in excess of 1,700 miles per hour . . . [and to have] a large ordnance carrying capacity.[15]

These were the characteristics which defined the Air Force missions of interdiction, air superiority, and ground support. In addition, the Navy wanted a plane for fleet air defence. For this, the plane had to be able to circle "a fleet of ships at high altitudes for long periods . . . [and] to locate and destroy up to twenty miles away any enemy aircraft approaching the fleeet."[16] It turned out to be very difficult to make one plane which could do all these things well, and in the end, the Navy version was cancelled.

The British cruiser *Invincible* and its sister ships *Indefatigable* and *Ark Royal* are expected to combine the roles of command, control, and coordination of British and NATO maritime forces, the deployment of anti-submarine warfare aircraft, and the capacity to carry one thousand commando troops—tasks which were formerly carried out by several different ships. The European Multi Role Combat Aircraft, which is jointly developed and produced by Britain, Germany, and Italy, has been described as the "egg-laying, wool-producing, milk-giving sow."[17] Britain wants MRCA for long-range strike and strategic air defence (against bombers). Germany wants MRCA for close air support. Italy wants MRCA for air superiority (against fighters). As we shall see in a later chapter, these requirements are not easy to reconcile; MRCA has ended up primarily as an expensive low-level bomber for nuclear strike.

These features of baroque technical change—trend improvement and multiplication of roles—are designed to preserve the military-industrial structure. But technical change demands organisational change. What occurs is a kind of regroupment for survival. More and more men are required to produce and operate a particular type of weapons system, increasing the size of military and industrial teams, as well as the degree of individual specialisation. As the variety of weapons systems declines, the tactics of different military missions, and even the broader land, sea, and air strategies, are more closely integrated. The number of prime contractors for each type of weapons system falls and the interdependence of companies is increased through mergers, collaboration, and an interlocking set of contractual relationships. The smaller subcontractors become more fragmented and more specialised; duplicate suppliers for particular components are squeezed out, while the total number of components increases. Essentially, these changes mean greater hierarchy and less individual autonomy; a narrowing of the apex of the pyramid in both military and industrial spheres. Transnational projects like MRCA or the Anglo-French Jaguar, or even the American and German attempt to achieve "commonality" in tank design, represent the development of multinational forms of military and industrial organisation.

The consequence of this elaborate combination of conservatism and technical dynamism is what economists call "diminishing returns": more and more effort is expended for smaller improvements in military effectiveness. As military and industrial teams grow bigger and more hierarchical, the relationship of the individual to the whole is at once narrower and more remote; the inability to see beyond the design of a component, the repair of a part, or the wrath of an immediate superior may impair the ability to consider the industrial technology or the military mission in its entirety. Conflict and compromise are increasingly built into the design of weapons systems as formerly competing users and producers join in a single project. A former Litton employee describes the problems that were encountered when two hundred people were assigned the task of preparing a proposal for the series production of Spruance class destroyers for the Navy:

> Scarce top engineering talent was siphoned into management roles, from which positions they had little time to actually work on, or even think about, the actual problem. Instead, they became embroiled in jurisdictional fights and empire-building. If a job got behind, the group involved automatically claimed it didn't have enough people. More people were supplied, and management problems compounded.
>
> Efforts at communication took up much of the time. This was aggravated by the fact that group managers sometimes withheld information if this was judged to be in the individual group's parochial interest . . . Thus a technical mistake . . . could proceed for some time without being noticed . . .
>
> Finally, a group this size presents severe problems in motivating the people who actually do the work to operate in accordance with the goal of the overall project. The people who actually did the work were so far removed from the corporate reward system that their own goal became minimizing the risk that their individual subsystem be judged infeasible . . . The result was consistent overdesign and conservatism. The lowest level would design an individual system element with plenty of margin, his boss would throw in another margin just to make sure, and so on.[18]

The problem was compounded by the size of the Navy evaluation team:

> Litton realized that whatever the merits of its basic concept, unless the proposal defined such subsystems as, say, the galley in great detail, whoever was evaluating the galley part of the proposal would give the proposal low marks. Since there were many such subsystems, a disproportionate amount of Litton's effort was devoted to routine subsystem design.[19]

Similar problems have been recounted for the design of other systems. On the F-111, for example, Graham Allison, in a summary of a study by Robert Coulam, describes how the contractor and the Air Force organised their engineering teams "in parallel fashion with horizontal communications quite strong between counterpart contractor and Air Force civilian engineers." This greatly hampered the ability to make technical trade-offs.

> If results at one level of design indicated the need to trade among higher order objectives, the whole elaborate hierarchy of specification detail—detail which coordinated the engineering efforts of thousands of contractors and government officials—stood in the way.... Even relatively minor reformulations would require the concurrence of layer upon layer of contractor and government authorities.[20]

The outcome of this contradictory process, in which technology is simultaneously promoted and restrained, is gross, elaborate, and very expensive hardware. The Trident programme will cost the American taxpayer over $30 billion (in 1980 prices). The latest nuclear-powered aircraft carrier, the subject of controversy between Congress and President Carter, will cost, together with its associated ships and aircraft, more than $60 billion. An Air Force F-15 fighter costs $19 million; the Navy F-14 costs $22 million. The Air Force F-16 and Navy F-18, which were originally designed as cheap, lightweight fighters, are currently estimated to

cost $11 million and $18 million respectively. These costs are
several times greater than the cost of World War II predecessors,
even when inflation is taken into account. One well-known estimate suggests that if current trends continue, the U.S. Air Force
will be able to afford only one plane in 2020.[21] Bombers cost two
hundred times as much as they did in World War II. Fighters cost
one hundred times or more than they did in World War II. Aircraft carriers are twenty times as expensive and battle tanks are
fifteen times as expensive as in World War II. A Gato class submarine cost $5,500 per ton in World War II, compared with $1.6
million per ton for the Trident submarine.[22]

These costs primarily reflect amazing sophistication and technical complexity. And complexity means thousands and thousands
of parts, each part a servicing and logistical problem. The F–4,
for example, the predecessor to F–14 and F–15, required 70,000
spare parts. In Vietnam, despite the most extensive logistical operation ever mounted, there were always shortages. All military aircraft are much less reliable than commercial aircraft. They break
down more often; they require more maintenance, more repairs,
more spares, and more fuel. Tanks are much less reliable than
tractors, and warships are much less reliable than merchant ships.
As weapons systems become complex, particularly as they incorpo-
rate more electronic equipment, reliability declines and operational
costs increase at an exponential rate (despite the increased reliability of solid-state devices and improved automated maintenance). According to Captain O'Rourke, a U.S. Navy officer:

> *Expensive airplanes are complex airplanes, and complex air-
> planes, over the past ten to fifteen years, have been the bane
> of our existence. The costs of keeping a stable of these complex
> machines in fighting trim is astronomical—in terms of people.
> Our maintenance and support people have repeatedly fallen
> behind the heavy demands which these complex, sophisticated
> systems have made. The Navy supply system; bound up in red*

tape of its own space age bureaucratic computerdom, has rarely
been able to stay apace with the ever-increasing demands for high
cost, one-of-a-kind spare parts for the sophisticated systems.[23]

Complex weapons systems are also complex to operate. And yet
training hours, combat exercises, and firing practise are reduced
because of high operating cost as well as the risk of an expensive
accident. And families of weapons systems are increasingly dependent on complex systems of communication which are also
costly to operate and maintain.

Nor is it at all clear that cost and complexity are justified by
increased performance. First of all, measurable improvements in
performance characteristics are rarely proportionate to the increase
in costs. In particular, all-roundedness, as we have seen, tends to
reduce the efficiency of any one role. Second, improvements in the
accuracy and lethality of munitions have greatly increased the
vulnerability of all weapons systems and their associated communication and support systems. As a result, many of the performance
characteristics so dear to the services and contractors have become
irrelevant in modern warfare. The classic examples are aircraft
speed, which reduces the accuracy of pinpoint bombing, and speed
of surface vessels, which cannot reduce vulnerability to aircraft
and submarines. A recent Pentagon exercise, known as Air Missile
Intercept Evaluation, demonstrated that numbers were more important than sophistication in air warfare. In close engagements,
F–5s, F–14s, and F–15s consistently destroyed one another. Major
General Frederick C. Blesse (USAF ret'd), who observed the
exercise, explained: "it doesn't make much difference how fast
your airplane is or how high it will fly. Once you get inside your
enemy's missile envelope, you're not likely to escape."[24] The more
sophisticated aircraft, F–14 and F–15, imposed great strain on the
pilots, who were unable to make use of the many theoretical
capabilities of the planes.

The Trident, perhaps, is the best example, because most people
would think that nuclear-firing missile submarines represent just

about the best that modern military technology has to offer. The Trident submarine is huge. It is 560 feet long, longer than the Washington Monument, and six inches too deep to get out of the Thames Channel in Connecticut from its building site to the sea. It is faster than its predecessors, the Polaris/Poseidon submarines. It carries more missiles with a longer range. It has a natural circulation nuclear reactor which is significantly quieter at normal patrol speeds. Its size and its large complement of missiles, however, may actually increase its vulnerability, since it will be easier to detect than its predecessors. Its top underwater speed (25 knots) is still significantly lower than that of attack submarines (30 knots), and in any case, it is so noisy at top speed that it would have to go slowly to escape detection. The increased missile range is of dubious advantage since, for the foreseeable future, Soviet anti-submarine warfare forces cannot detect submarines within the operating area of the current Poseidon submarine.

Similar criticisms can be made of the main systems now under development in the United States: the XM–1 Main Battle Tank, the new MX intercontinental missile, the new class of Air Force and Navy fighters, the cruise missile carriers, and the latest aircraft carriers. William W. Kaufman, an adviser to James Schlesinger when he was Secretary of Defense, said of the aircraft carrier that

> no more costly method of keeping a limited number of airplanes at a forward base has ever been devised by the mind of man. The Navy cannot define circumstances in which these very expensive sorties will make a significant difference in a situation where we care.[25]

It is equally difficult to explain why some of the European systems like MRCA or Invincible will be better than their predecessors.

In short, the weapon system, in perfecting itself along the lines projected by users and producers, seems to have overreached itself. It has become big, costly, elaborate, and less and less functional. It serves a certain social purpose, in creating an ever more complicated set of connections between soldiers, sailors, officers, managers, designers, workers, and bureaucrats. And it retains a certain grandeur, a certain ability to instill social awe, that is often to be found in the baroque, whether art, architecture, or technology—a grandeur that may portend degeneration.

2
Vickers

Modern industry joined the enterprise of warfare in the late nineteenth century. The new partnership between industry and the military was crystallized in the battleship. The battleship could be described as the first modern weapons system. Its story and the story of its most famous manufacturer, the British firm Vickers, foreshadows the story of the Trident submarine, the XM–1 tank, and the Multi Role Combat Aircraft, and of General Dynamics, Chrysler, and Panavia. What happened to Britain as a result of its investment in battleships may tell us something about what could happen to America.

Vickers was one of the greatest armourers of modern times. It was comprised of the two most important early-twentieth-century gunmakers, Vickers and Armstrong, whose only real rival was Krupp of Germany. At its height in World War II, Vickers produced the whole range of military equipment, from the hand-held machine gun to the capital ship, from the Valentine tank to the Spitfire fighter. Today, most of its armament plants have been run down or nationalised. All that is left is the Elswick works in Newcastle, which still builds tanks for Middle Eastern potentates. Ironically, it is the very same plant where it was all begun by William Armstrong in the 1850s.

The Rise of Vickers

The middle of the nineteenth century, like the first half of the twentieth century for America, was the most dynamic period of British industrial development. Shipbuilding, engineering, iron and steel were the most rapidly growing industries, and it was then that the companies later to enter the arms business came to industrial prominence. Vickers, based in Sheffield, was one of the earliest and most successful steelmakers, with a substantial market in America. Armstrong manufactured hydraulic machinery in Newcastle. Military spending was low during this period, both absolutely and as a proportion of national income; civilian technology was much more advanced than military technology. For the most part, manufacturers were not interested in the military market. Armstrong's breech-loading rifled gun, invented during the Crimean War, represented an isolated attempt among private entrepreneurs to rectify the backwardness of the British armament techniques.* As we shall see, United States military spending up to World War II was similarly low.

From about 1870, the rate of British economic growth declined. According to the economic historian David Landes,

> change was built into the system and innovation was, if anything, more frequent than ever. But the marginal product of improvements diminished as the cost of equipment went up and the physical advantage over existing techniques fell.[2]

All technologies seem to follow a similar cycle, with what economists call "increasing returns" in the early phases and "diminishing returns" in the later phases. That is to say, as new technologies develop, every additional sum invested results in bigger improvements, and as old technologies decline, every additional investment

* Armstrong's studies of the science of destruction were a product of the engineering enthusiasms of the time. A colleague, Alfred Cochrane, wrote: "All this time, Mr. Armstrong had been investigating problems entirely new to him with his usual thoroughness against the opposite hillside and the numerous adventures which he met with during these firing trials, as well as narrow escapes he had of blowing himself to pieces, were most exciting. In those days there was no science of artillery such as there is today—nor was there any knowledge of what pressure metals would stand, and our illustrious founder deserves some credit for his physical courage in wrestling with this unknown and perilous subject."[1]

results in less improvement. Very often technologies are bunched together in groups of industries; in the early stages of industrial development, an advance in one technology spurs on advances in others, and in the late stages of development, outdatedness in one technology fetters the attempt to improve others. Schumpeter argued that such "bunching" of technologies explains the tendency for long waves in capitalist history. British industrial development had been based on a series of related inventions—the steam engine, new methods of coal mining, new iron and steel processes, the railway, and, above all, machinery. Industries based on these inventions were at their zenith in the mid-nineteenth century. After 1870, their existence, embodied in brick and steel and human skills, gradually became a liability to the newly developing technologies of chemicals, electricity, and automobiles. For the first time, Britain faced serious commercial competition from new industrial rivals in Germany, France, and America. Economic growth, according to Landes, gave way to economic struggle.

> Optimism about a future of indefinite progress gave way to uncertainty and a sense of agony, in the classical meaning of the word. All of which strengthened and was in turn strengthened by sharpening political rivalries, the two forms of competition merging in that final surge of land hunger and that chase for "spheres of influence" that have been called the New Imperialism.[3]

From around 1880, British military spending began to rise. The reason for the increase was the developing imperial rivalry. But the form of the increase, the emphasis on bigger and better and more expensive warships, was a consequence of the stage of industrial development and the organisational structure of the Army and Navy.

During the 1880s, military contracts were first extended on a significant scale to private manufacturers. Earlier, most military equipment needs had been met by British government arsenals and dockyards. During this period, some of the most dynamic companies—steel makers like Vickers, John Brown, Beardmores, Cammells, and Firths; shipbuilders like Fairchilds, J. & G. Thompson (later to become John Brown), Yarrow & Co., Palmers, or engineers like Armstrong—turned to the military market as an alternative outlet to the depression in trade. For the steel companies, it was the loss of the American and German markets as a consequence of protection and emerging local competition, combined with the general recession, that motivated this strategy. Tom Vickers wrote that his company was fortunate in having found this means of escaping from "a serious falling-off in trade . . . and the reduction in prices consequent upon severity of competition."[4] For the shipbuilders, it was the decline in the market for passenger liners, as a consequence of amalgamations among the shipping lines and growing German competition. William Pearce, the chairman of what was to become Fairfield Shipbuilding and Engineering Company, stood for Parliament in the election of 1885. His policy was to disperse Admiralty contracts from the Royal Dockyards to commercial firms. A few days before the election, his company was reorganised and renamed Fairfields "to enable it to execute Government contracts in the event of Mr. Pearce being elected to Parliament."[5]

Military contracts were extended to private manufacturers, on the grounds that the companies constituted a national asset, a potential reserve for producing armaments in time of war. A government committee, chaired by John Morley, which recommended this course of action argued:

> Not only does it [the system of private manufacture] stimulate inventors and manufacturers to vie with one another in producing the best possible articles, but it tends also to widen the area of production so that in time of pressure the requirements of the Service would be more readily supplied.[6]

The argument was to be repeated often, whenever, in fact, the arms companies faced a depression in trade. Trevor Dawson, a leading figure in Vickers, suggested in a deposition to the War

Office in 1904, when the company faced a severe slump owing to
the fall in orders after the Boer War, that

> the government . . . might perhaps consider it only necessary
> to keep the ordnance factories as a reserve in time of war espe-
> cially, and to employ such facilities as now exist in the trade
> for their main requirements.[7]

And in 1907, the Government Factories and Workshops Committee, chaired by Sir Gilbert Murray, recommended that military
orders be concentrated on private firms rather than on ordnance
factories:*

> Whereas the maximum productive power of the Arsenal is
> something with definite and ascertainable limits, that of private
> trade is not. The resources of private enterprise in this country
> are capable of almost indefinite, though not of immediate, ex-
> pansion. Demand discovers or creates new sources of supply, and
> the result of an increased demand upon the trade in ordinary
> times would, therefore, probably be to create an additional re-
> serve of power in an emergency.[8]

As we shall see, this argument for preserving defence industrial
capacity has been used repeatedly in the postwar period. It was
used to justify the procurement of aircraft in the late 1940s and
it is used to justify the acquisition of whole families of weapons
systems today. It has become the rationale for what is known in
the business as the "bail-out imperative."

During the 1890s and early 1900s, the new private contractors
formed themselves into a formidable group of armament specialists. Armstrong had already built a naval shipyard at Elswick.
Now Vickers acquired a shipyard and engineering works at Barrow
and the machine-gun works of Maxim Nordenfeldt. John Brown

---

* That same year, Bernard Shaw published his play *Major Barbara*. The
Professor of Greek, Adolphus Cusins, who is so impressed by the power of
the arms manufacturer, was modelled on Shaw's friend Gilbert Murray. Major
Barbara was a portrait of Murray's wife.

and Cammells acquired Scottish shipyards. Armstrong merged
with the Manchester gunmaker Joseph Whitworth. And similar
manoeuvres were undertaken abroad by Krupp in Germany and
Creusot in France. The main aim of each of the manufacturers,
which was only really achieved by Vickers and Armstrong, was, in
the words of Albert Vickers, "to supply ships with their engines
complete and equipped with Guns and Armour Plate, entirely
manufactured by the Company in its own works."[9]

The warship was the perfect expresşion of the competitive dynamism of nineteenth-century industry and the traditional conservatism of the armed forces—a foretaste of the relationship between
modern armourers and the military that has produced the weapons
system of today. Although the late-nineteenth-century battleship
incorporated immense technological advance, as wood gave way
to iron and steel, sail to steam, and as ships and guns got bigger
and more powerful, in form and function it was still recognisable
as the capital ship of Nelson's day. In relation to the development
of warships in the United States, Elting Morison has written that
the Navy

> sought to contain the new machines and new forces that had
> produced a novel and unrecognized potential within a familiar
> pattern. Whatever the design and intended purpose of the new
> vessels, they were sent out on the old cruises and missions of
> the ships of the line.[10]

The new warships did not entail any change in the lines of naval
command, in ideas about naval warfare, and they represented a
visible affirmation of past naval victory, of British power at sea.
"On them as we conceived," wrote Churchill, "floated the might,
majesty, dominion and power of the British Empire."[11]

The battleships were symbols of the British victory at Trafalgar,
just as now the modern equivalents of the battleship serve as a
reminder of the battles which were won in World War II. And
just as now, as we shall see, new nations attempt to climb the
international hierarchy through the acquisition of military sym-

bols, so Germany, and other countries, adopted a policy of naval expansion to be used as a "political lever against British hegemony."[12]

Nothing so appropriate was invented for the Army. The heavy rifled breech-loading guns developed at the end of the nineteenth century, which were so much more powerful and accurate than the traditional smooth-bore muzzle-loading guns, and the deadly machine guns threatened to change the whole nature of land warfare and with it the whole organisation and ethos of the Army, centred, as it was, on the conception of heroic infantry attacks and cavalry charges. As a result, the Army developed a strong resistance to the products of modern industry.

> The ability of Armtrong's gun to put a concentration of shells into a small area was considered by one senior officer to be a disadvantage; if he were faced with such a gun, he argued, all he would have to do would be to keep out of the area that was being shelled, whereas with the old guns one was in danger anywhere.[13]

The resistance to the machine gun is even more instructive. An officer, Captain Fosberry, who saw the potentialities of the machine gun, explained, in 1882:

> A most ably conducted and exhaustive set of trials has already determined that we have a system of machine guns by which one or two men can do as much destruction as, say, forty ordinary soldiers . . . And yet, though it is certain that an enemy will always do the unexpected thing, and if a European one, use machine guns against us, we neglect to acquire them for the army because the exact tactical place for the weapon is as yet undiscovered.[14]

When machine guns were acquired, they were classed as artillery; they were mounted on cumbersome gun carriages and were outranged by heavy guns.

> The artillery were happy to hang on to the machine gun at any
> price, even if it meant making of them a tactical absurdity. The
> other arms were equally happy to surrender control as long as
> this meant that their effectiveness on the battlefield was almost
> nullified. The vested interests of both sides came together to
> ensure the continued neglect of the machine gun.[15]

The effectiveness of the machine gun was demonstrated repeatedly
in Africa,* and the Boer War showed

> that . . . the possession of heavy artillery firepower was essential,
> that small calibre automatic weapons were of great value, that
> immense supplies of shell with serviceable fuses were required.[17]

Yet those lessons were never absorbed and naval expenditure continued to rise much faster than spending on the Army. When
World War I broke out, there were shortages in all categories of
modern land weapons. The British Army, for example, had only
two machine guns per battalion.

There are striking parallels to be drawn, not only between the
warship and the present-day weapons system, but also between
the attitudes towards the machine gun and current views about
what are known as Precision Guided Munitions (PGM). The
experience of Vietnam and the Middle East have been absorbed,
as I shall argue in a subsequent chapter, no more than was the
experience of colonial wars in Africa before World War I.

The naval bias of military expenditure suited Britain's arms
manufacturers as well. Warships were much more lucrative than
other types of military equipment; they combined the various
capabilities of the armourer in a single hull; they required a long
production period. In theory, readiness for war involved "the an-

---

* John Ellis describes the terrible slaughter that occurred in colonial wars.
For example, at the Battle of Omdurman in Sudan in 1898, which was "not
a battle but an execution," twenty British and twenty other Europeans were
killed as against eleven thousand dervishes *dead.*[16]

nual accumulation of a few very capital-intensive units in a pre-war situation."[18] In contrast, the rapid industrial mobilisation demanded by Army requirements in wartime was quite unsuited to the industrial environment that created the specialist arms companies. Today, it is PGMs, the products of electronic companies, which threaten the position of established arms manufacturers—shipbuilding, aircraft, and automobile companies.

Competition between the arms companies in the period before World War I, which reflected and reinforced Anglo-German rivalry, took a technological turn with ever greater improvements in destructive power, speed, and protection, culminating in the Dreadnought building programme, which began in 1906. Whenever national orders slackened, the arms companies sought export markets, and the technical ingenuity of the products they offered to foreign governments often called forth a domestic response. At the turn of the century, some South American countries were spending a quarter of their national income on battleships, such was their perceived international political prestige. And British manufacturers dominated the world market, accounting for over 60 percent of exports in the period 1900–14, compared with around 9 percent each for France, Italy, and the United States, and only 8 percent for Germany.[19] It was the ability "to offer the technically flamboyant and eye catching design, the bigger Dreadnought, the extra turrets or the ultimate cannon"[20] that made the British companies, notably Vickers and Armstrong, so successful. For example, the

> contract for Rio de Janeiro, later shared between Barrow [Vickers] and Elswick [Armstrong] was landed by d'Eyncourt's [Armstrong's naval architect] ability to redesign her on the spot as the largest warship of the pre-1914 world outbidding entirely the Kaiser's personal protest that not even the Imperial Navy, let alone the Brazilian Navy, needed leviathans of these proportions.[21]

And these technical "improvements," aided by periodic public
outcry about real or presumed German naval construction,*
further speeded up the naval build-up. In some cases, the Admiralty actually requisitioned technically advanced ships built for
export, and in other cases, the Admiralty was induced to order
comparable units. The competitive process that underlay the
Anglo-German naval arms race was described by Engels in terms
that anticipate post-1945 developments in weaponry:

> The modern warship is not only a product but at the same time
> a specimen of modern large-scale industry, a floating factory—
> producing mainly, to be sure, a lavish waste of money . . . in this
> competitive struggle between armour-plating and guns, the war-
> ship is being developed to a pitch of perfection which is making
> it both outrageously costly and unusable in war.†

Battleships explicitly came to be seen as deterrents. As they
became bigger and as firepower increased, they became more
vulnerable. And as they incorporated more and more extravagant
features, they became more and more of a liability. When war
came in 1914, the big battleship played a marginal role. It was
vulnerable not only to the guns of other battleships but more importantly to new weapons—submarines and greatly improved tor-
pedoes and mines. Except for the battle of Jutland, an example of
gingerly naval manoeuvring, neither side dared risk the use of the
battleship in combat. "The battlefleet," writes one historian,

> was the king on the chessboard; its loss would be fatal but its
> strategic role was limited. In fact, by absorbing resources like

* Philip Noel-Baker describes in his book *The Private Manufacture of Arms*
how the Mulliner Panic of 1906–9, in which fears of a German naval build-up
were based on the allegations of the managing director of an idle armaments
firm, led the British government, against the inclination of most of its min-
isters, to accelerate the naval building programme. The story anticipates the
missile and dollar-gap panics of recent times.
† It is interesting that Engels correctly predicted that the development of
the "self-propelled torpedo" would mean that "the smallest torpedo would be
superior to the most powerful armoured warship."[22]

escorts and destroyer screens, it even increased the menace of
the new warfare.[23]

And this is equally true of some present-day baroque weapons
systems, whose loss would be literally disastrous.

Military spending remained a relatively small proportion of
national product up to 1914. It reached a peak of 4 percent during
the Boer War. Nevertheless, it was significant because it was concentrated in some of the largest companies in the country. In
1905, the arms companies represented 10 percent of a list of
Britain's largest industrial companies compiled by P. L. Payne.[24]
They tended to dominate groups of smaller companies in related
trades and particular regions, like North-East England, the West
of Scotland, Northern Ireland, Sheffield, and Birmingham, so that
the effect of military contracts, as is the case today in the United
States and Western Europe, was probably much more pervasive
than the figures suggest. By 1914, most of the arms companies had
become dependent on government support. Vickers, Armstrong,
and Beardmore's had become professional armourers, and although
they continued to build merchant ships, their yards, like those
of other shipbuilders, could not have survived without "generous
topping up of the order book with naval contracts."[25]

The dependence on arms, it can be argued, was directly related
to the growing stagnation of the British economy. The slowdown
in economic growth which occurred after 1870 was a consequence
of the stage reached by the shipbuilding and heavy engineering
industries of the mid-nineteenth century, the end of a long wave
of growth based on these industries. But the slowdown was not
reversed, as it was in other countries in the last decades of the
nineteenth century, with the development of the new set of industries, sometimes described as the second Industrial Revolution.
David Landes explains the British failure in terms of the "burden
of interrelatedness," the fact that "no piece of equipment works
in a void," that any act of innovation calls forth a series of related
acts in the industrial, technical, and social environment, so that

any one obstacle to innovation multiplies itself. "All of British industry," Landes writes,

> suffered from the legacy of precocious urbanization; the early cities of the nineteenth century were not built to accommodate the factories of the twentieth . . . Steel plants, especially with cramped, ill-shaped sites, found it difficult to integrate backwards to smelting and forward to finishing, and lack of integration in turn inhibited adoption of a number of important innovations . . . Similarly, railways and colliery owners were long unable to agree on the adoption of larger freight trucks . . .[26]

This "mummification," as Landes calls it, of the industrial structure prevaded all human and social capital—the composition of skills, the style of living, education, transportation, etc. The increasing social hierarchy and the rigidity of class divisions which tends to develop in a "mature" industry limited the creativity that was characteristic of the early period of industrialisation. Britain was, as it were, stuck in the industrial culture of the mid-nineteenth century.

It can also be argued, although Landes does not, that these obstacles to innovation set in motion a circular process of decline in which domestic investment slowed down, thus reducing the possibilities for transforming the social and material infrastructure, while increasing overseas investment helped to increase the competitiveness of Britain's economic rivals and to widen further the gap in innovatory activity, thus further reducing the opportunities for profitable investment at home.[27]

Military spending played a role in this process, for it enabled some of the most important companies of the period to grow and innovate within the confines of the established institutional structure. Hence, it reinforced the "mummification" of British industry and put off the day when the necessary structural adjustments would have to be made. To be sure, the arms companies generated some of the most important innovations of the period. The assembly line was first introduced for the manufacture of small arms.

New steel processes were developed for use in armour plate. The navies were among the first to make use of the turbine engine. Aircraft and automobile companies, in Britain at least, were by and large offshoots of the armament manufacturers. Similar examples of "spin-off" can be found today: many U.S. electronics companies originated in response to a military demand. But all these innovations were fettered by the nature of the military market. Apart from small-arms manufacture, they were shaped by the demand for custom-built products and by the capabilities of the craftsmen who jealously guarded their autonomy. They were never even conceived of as appropriate to the mass market and controlled manufacturing processes that are the requisite for industrial success in this century. Arms did not simply postpone the kind of restructuring necessary for the survival of old industries; they also removed the necessity of entering new ones. Armstrong had a plan in 1906, two years before the Model T, to mass-produce six thousand cars. The proposal was rejected by the directors on the grounds that "the profit would be less than on a single river gun boat."[28] In the end, it was largely foreign countries that were able to benefit from such examples of spin-off and so lead the way in the next stage of industrial development, which largely bypassed Britain. As I shall show in the next chapter, today's spin-offs have suffered a similar fate.

It was not just that armaments manufacture absorbed some of the finest engineers and scientists and distorted their concepts of what constituted technical advance. Military spending also absorbed funds that might otherwise have been available for investment in civil industry. And the failure to invest and restructure was self-reinforcing because it increased the tendency to seek military contracts as an alternative to stagnating civil markets. This tendency was compounded by the sense of insecurity engendered by economic stagnation and the notion that growing German power, which was of course largely economic, could be countered with bigger and better warships, the symbols of British industry and power. And, in a circular fashion, naval expenditure channelled innovation and investment further into a technological cul-de-sac, preserving and perfecting an outmoded nineteenth-century industrial structure and denying the emergence of more modern markets and methods of manufacture.

The Decline of the Armourers

Vickers and Armstrong, like the other arms producers, underwent an enormous expansion during World War I. Employment at Elswick alone reached 20,000. At Vickers Crayford works, where Vickers machine guns were made, employment rose from 300 to 14,500.

After the war, the companies began to seek alternatives in the commercial market. Vickers set up a Peace Products Committee, which put forward a whole range of proposals, from traditional products, like locomotives, merchant ships, engines, boilers, steel products, and sewing machines, to new products, like automobiles, aircraft, and electricity. Initially, the company benefitted from the surge in postwar demand for traditional products, but on the whole, the products were too elaborate and expensive to compete in commercial markets. Barrow had extensive plans for locomotive production, as did the Elswick and Scotswood plants of Armstrong. But, according to the official historian of Vickers,

> *Just as in wartime, when firms outside the industry had been brought in to manufacture weapons, they found that the standards of robustness, accuracy and safety that were required were something quite outside their ordinary experience, so now in peacetime the company found it extraordinarily difficult to get down to the lower standards which were acceptable—which were indeed all that could be afforded—in civilian use.*[29]

In the new spheres of production, Vickers and Armstrong were relatively successful so long as they confined themselves to military products. Many of the new aircraft manufacturers were subsidiaries of the arms companies—Vickers, Supermarine, Armstrong, Whitworth, and English Electric. Barrow was at the forefront of submarine design. And the tank division at Elswick, established in 1927, was unique in the world in the design and development of tanks during that period. The official historian of British war production commended the tank designers at Vickers-Armstrong for their "solitary and pioneering efforts."[30] Vickers tanks were to provide the basis for tank developments all over the world. The tank sold to the Soviet Union in 1931, with the cynical name of the English Workman, is the direct progenitor of nearly all subsequent Soviet tanks.

But in related civil fields the companies were not nearly so successful. Ronald Miller and David Sawers, in their seminal study of the technical development of aviation, argue that if

> the British [aircraft] industry had not been dominated by a few men whose most memorable experience was the 1914–18 war, and if the staff of the government research establishments had not appeared strangely conservative, it might have been better placed to use the ideas of its many able designers . . .[31]

Woleseley and Armstrong–Siddeley, the automobile subsidiaries of Vikers and Armstrong, faced similar problems, obsessed as they were with the idea of luxury cars for staff officers. J. D. Scott says that

> Woleseley had built costly showrooms in Piccadilly before finding that the police would not let them bring cars across the pavement, and the incident was not unrepresentative.[32]

But the maddest scheme of all was Armstrong's Newfoundland paper mill. This was conceived soon after World War I. The company was to develop a large forest area on the west coast of Newfoundland with a new paper mill, hydroelectric power station, and port. Construction work, shipping, etc., were to provide employment for Elswick and Openshaw (the old Whitworth plant in Manchester). The Board underestimated the harshness of New-foundland conditions and the cost of production. By 1926, the company was heavily dependent on borrowing from the Bank of England.

The "bail-out imperative" came to the rescue. The "Admiralty in particular were alarmed" that this "might put Armstrong's capacity out of operation,"[33] and a merger was arranged with Vickers, with the help of the Bank of England. Churchill had earlier refused to provide financial assistance.

Admiralty alarm was typical of the government's response to the problems faced by arms companies during the interwar period. "There are . . . all over the country," the Financial Secretary to the Admiralty told the House of Commons in 1928, ". . . great new building establishments which in the interest of the country must be kept going . . . We have to keep the Dockyards in a state of efficiency and not let the private yards go out of use."[34]

Because of the failure to adapt to modern industry, the arms-producing areas were those worst hit by the Depression. The great shipbuilding companies did build some merchant ships, but their share of world output declined, largely because they were not able to keep up with the new developments, such as the wide-spread introduction of electricity, electric welding, and the internal-combustion engine. The closure of Palmers shipyard at Jarrow was one of the catastrophes of the Depression; it was the very same shipyard that had produced the first iron warship, HMS *Terror*, in 1854. But, by and large, the yards did not close. They were kept open by a trickle of Admiralty orders and foreign contracts and the anticipation of rearmament, so that even the Depression did not produce the kind of massive inducement to structural change that might have been expected. The arms companies survived, even if their employees suffered, and when World War II broke out, they were able to expand even beyond the grandest expectations of the late nineteenth century.

But World War II, even more than World War I, marked the end of the nineteenth-century approach to arms manufacture. For it decisively marked the end of the capital ship: "The nineteenth century revolution" in armaments, J. D. Scott has written,

> had been a revolution in favour of heavy industry. The change that occurred during the Second World War with the advent of radar, the birth of homing devices, and atomic warfare was a change in the direction of an alliance of "pure" science and light industry. In the birth of this new warfare, Vickers played very little part. Both Vickers and Armstrong had assumed their characteristic shape in response to the needs of a big ship navy, and they were too deeply committed to them to be permitted to make much change. In the end of the big-gun ship we see more than the end of a phase in the history of Vickers; we see the end of the epoch which had begun in 1897 [when Vickers acquired the Barrow shipyard].[35]

The lessons of World War II do not, however, seem to have been appreciated at Vickers House. At Barrow and Newcastle, for example, the shipyards were reorganised on flow lines for standardized production during the war. After the war, Vickers spent £8 million on "modernisation," so that they could revert to the production of custom-built ships. The same search for new products that had occurred after World War I was set in motion. And the same problems were encountered. Part of the difficulty was the unwillingness to view commercial products as anything other than "fillers-in" until the facility should be needed again for armaments. When the Korean War broke out, J. D. Scott writes,

> civil products at Barrow and Elswick in particular were abruptly stopped and thrown off the production lines; negotiations for new engineering products, which had been delicately nursed for months, or even for years, were cancelled overnight, and some disgruntled customers never came back.[36]

Barrow and the great engineering works of the North-East were regarded as jobbing shops and faced an endless series of different civil products—sugar-beet crushers, sulzer engines, moulds for pre-fabricated houses, electric furnaces, car presses, car dies, deck machinery, printing presses, mining machinery, recycling equipment, variable speed gears and delivery pumps, rubber processing equipment, pulverising plant, strip wound pressure vessels, etc. More fundamental, however, was the inability to adapt technical abilities to the civilian market. The tractor scheme at Scotswood, in Newcastle, represents a real attempt to provide a lasting alternative to tanks and guns. It was designed with a Rolls Royce engine at a time when the market for heavy earth-moving equipment was rapidly growing. According to Jim Hendin, chairman of Vickers Engineering Group, "This was looked upon as a very major step forward in that we were really building for peace now." But the problem was the bias of the tank designers and the failure to establish user needs at an early stage.

> By the time we had our prototypes out in the early 50s, we ran in quite a lot of problems because a tractor is a different animal to a tank. A tank is very well maintained, it has a low service life, they change the tracks very frequently and all the rest of it, whereas a man buying a construction machinery tractor, he expects the tracks to last a fair long time, I should think from memory four or five thousand hours, against about four or five hundred for a tank, and so on. And we ran into a lot of trouble with these tractors, unfortunately; design problems and the rest of it and we got to the stage that we had a lot of tractors in the field and the Chairman of Vickers-Armstrong Ltd., as it was at that time, Sir James Reid-Young, made the bold decision that we'd pull them all back and we would recompense the user for all the hours they had used the tractor, and we stopped production.[37]

At its peak, the scheme employed about a thousand people. It folded in 1960, after a loss of £8 million. Similar problems were encountered in the commercial-aircraft division; the only postwar commercial aircraft to make a profit was the Viscount.

As we shall see in subsequent chapters, many American defence companies which have attempted to diversify into civilian products have faced the same difficulties. The emphasis on performance rather than reliability, the preoccupation with product improvement rather than process improvement, the custom-built approach, the neglect of costs, have all been cited as reasons for their difficulties. Ambitious solar-energy schemes, space programmes, and urban-transit systems have succeeded only where tractors and Newfoundland development failed, because, despite their evident shortcomings, they have been financed by the state. They have preserved what people in Britain describe as the "service" attitude, the cosy relationship with the government, the idea of the arms companies as national institutions.

The underlying weakness of Vickers did not seriously affect the company until the late 1950s. Korea and the postwar boom, before the recovery of Germany and Japan, kept the factories open with fillers-in and the odd military contract. But by the early 1960s the traditional arms-producing industries began to face severe problems. In the west of Scotland a similar process was occurring; the "structural weaknesses of the [shipbuilding] industry" were "disguised and reinforced" by naval construction before World War I by the "artificial conditions" of war and "the 1950s boom, characterized by the absence of significant foreign competition and the temporary revival of the liner market."[38] For example, the shipyards were built for nodal production and were inappropriate for modern flow-line methods of production.

The Clydebank and Fairfield yards were laid out principally to build passenger and naval tonnage, with the building berths and plater's sheds on the flanks and the fitting out and engine building facilities in the centre. This was a sensible arrangement when fitting out and engine building was elaborate and costlier than hull construction. Now with the cessation of passenger and naval work, and engine construction, the yards are poorly equipped for the efficient throughput of materials.[39]

As a consequence of the situation in these industries, the government took a series of rationalisation measures which culminated in the nationalisation of steel in 1965 and of aircraft and ship-building in 1977. At the same time, one of Vickers institutional shareholders, the Prudential Life Insurance Company, took the then unprecedented step of interfering in Vickers management and introducing strict financial control. The result was the transformation of Vickers, as a company, into what might be described as a multinational financial holding—a transformation which reflected the rentier character of British capitalism. Vickers entered new fields: office furniture, bottle washing, and, above all, property (which now represents a third of Vickers assets), through the takeover of existing plants, often overseas, rather than through new investment. Increased profits were achieved in the short run through the elimination or run-down of older plants, rather than through modernisation and innovation. The consequent expansion of Vickers output was thus merely fictitious, representing an increase in the share of national output controlled by Vickers rather than an absolute increase. Between 1967 and 1977, trading profits increased threefold as a percentage of sales and sixfold in absolute terms, while employment fell by 10 percent, a reduction of 6,000 people. If one takes into account the fact that acquisitions during the period added about 9,000 people to the total labour force—a period in which there were no nationalisations—the total loss to the labour force was probably 15,000. This strategy is evidenced in the composition of foreign sales. In the highly competitive advanced industrial markets of West Europe, North America, and Australia, increases in sales have been achieved through the establishment of overseas subsidiaries. Indeed, the *entire* increase

in sales of overseas subsidiaries has occurred in these regions.
In contrast, exports have been stagnant in real terms. Such increase as there has been has mostly gone to the underdeveloped
markets of Asia and South America (probably consisting of Barrow
ships and Elswick tanks), in countries where technically backward, cheaper products are more likely to find a customer.

Elswick[40]

Elswick is the only arms-manufacturing plant that remains within
the new streamlined Vickers financial empire. It produces tanks—
the Chieftain, the Vickers Main Battle Tank, an armoured recovery vehicle, and an armoured-vehicle-launched bridge—for
countries like Iran, Kuwait, Kenya, and India. Its success in the
export market is the consequence of another recent government
measure designed to aid the traditional industries—the intensive
effort to promote arms sales undertaken by the British Ministry
of Defence.

Elswick is a perfect example of nineteenth-century engineering.
Building a tank is rather like building a ship; many of the concepts
of tank manufacture were drawn from the experience of shipbuilding. The chassis is known as the "hull," and the early tanks
were classified as "cruisers" and "battle tanks."

Elswick is built on top of a coal mine, between the river and
the railway line—an ideal nineteenth-century site; but today its
past is a liability. The factory uses electricity as a source of power
and the mine constitutes a safety hazard. Road access is limited
to a tunnel beneath the railway which is too small to take heavy
traffic. River access is confined by the swing bridge, built, ironically,
at Elswick a hundred years ago to facilitate seagoing traffic.

Elswick does very little design work now. Most tank design is
undertaken at the government establishment at Chobham. Until
the mid-1960s Vickers maintained a large design team which
designed the Vickers Main Battle Tank especially for export. But

with the decline in government orders and uncertainty about the future of plants like Elswick, the design team was largely disbanded. No attempt was made to reorient or recruit designers for commercial work. There are now two empty floors at Elswick's head office.

Tank production is organised along the principle of what Germans call *Platzarbeit*, although this has long been superseded by the assembly line. During World War II, a tank shop was built to accommodate more efficient assembly-line manufacture, based on the example of automobile production. But when production of the Centurion tank was completed in the late 1950s, the tank shop was sold, and production is now dispersed in several different shops, each organised around a particular stage of tank manufacture—fabrication, big machining (on the hull and turret), small machining on parts, and fitting and final erection. The tank moves back and forth through six or seven shops, carried on heavy tank transporters.

The skills of the workers involved have not changed much since the nineteenth century. They include burners, sheet-metal workers, boilermakers, whitesmiths, platers, welders (which replace the nineteenth-century riveter), grinders, borers (vertical and horizontal), millers, plano-millers, plumbers, electricians, painters, rough painters, and leather workers. Whitesmiths are a Vickers specialty. They work in cold metal, as opposed to blacksmiths, who work in hot metal. They were introduced in the 1920s to counter the militancy of the boilermakers, who do approximately the same job. They belong to a separate union, the National Union of Sheet Metal Workers and Domestic Engineers.*

There are also ancillary workers—handymen, craners, slingers,

---

* Industrial memories are long. When I was at Elswick I got involved in a heated debate between a boilermaker, who argued that Lord Armstrong was the greatest villain that ever lived, and a whitesmith, who argued that, on the contrary, Lord Armstrong was the greatest philanthropist that ever lived. Each supported his case in minute detail on the basis of events that took place in the nineteenth century.

and labourers—who do odd jobs, such as carrying parts from one section to another. Then there are a great variety of overhead people, popularly known as "hangers-on." These include the progress people, who are supposed to make sure that equipment is in the right place at the right time, the store people, the rate fixers, the inspectors, the foremen, and, of course, management.

Production of a tank takes about eighteen months; testing starts between twelve and fourteen months. But these schedules are subject to great variation. There are enormous problems in programming the work, and when these problems are not quickly overcome, there is a good deal of waste—of space, of capital equipment, and, above all, of people. It is not just the inefficiency resulting from the dispersal of shops, though this presumably adds to the problem. Workers are always waiting around; sometimes waiting for orders; sometimes waiting for work from other sections; on new orders, the fabrication shops may be working flat out while the finishing trades are on short time. The problems are easier to manage if the contract is big, if there is enough work for all sections, and subcontracting can be used to maintain an even flow of work. But a major source of the difficulty is the absence of planning; planning is very difficult when information has to pass through layer upon layer of social hierarchy, each layer unwilling to admit a mistake or a delay. This is a problem well known to students of modern weapons acquisition.

Elswick remains, caught by armaments, in a moment of nineteenth-century history. It is probably typical of shipyards and engineering works throughout Britain that have preserved their traditional forms through military contracts. Nevertheless, change cannot be put off forever, and as we have seen, the military sector is ultimately affected by new technology. The manufacture of tanks has been rationalised and an increasing quantity of electronic equipment is needed to improve the accuracy of the gun. Before World War II, Vickers built the complete tank, including the gun, the engine, the armour plate, and so on. Now only 18 percent of the value of a tank is made at Elswick. Although the value of

tanks produced at Elswick may well have risen, the work done at
Elswick has declined considerably. Furthermore, the introduction
of numerically controlled machines has replaced many jobs. This
is why there are only 2,000 people at Elswick, compared with
5,000 in 1963 and 12,000 in 1939.

In the 1890s, it is estimated that 70,000 people were directly
dependent on the Elswick works. A contemporary observer, R. W.
Johnson, wrote in 1895:

> Consider that the Elswick works began forty-eight years ago on
> the verdant banks beyond the western limits of the town with
> a handful of mechanics headed by a scientific dreamer of im-
> mature age and no experience. Consider that today those same
> works are a national glory, employing 13,000 men, dictating the
> methods of the world's warfare and having a reputation which
> has reached the ear of every intelligent man in Europe and
> America and then ask if this is not romance in hard fact. The
> place is one of the sights of England . . . Their size, their com-
> pleteness, their tremendous productive energy, their variety of
> blast furnaces, foundries, machine shops and chemical labora-
> tories, teeming with human life, reverberating with the shriek
> of steam, the clang of hammers and the whirr of machinery, over-
> hung by a pillar of cloud by day and of fire by night, present a
> picture of concentrated industrial activity which overwhelms
> and astonishes the average observer.[41]

Today, the ruins of the gun shops, with their imposing arches,
can be seen from the river. Many of the factories have been turned
into warehouses, and the houses and pubs that lined the Scotswood Road have been pulled down and replaced by vacant spaces.
Old people can still remember when "tides of men" trudged up
the streets from the Elswick works at the end of their shifts.[42]
There used to be fifty pubs along the Scotswood Road, with names
like The Rifle, The Gun, or The Ordnance Arms. Now there are
only six. The main impression is of emptiness.

Is this the future of Southern California, Massachusetts, or

Seattle? Can the MX missile or the F-14 aircraft be compared to the Dreadnought? What does the Vickers story portend for the United States and the growing number of other countries committed to the manufacture of baroque armaments? The next chapter is about recent American experience.

3
The American Era

By the end of World War II, the United States was producing more aircraft and tanks than all its allies and enemies combined, excluding the Soviet Union. Allied victory was a victory for the internal-combustion engine and the assembly line. More than anything else, it was this combination, pioneered by Henry Ford, which underlay the modern American industrial strength built during the first few decades of the century. At one time during World War II, the monthly aircraft output of a single plant, Ford's Willow Run factory, was half the peak monthly output of the entire German aircraft industry.

But if World War II saw the culmination of American economic development, it was also the limit. It created American military power and drew the energies of American enterprise into the organisation of war. World War II crowned a triumphant moment of American industrial history; its institutions and ideas have never quite escaped from that experience. Something like what happened to Britain between 1880 and 1914 can be said to have happened to America in four years.

Origins

In the early part of the nineteenth century, military technology played a stimulating role in American development. The techniques of mass production and the concomitant development of the American machine-tool industry had their origins in the manufacture of firearms. However, after the American Civil War, the participation of private industry in American arms manufacture virtually disappeared and the techniques of mass production were applied and extended in the manufacture of commercial products like sewing machines, bicycles, and eventually automobiles. The assembly line, as instituted with Ford's Model T, involved extensive mechanization and carefully calculated fragmentation and timing of labour. The phenomenal growth of the automobile industry occurred between 1900 and 1929. During this period, sales of motor vehicles rose from $4 million to $3,412 million.[1] And the growth of the industry revolutionised other industries, steel and petroleum, plate glass, rubber and lacquers. New roads and highways were constructed—indeed, this was the second-largest item of government expenditure during the 1920s. The 1920s also marked the beginning of suburbia, the proliferation of service stations, drive-in cinemas, and motels. This bunching together of new industries and patterns of consumption constituted what could be called a new long wave in industrial history, which succeeded the earlier long wave, based on shipbuilding and engineering, described in the last chapter. The new long wave was based to a large extent on the automobile, although chemicals, electricity, and aircraft were also important. And it created a new industrial culture in America.

The development of the aircraft industry occurred much later than the development of the automobile industry. The period of maximum growth was between 1927 and 1933. The Depression inhibited civil expansion; nonetheless, as we shall see, many aircraft manufacturers planned for a sufficiently large volume of civil orders to justify mass-production techniques after the design of aircraft began to stabilise in the mid-1930s. However, war broke out before these plans could be realised. Thus, in the late 1930s, the aircraft industry was still basically design-orientated rather than production-orientated. The injunction "Design or die" was

> virtually axiomatic. Superior performance expressed in higher speeds, greater ceilings, heavier loads and longer ranges wins contracts. To stay in business, manufacturers soon learned that

they must maintain engineering staffs capable of exploiting the
latest findings in aeronautical science, translating theory into
practical designs.[2]

The American automobile and aircraft industries were far more
successful than their European equivalents. By 1913, the United
States had three times as many cars registered as Western Europe,
and by 1921 this ratio had risen to thirteen to one. By 1930, the
United States had more passenger air traffic than the rest of the
world combined, and by the late 1930s, American airlines had
become big business. Several commentators have attributed the
early American success to the size of the commercial market and,
pari passu, the absence of military influence. According to James
Flink:

> The governments of France, Germany and England had real-
> ized the military potential of the motor vehicle by the mid-
> 1890s. They conducted extensive experiments with motor
> vehicles and offered substantial subsidies to encourage the de-
> velopment of motor vehicles suitable for military purposes. The
> early governmental subsidization in Europe delayed the manu-
> facture of light cars for the family driver by emphasizing the
> development of heavy towing cars and trucks that were better
> suited for officers' staff cars, weapons carriers, and transporting
> troops and supplies.[3]

Similarly, European aircraft manufacturers are said to have been
"hampered by the predominance of military influence on the industry at the time [interwar period]."[4] While American manufacturers were designing aircraft especially for civilian markets, the
Europeans tended to regard airliners as inefficient bombers.

Before World War II, American military spending was very low.
It averaged around 1 percent of GNP during the interwar period,
compared with 3 or 4 percent for most other industrialised countries. Armaments, such as they were, were largely manufactured
in government arsenals and dockyards. There were also a few

private shipyards. With the important exception of World War I, the military aircraft market was limited and concentrated on a few companies. The automobile industry also produced military equipment during World War I, but it was the smaller, less profitable companies that were most involved. In the United States, as in Britain in the mid-nineteenth century and Japan in the postwar period, the crest of the long wave, the most dynamic phase of industrial development, was ridden without the participation of armaments. In all three cases, military spending and military production were minimal.

The depression of the 1930s, like the depression of the 1880s, increased national rivalries in Europe—rivalries which had been left unresolved by World War I—and created new pressures for military spending. Just as the depression of the 1880s had been a depression of shipbuilding and engineering, above all, so the depression of the 1930s most deeply affected the automobile. In Detroit, the centre of automobile manufacture, two-thirds of the working population was unemployed. When U.S. military spending did begin to rise in 1939, it was thus not surprising that the contracts should be let to America's most successful and most depressed industry.*

World War II has been described as the war of the "internal-combustion engine." It was a war of mobility in which military forces everywhere depended on millions of cars, trucks, armoured vehicles, aircraft, and ships, all using internal-combustion engines. The glamour weapons of the war were aircraft and tanks. "More than any other weapon of land warfare," explains one of the official histories of the war,

> the tank in World War II captured the imagination of soldier and civilian alike. Its roaring motors, inscrutable armor, and smoking guns added a new and terrifying element to the al-

---

* In fact, the auto companies were actually unwilling to undertake war production because increased military spending had generated a new demand for cars.

*ready grim life of the battlefield. It symbolized for the ground
forces, as did the sleek bombing plane for the air forces, the
revolution in warfare that sprung from the union of military
need with industry and technology.*[5]

Indeed, strategic bombing, especially the use of atomic bombs on
Hiroshima and Nagasaki, endorsed our awe of airpower, particularly the bomber, that was to be inextricably associated with
America's postwar hegemony. It was in much the same way that
seapower had become associated with the Pax Britannica—a symbolic expression both of military might and industrial capability.

The automobile and aircraft industries played the central role
in World War II. All the top prime military contractors were aircraft or automobile companies. The automobile industry spread
the techniques of mass production, while the younger aircraft
industry emphasised the significance of design improvements in
response to battlefield experience and scientific advance.

During the war, the automobile industry accounted for one-
fifth of total war production. In January 1942, the production of
automobiles for the civilian market ceased. Its wartime output,
valued at $29 billion, included 4 million engines, nearly 6 million
guns, 88,000 tanks, 3½ million cars and trucks, and 27,000 completed aircraft. But its influence extended further as the techniques of mass production were introduced into the aircraft and
shipbuilding industries. The aircraft industry's wartime role was
as important as that of the auto industry. Aircraft production increased from 1,000 aircraft a month in January 1941 to 8,000 in
December 1944. The increase was even more remarkable because
during the war aircraft became steadily heavier and more sophisticated. Productivity increased from 21 pounds of airframe per
employee per month to 96 pounds of airframe per employee per
month over the same period.[6] War production, in the words of
a Boeing executive, became "a crusade in which every rivet was a
lance." The highest productivity was achieved at Ford's Willow
Run Factory—an experiment which, as we shall see, was not uni-

versally applauded, because the rigid introduction of mechanisation led to inflexibility of design. Nevertheless, it is widely agreed that Ford set a critically important example to the aircraft industry.[7]

The construction of ships underwent a similar revolution in technique. In addition to naval vessels, shipyards built Liberty and Victory merchant ships on a huge scale. Special facilities were created at the cost of over $2 billion. At the Bethlehem-Fairfield yard in Baltimore, for example,

> a mass production system was adopted . . . resembling as closely as possible that of the automobile industry. Simplified standard drawings were issued to the shops. A minimum number of standard steel sizes were employed to increase interchangeability and to reduce the risk of material bottlenecks. . . . Labor was organized in gangs doing specialized jobs moving from ship to ship on definite schedules . . . the entire assembly operation thus consisted of high-speed consolidation of previously prepared sections.[8]

The production of artillery, ammunition, small arms, explosives, etc., followed the same pattern ("Raw material . . . came in at one end of the plant; millions of bright and shining cartridges came out the other end").[9] And above all, there were hundreds of thousands of different types of vehicles, and equipment which delivered and installed this matériel all over the world, giving rise to Churchill's remark that the war was won by a Dakota (DC–3) and a bulldozer.

The realities of war utterly changed conceptions of military power and the role of industry and science. Aircraft and tanks had replaced the battleship; the automobile and aircraft industries had established their industrial predominance. "U.S. industry," writes one historian,

> emerged from the crucible of war shored up by an American gold monopoly, by new and undamaged facilities, with a vast array of new experiences and techniques, and habituated to a

profitable symbiosis of military expediency and industrial power.
The release of long-pent frustration and the needs of war generated a flash of energy which almost eclipsed the long night
of the depression. . . . For the achievements of 1941–45 were
so dazzling that the links between patriotism, self-interest and
production were not seriously questioned for two decades, when
in the late 1960s the shadows of Vietnam eclipsed the bright
afterglow of the Great Crusade for Freedom.[10]

At the end of World War II, the military budget was dramatically reduced. Thousands of workers in the arms industry were
laid off. In one year, beginning in 1945, employment at Republic
Aviation, the company which produced P–47 fighters by the thousands, fell from 10,000 to 3,700. At North American, employment
fell from 102,000 to 9,000 in the same period. The automobile
corporations, as well as companies making domestic appliances,
chemicals, electrical equipment, etc., were able to move out of
the military business in response to a consumer demand which
had been in abeyance for over fifteen years. This was not possible
for the aircraft companies, the naval shipyards, and certain specialised companies, like Raytheon, which made radar and which
had developed in response to the special technological demands
of war. For a brief period, these companies were able to keep
going with accumulated wartime profits and with small, largely
military contracts. There were a few orders for merchant ships
from foreign carriers, often financed with United States aid. (The
U.S. Merchant Marine was swollen with Liberty and Victory
ships.) Many of the aircraft companies attempted to develop
civilian transports, but the market, already surfeited with surplus
war transports, was not large enough to encompass them all, and
only Douglas, at that time, made a lasting impact.

Essentially, what these companies maintained during this period
was a technical core, which could be said to represent their manufacturing capability. This core consisted of patents, top engineers,
and specialised facilities, such as testing equipment and labora-

tories. But it soon became clear that such a core could not be kept going without production contracts. For the corporations, development work had always been regarded as a form of investment; it was production that brought in the profits. For the government, it was difficult to justify development contracts in the absence of a firm commitment to procurement. Pressures began to build up for a new programme of military aircraft procurement.

The arguments were reminiscent of the arguments used to justify private contracts for warship building in Britain in the 1880s. The National Planning Association set up a committee composed of representatives from business, labour, and government, which reported in 1946:

> Unless a substantial volume of military production is maintained at this time, this country runs the risk of doing irreparable damage to its aircraft manufacturing industry, which is not merely a collection of plants, machinery, raw materials, and designs, but which is, first of all, a living organization of skills—research, engineering, labor and management. These skills inhere in particular individuals and companies.[11]

Similar sentiments can be found in the annual reports of the aircraft companies and in the evidence put forward by the Aircraft Industries Association to the President's Air Policy Commission (Finletter Commission) and the Joint Congressional Air Policy Board, which reported in 1948. The president of Republic Aviation, for example, argued that the decline in postwar markets has

> contributed in no small way to weakening the industry—financially—in loss of manpower and engineering—in the loss of subcontracts and facilities—to the point where not only is the possibility of quick mobilization questionable but the very existence of such a vital industry is threatened.[12]

And in his 1948 message to Boeing shareholders, William M. Allen, Boeing's president, wrote:

There is a growing realization on the part of the American public and government leaders that from the standpoint of national defense alone it is essential that this country have an industry capable of producing military requirements. There must be not merely an industrial mobilization plan to be put into effect on some future signal but a continuing program of development, perfection and proving of new experimental models, and continuing production of the required quantity of the latest accepted and operating types of aircrift.[13]

This, as we shall see, is exactly what happened.

The Finletter Commission, which considered this evidence, concluded, as did Congress, that airpower was essential for the defence of the United States. It was conceded that another war seemed unlikely.

However, we cannot be sure. The world situation is dangerous. A nation in the position in which the United States finds itself today has no choice but to follow policies which may lead to friction with other nations. There is, moreover, such a thing as blundering into a war. . . . Sometimes, events get out of hand and war happens when neither side wants it.[14]

The commission argued that the most important task was to protect U.S. air space against possible atomic attack. Further,

a strong aircraft industry is an essential element in the Nation's air power. Our air establishment would be useless unless backed by a manufacturing industry, skillful in technological application, efficient in production, capable of rapid expansion, and strong in basic financial structure.[15]

The commission, reflecting the opinion of the aircraft industry, argued against a reduction in the number of companies, on the grounds that there should be at least two sources for each type of aircraft in order to foster competition and to ensure dispersal of

manufacturing facilities. Because the industry was dependent on
the government, the government, through "proper planning, adequate volume and abandonment of uneconomic procurement
practices," would need to "create an atmosphere as conducive as
possible to profitable operations in the aircraft manufacturing
business."[16] Similar arguments were expressed, somewhat less vo-
ciferously, on behalf of the shipyards.

Following the report of the Finletter Commission, military procurement began to rise. Many of the important military contracts
for aircraft and, to a lesser extent, for ships were signed in 1948
and 1949 before the formation of NATO and *before* the outbreak
of the Korean War. "The acceptance by the United States Congress of the need for a 70-Group Air Force and an enlarged Naval
Air Service," wrote the editor of *Jane's All the World's Aircraft*
in the 1948 edition, "has resulted in the placing of contracts with
the American industry for many new types of jet aircraft."[17] This
was, for example, the period when Boeing received orders for
the B–50 Superfortress, the new B–47 bomber, and the C–97
Stratocruiser transport plane; North American went ahead with
development and production of the F–86 fighters of Korean War
vintage; and a series of carrier-based aircraft were ordered from
McDonnell Douglas, Grumman, and Vought. The Navy ordered
two new antisubmarine-warfare cruisers at $40 million a piece
(1949 prices); four new destroyers from Bethlehem Co., and Bath
Iron Works; and nine new submarines from Electric Boat New
York Shipbuilding Co., and Portsmouth and Mare Island Naval
Yards.[18]

Of course, these orders were not just a response to the problems
of the arms industry. They were part of a wider shift in American
policy, heralded by the Truman Doctrine of 1947 and based on
America's wartime experience, in which a vigorous economy, military production, and American world leadership were viewed as a
winning coalition for the postwar period. It was a decisive break
with the liberal, non-interventionist, isolationist conceptions of
the earlier New Deal era.

The Korean War seemed to confirm the wisdom of these decisions and, for a brief period, recaptured the energetic excitement
of World War II. The Korean War seemed to imply that the
techniques developed against the Nazis in Europe could be equally
well applied to Communists in Asia. Walt Rostow said that war
demonstrated how "industrial capital could to an important degree
be successfully substituted for manpower against an Asian land
army."[19]

The Military-Industrial Complex

After the Korean War, the military budget declined somewhat,
but it never returned to its prewar level. The Army and the Navy
experienced the main impact of defence cutbacks. The strategy
of massive retaliation initiated by the Eisenhower Administration
in 1954 confirmed the emphasis on air power and ensured a steady
flow of orders to the aircraft industry, soon to become the aerospace industry.

THE FOLLOW-ON SYSTEM

The argument that procurement was necessary to maintain a
capacity to design, develop, and produce weapons became institutionalised in the follow-on.* Essentially, this means that as soon
as work is completed on one weapons system, work begins on its
successor. Hence, Boeing produced the B–47, followed by the
B–52, followed by Minuteman ICBM. Lockheed produced the
F–80 and the F–104 fighters, and a famous series of heavy transports. North American produced the P–51 Mustang, followed by
the F–86, followed by the F–100. As one Air Force colonel said,
"there is always someone working on the follow-on at the Pentagon, it's an article of faith."

During the Second World War, there had always been a tension

---

* The idea of the follow-on imperative as an intellectual concept was originated by James Kurth.[20]

between quality and quantity, between the design orientation of the aircraft industry and the production orientation of the automobile industry. It is probably true to say that it was quantity that won the war. Certainly, it is often said that American weapons were qualitatively inferior to British and German weapons, engineered as they were for quantity production. Nevertheless, continual design modification was of critical importance and, afterwards, when neither the budget nor attrition could justify high volume production, this aspect of wartime experience became more prominent. In wartime, as one of the official histories put it,

> continuing superiority required continual change. Every innovation introduced by the enemy must be outmatched. Superior performance in aircraft is the sum total of many components—range, speed, climb, maneuverability, firepower and the like—each conditioned by thousands of features of design: here a change in engine cowling to improve cooling and increase horsepower, there a better gun mount to enlarge the field of fire and so on in an endless procession suggested by experience in the field and innovations on the drawing board. When one is pitted against an aggressive and determined foe, to maintain superiority is to accept the absolute necessity of frequent change, modification of existing designs to incorporate improvements wherever possible and, ultimately, replacement of old models with new ones, fluidity of design is a requisite for superior weapons.[21]

It was fluidity of design that justified the follow-on system. The useful life of a weapon was much shorter than the physical life because of the seemingly inexorable process of obsolescence. Yet design changes, in peacetime, were almost entirely introverted. Russian weapons, for most of the period, as we shall see, were considered technically inferior to American weapons. Hence, design improvements were measured against an imaginary foe, a concept, which was by its very nature subjective, of what an enemy's advanced weapons might be like. This was the essence of the "worst case analysis," in which weapons were designed to match the most advanced weapons which an enemy might be capable of designing at some specified future date. Inevitably the concept of technical advance as well as ideas about the future capabilities of an enemy were shaped by the experience of the designers and the users. It practice, it was a kind of extension of World War II. It was as if a phantom German Army had continued to design and develop weapons in a linear extrapolation of the past. The criteria of technical advance which had seemed important in the war, like aircraft speed or tank armour, continued to occupy a prominent position in the design of weapons. This is the thinking that gave rise to baroque technology.

The follow-on system is often explained in bureaucratic terms. The mission of each military unit and the organisation of its officers and men is built around a particular weapons system. When the weapons system comes to the end of its useful life, the military unit needs a successor to justify the unit's continued existence. While this explains the attachment to particular types of weapons systems and particular performance characteristics, it does not explain the pace of technical advance, the length of the useful life, the emphasis on "quality" rather than quantity, the "cost and complexity" syndrome. There are, after all, many military men who favour numbers and simplicity and a slower rate of replacement. For the corporations, however, it is continuous development of weapons systems, rather than continuous use, on which their existence depends. Hence, there are reasons for supposing that it is the corporations that have had a decisive influence on the pace of the follow-on system.

A major study of the weapons-acquisition process was undertaken at the Harvard Business School by Professor J. R. Fox, based on his personal experience at the Pentagon, extensive interviews, and documentary research. The critical importance of continuous development and procurement contracts was confirmed by the study:

When the major share of a company's business is defense work, the drive for new contracts becomes compelling. One reason is that technical and management personnel who have worked on defense programs are now geared for advanced technology and complex equipment. Also, since the Department of Defense handles its own distribution, defense contractors do not develop a phase of their operations vital for commercial business. By the time a firm has developed the personnel, facilities and equipment to handle programs budgeted for hundreds of millions or billions of dollars, management must keep the company operating at or near full strength or risk serious losses. During our interviews with industry managers, this concern seemed to outweigh all others. The fact that profits in the defense industry are almost solely a function of the level of costs seemed of secondary importance.[22]

That the procurement policy is a response to these imperatives is suggested by the fact that the useful life of weapons systems tends to correspond to the manufacturing cycle. As development ends on one weapons system, development begins on another, and as production ends on one system, it begins on another. It seems unlikely that the corporations adapt their development and production schedules to meet military requirements, since this would imply considerable flexibility and a foreknowledge of five to ten years of military plans. Rather, it seems that, at least for aircraft, the development cycle is paramount. For any particular corporation, given the equipment and core engineers, there tends to be an optimum time period in which an aircraft can be developed. This can be defined as the shortest possible time before administrative inefficiencies (from too many people) sets in.* Pro-

* In fact, of course, administrative inefficiencies do set in. Ernest Fitzgerald, a former Pentagon official, argues that defence corporations operate according to the so-called Ape Theory of Engineering; i.e., "If enough chimpanzees could be put to work at enough typewriters, one of them would eventually reproduce the works of Shakespeare": problems will be solved more quickly if more people are put to work to solve them.[23]

duction schedules are much more flexible. The production of aircraft requires little more than floor space, which can easily be adapted for other uses, and unskilled workers, who can be hired and fired with surprising ease. This is not true of the production of naval vessels. Shipworkers are highly skilled and cannot easily be laid off on a temporary basis, and production facilities are fixed.

To ensure continuous work, all defense companies have planning groups, whose sole function it is to choose suitable successors for the weapons that are currently being produced and who work closely with similar groups in the services. The planning group is supposed to predict what a particular branch of the armed forces might require when current projects come to an end, and the various ways the corporation might meet that requirement. Because of the relationship with the armed forces, particularly during the so-called concept-definition phase, the prediction tends to become a self-fulfilling prophesy. As one corporate vice president said, the government "depends on companies like ours to tell them what they need."

A handbook on defense/space market research compiled by a group of defense-industry executives in the early 1960s emphasised that

strong competition in the defense/space market necessitates close working relationships with the customer. It means not only frequent contacts but considerable participation with the customer in development of his performance and product requirements. It is necessary to attempt to work with the customer on study contracts and feasibility studies in order to help analyze the required characteristics of products and performance for which the customer issues requests for proposals. Market research activity must provide sufficient lead time to guide research and development efforts in the directions in which requests for proposals are likely to be forthcoming. Hence, considerable contact with the customer during the formulation of product requirements is an extremely important function of market research activity in the defense field.[24]

Professor Fox, in his study, found that this advice is acted upon as a matter of course:

> Our discussions with Defense Department and industry personnel, and a review of the case histories of ten current defense programs, revealed that defense contractors are profoundly influential in the origination and development of new program ideas. Private firms often assist government staffs in writing the Requests for Proposals that are eventually issued to potential contractors. Industry officials research areas to which their particular companies' skills might be applied and identify key government offices that will welcome their proposals. They also attempt to find out what funds are actually or potentially available for particular programs. According to the industry executives we interviewed, intelligence information concerning defense funding is a major factor in the preparation of cost estimates submitted to the Defense Department.[25]

Despite these efforts, the follow-on system does not function smoothly. If it did, the efforts would be unnecessary. Indeed, interruptions are a paradoxical consequence of the workings of the system. The struggle for continuous employment of industrial capacity also entails the tendency for continuous expansion. As competition spurs further "improvements" in design, so the weapons system becomes bigger and heavier, more expensive and more elaborate. Teams of engineers expand and additional layers of management are inserted. Each engineer pushes his own idea, each manager competes to attract more funds for his own section, and so more improvements, in a self-perpetuating manner. In war, the acid test of battle proves which improvements are useful and which are not. In peacetime, the only limits to the improvements that can be offered are the available technology and the size of the military budget. In fact, those limits are consistently over-reached as the advocates of particular programs—the defence contractors and their military allies—underestimate the cost of their program and overestimate the technological possibilities. This is why cost overruns which, during the 1970s, *averaged* 100 percent, are a permanent feature in defence contracting.[26]

As the cost of individual weapons systems increases, the capacity needed to design, develop, and produce the weapons system also tends to increase. This capacity can be defined as the resources—plant, equipment, and people—required in a given time. The time taken to design, develop, and produce weapons systems has, in fact, increased by several years, as a result of delays in decision-making and budgetary limits on procurement.[27] But this increase has not been as great as the increase in the cost of weapons systems. Hence, each new weapons system has tended to entail an increase in required industrial capacity.

Given other claims on national resources, however, the defense budget has not kept up with the rise in costs. With ups and downs, American military spending has been more or less stable in real terms since the end of the Korean War. Although, as we shall see, there are still many small programs—like anti-tank weapons—the number of different types of major weapons systems has been reduced and prime contracts have got fewer and larger. In the years 1957–59, for example, the U.S. government bought twenty-three different types of combat aircraft, seventeen helicopters, seven air transports, and twenty-one ASW, utility, or trainer types of aircraft. Twenty years later, the U.S. government was buying eight different types of combat aircraft (including a cruise missile carrier), five helicopters, two air transports (together with modifications to existing planes), and seven ASW, utility, or trainer types of aircraft. Similar reductions have occurred in the variety of fighting vehicles and warships. The number of different types of missiles, which include many new small programs (discussed in a later chapter), has remained roughly constant. In Europe, the decline in the number of major weapons systems has been even more dramatic. Indeed, no single European country will be able to afford to develop and produce the next generation of combat aircraft.

Military contracts have thus got bigger and fewer, and the impact of military spending has consequently become much more uneven. Industrial capacity has correspondingly expanded and contracted so that excess capacity has become the perennial problem of the arms manufacturers. Each prime contractor now has one or two prime contracts where formerly it might have had four or five. Douglas and Lockheed no longer make bombers. Grumman and Convair no longer make military transports. Some prime contractors have merged; like McDonnell Douglas or Republic and Fairchild. All the primes undertake much more subcontract work from each other than in the past. Hence, the competition for any one prime contract is all the more intense and the "improvements" offered all the more extravagant.

The role of industry in determining the shape of armaments is also apparent in the effects of the changing composition of the industry. Throughout the 1950s, the Air Force and Navy aircraft dominated the military budget and the aircraft industry dominated military production. As technical advance proceeded, the electronics industry played an increasingly important role, but nearly always as a subcontractor to the aircraft industry. When guided missiles were introduced, the aircraft companies became the prime contractors for all except the smallest missiles, despite the fact the electronic equipment accounted for two-thirds the cost of a missile. Similarly, the Air Force established hegemony over land-based missiles, despite the moot question as to whether they should be treated as bombers or artillery. The issues were vividly illustrated in the Thor-Jupiter missile controversy of the 1950s. Both were intermediate-range ballistic missiles. The Jupiter missile was designed at the Army's Redstone Arsenal (this form of design was known as the Arsenal system) under the leadership of the German wartime scientist Dr. Werner von Braun, and was to be produced by Chrysler in government-owned facilities. The Thor missile, which was eventually the winner, was one of a series of Air Force missiles whose

> complexes included 18,000 scientists and technicians in universities and industry, 70,000 others in 22 industries including 17 prime contractors and over 200 subcontractors as well as innumerable smaller suppliers. This broad industrial base constituted a significant political asset to the Air Force.[28]

The Air Force victory was widely viewed as a victory for the aircraft industry.

> At that time, the industry was in the unhappy state of a producer falling upon evil days with but a single buyer—the government—and facing competition from new sources—the Army and Navy and their industrial affiliates. If the Air Force was interested in excluding the Army from missile and space missions, the airframe industry was equally desirous of eliminating competition from the automobile industry and liquidating the competition emanating at that time from the Redstone Arsenal missile engineering team. They also wished to discredit the concept of weapons development implicit in the Army's Arsenal system.[29]

During this period, the unit cost of aircraft rose much faster than the unit cost of ground vehicles and ships. Further, the large cost overruns of the 1950s largely applied to aerospace systems. Merton J. Peck and Walter Scherer, in a study at the Harvard Business School on the weapons acquisition process published in 1962, showed that on twelve major weapons systems of the 1950s, final costs were 2.3 times greater than original estimates.[30] A study undertaken at around the same time concluded that cost overruns, and hence the overall rate of cost increases, were related to the degree of technical advance sought, i.e., the "improvements"

offered. The study found that cost estimates for equipment re-
sembling commercial equipment (i.e., cargoes or tankers), tended
to be fairly accurate because the design did not push the state of
the art.[31] A similar conclusion was reached in a later Rand Corporation study.[32]

THE McNAMARA ERA

The dominant role of air power was somewhat checked by the
Kennedy Administration, which introduced the strategy of flexible
response and increased the budget for conventional weapons. The
conditions which brought forth this change of policy were characterised by the same interrelated combination of insecurity and
industrial depression that had, on a larger scale, characterised previous impulses for increased military spending. As the postwar
boom came to an end and as America's industrial competitors re-
covered from defeat, American economic growth began to slow
down. America experienced the first balance-of-payments deficit in
1957; the balance of trade remained in surplus, but it was not large
enough to finance overseas military spending. Economic insecurity
was compounded by new challenges to American hegemony. These
came not merely from an increasing assertion of independence by
industrialised countries, particularly the newly formed Common
Market countries, but also from increasing violence in the Third
World, especially in Southeast Asia and Latin America. The realisa-
tion that massive retaliation could not contain revolution was the
main reason for the new doctrine of limited conventional war. But
the emphasis on increased purchases of conventional weapons also
had to do with the situation of the arms-producing industries.

With the at least temporary slowdown in the growth of the
American domestic consumer market, particularly for automobiles,
and the declining American share of world trade, many companies
sought alternative outlets. Overseas investment was one alternative,
and this was the period when American corporations began to
move abroad on a massive scale. Defense was another. The defense-
space market-research study quoted above explained that

in the ten years following World War II, consumer and industrial markets provided a large backlog of demand that made it
profitable for manufacturing companies to concentrate on commercial products. During recent years, many of those markets
have become saturated, and profit margins on commercial lines
have fallen. In consequence, defense business, which tradition-
ally has a moderate profit margin, has come to appear more
attractive.[33]

The Kennedy Administration was part of the first political postwar generation; it reflected the enthusiasms of World War II and
the belief that mass production, advanced technology, private
enterprise, military efficiency, and economic well-being were a viable
combination. McNamara, the Secretary of Defense, together with
his systems analysts, entered government at a time when the
follow-ons ordered in the 1950s were coming to fruition and the
pressure on the military budget was already large. He increased the
Navy and Army budgets and extended the methods of aircraft
procurement to the procurement of vehicles and ships. Design
work, which had previously been undertaken in-house by the Navy
and Army, was contracted out to shipbuilders and automobile
companies. He also attempted to encourage series production by
reducing the number of weapons systems both developed and produced. In the end, McNamara simply added new dimensions to
the military-industrial complex. Ships and tanks increased in cost
and complexity. Companies compensated for reductions in the
number of contracts by cramming more new technology into a
single system, and this accelerated the growth of unit costs. Members of the Kennedy Administration believed they could impose
"rational" and efficient solutions on defence problems. What they
failed to understand was that the underlying institutional structure
of defence perverted the notion of military rationality.

In shipbuilding, for example, a number of aerospace companies
and other corporate giants purchased shipyards in anticipation of
new orders and new ways of doing things. Lockheed, General Dy-

namics, and Litton all entered the shipbuilding business. Under
pressure from McNamara, the Navy embarked upon a number of
ship-construction programs, according to which the warships were
to be designed by the shipyard (following aircraft practise) and all
were to be built in one yard (in order to realise production savings).
A recent post-McNamara example of these programs was the order
for thirty destroyers to be built by Litton. The government built a
brand-new mass-production yard for the purpose. The target price
was $1.79 billion for thirty destroyers and the ceiling price was $2.1
billion. By 1977, only ten had been completed and the estimated
price had risen to over $3 billion. There were constant changes in
design which made nonsense of the automatic production line, and
an extraordinary proliferation of control procedures. Others in the
shipbuilding business argue, though they probably exaggerate, that
under the old methods of Navy procurement, where contracts,
based on a standard Navy design, were let out to a number of shipyards, to be built with existing facilities, the ships could have been
built for $950 million and completed by 1972 or 1973.[34] During the
1970s a number of shipyards experienced major cost overruns on
naval programs, and a series of claims against the Navy for cost es-
calation, allegedly due to customer-induced design changes, created
a major public controversy. Many commentators argued that the
problems arose from the Navy's addiction to "buying the most technologically advanced ships,"[35] in particular, Admiral Rickover's
attempt to create a "nuclear-powered Navy," and the emphasis on
very sophisticated equipment. But it is interesting that this addiction was not really significant until the 1960s, when the shipyards
were given the opportunity to compete in realising every sailor's
technological fantasy.

The same philosophy was applied to the production of tanks. In
order to increase the volume of production, McNamara decided
that the next tank had to be a joint United States–German project.
To make best possible use of private enterprise, the contract was
awarded on the basis of a design competition between General
Motors and Chrysler. GM won the competition, despite the fact

that Chrysler was the traditional tank contractor. The MBT–70, as the tank was called, was a total contrast to previous tank designs, which were characterised by "evolutionary" improvements. Since World War II, unit costs for tanks had risen by 4 percent a year, compared with an average of 20 percent for other types of weapons systems.[36] The MBT–70 pushed the state of the art in every system and subsystem. Costs soared and the project was finally cancelled by Congress in 1972, because it was too expensive and had too many extravagant features. (The Germans had pulled out in 1968.) In 1972, the cost was estimated at $850,000–$1 million per tank. The MBT–70 was succeeded by the XM–1, which was supposed to be a cheaper, simpler version of an austere version of MBT–70 known as XM–803. Chrysler was selected as prime contractor, in competition first with Germany and then with GM. Chrysler offered greater "commonality" with the German Leopard tank. The 1978 estimate for the unit cost of the XM–1 was $1.46 million, which was already 2.3 times greater than the most advanced tank in the American tank inventory.[37]

Two other famous examples of the McNamara approach are the TFX combat plane, better known as the F–111, and the C–5A aircraft. The TFX was McNamara's attempt to reduce the number of different types of weapons systems produced by persuading the services to share a combat plane. It was an extreme example of squeezing too much technology into a single piece of hardware. The Army pulled out at an early stage. The contract was awarded to General Dynamics and Grumman, despite Air Force and Navy preference for Boeing. McNamara favoured the General Dynamics–Grumman team because they offered greater commonality between the Air Force and Navy versions, that is to say, the two versions had more common parts. The original program, including orders from the U.K., anticipated a production of 1,700 planes at a unit cost of $3.4 million. In 1968, both the Navy and Britain cancelled their versions because of poor performance. Many F–111s crashed in Vietnam, and in the end, those that remained were grounded. By 1976, production was completed with 562 F–111s. The unit development and production cost was estimated by the General Accounting Office at the time to be $14.9 million.

The C–5A was an attempt to reduce the number of different systems under development. Under previous weapons-system-acquisition methods, competition took place at the development stage after several different prototypes had been constructed. This was considered a costly approach, especially since it was difficult to cancel a program after it had reached the development stage. (Interestingly, the "fly before you buy" approach was reintroduced by David Packard in the 1970s. The consequence was the acquisition of both the F–16 and the F–18 fighters, which were originally designed as competing prototypes.)

McNamara negotiated with Lockheed a so-called Total Package Procurement contract for the C–5A at the design stage. The price was fixed. Lockheed ran into considerable problems with the plane, the most serious being overweight. In order to meet the specifications of the Department of Defense, Lockheed had to remove about 14,000 pounds from the airframe structure, mostly the wing. This proved immensely costly. The resulting $2 billion cost overrun brought Lockheed to the verge of bankruptcy. The order for the planes was reduced from 180 to 81, and the removal of weight so greatly weakened the wing joint that after five years the wings began to crack. Currently, the government is proposing to retrofit a "new" wing at a cost of more than $1.3 billion (1977 prices), which will, ultimately, reduce the range and/or carrying capacity of the aircraft.

Vietnam

The limited war doctrine which underlay the strategy of flexible response and the procurement of conventional weapons found expression in Vietnam. The realities of a capital-intensive war, and the military consequences when the subjective and somewhat nostalgic thinking of military designers was called to account in war, are discussed in a later chapter. From the point of view of the industry, the Vietnam War was a boom period. The war mostly affected ordnance, which was produced in government arsenals and by the automobile industry; there was a regional shift of defence procurement from California and Massachusetts to the Midwest[38] and increases in the defence sales of automobile companies. Large numbers of helicopters were also purchased for the war effort. In addition, the war coincided with a boom in commercial air transportation and in space exploration (1968 was the year of the moon landing); this came to an end, even before the war was over. In the early 1970s, the defence industry experienced a recession unequalled since 1946. In the aerospace industry as a whole, employment fell from 1,402,000 in 1969 to 922,000 in 1973. For some companies, the fall was even greater. At General Electric's Missile and Space Division, employment fell from 103,000 to 35,000 between 1968 and 1972. At Boeing's Everett plant in Seattle, which was built especially for the 747, employment was reduced from 25,000 to 10,000 and the plant was still producing seven planes a month. Indeed, such was the dependence of Seattle on Boeing that a large poster was erected on the main highway out of Seattle, with the legend "Will the last person to leave Seattle please turn out the lights?" The Japanese sent food parcels to unemployed Boeing workers. At the C–5A plant in Georgia, Lockheed had to fire some of its most prized engineers. The Vice President of Research and Development is said to have decided in 1968 to identify a technical cadre in case Lockheed should have to retrench. He had just completed the exercise when the C–5A program was terminated at 81 instead of 180 planes. The resources of the Marietta-Georgia plant, which covered 30,000 people, were drastically cut, and this included the technical cadre.

But the real victims of the recession were, in addition to workers, the subcontractors: small companies, often with fewer than ten employees, and often created by the big corporations in order to produce a specialised piece of equipment at lower cost. The advent of the recession led the primes to "pull back" as much work as possible from the subcontractors, who often accounted for over 50

percent of the work on a particular project. Thousands of subcontractors went bankrupt in 1969 and 1970, and by 1972, the
failure was about 2 percent a month.[39]

Clearly this situation could not last long. The defence companies,
stripped to a bare minimum, could not survive without defence
contracts. At the time, many corporations believed that there
would have to be a shake-out and one of the primes would have to
go under. Lockheed was considered the likely candidate. But Lockheed merely illuminated the strength of the industry's political
position. The C–5A scandal, together with problems of the Tri
Star commercial transport, threatened to bankrupt Lockheed unless government assistance was forthcoming. The Air Force would
probably have been prepared to sacrifice Lockheed so long as a
production line for military-transport aircraft continued to exist;
their concern was with Lockheed as a production line rather than
as a company. Lockheed's Missile and Space Division at Sunny-
vale, California, was very important to the Navy, but it could have
been re-created as an independent company. Lockheed's appeal for
government assistance was a fail-safe mechanism. If it succeeded,
as it did, Lockheed maintained its capability in transport aircraft.
If it failed, Lockheed would merely have to reorganise itself around
its profitable parts. The vote in Congress was an open demonstra-
tion of the strength of the California lobby, and an example of the
"bail-out imperative."

There has been a revival of the traditional argument about the
need to maintain excess capacity for mobilisation in time of war.
The Pentagon has come up with a new version, which avoids the
pitfalls of envisaging arms production on a large scale in the event
of an all-out nuclear war. This is the notion of a "surge" capability.
Jacques S. Gansler, the former Deputy Assistant Secretary of Defense, whose name has been associated with the idea, told the
Joint Committee on Defense Production:

We have become aware that our previous planning was more
in terms of first, just normal peacetime procurement, and sec-

ond, all-out mobilization with total impact in fact on the civil
sector. It is the part in between which has not been properly
planned for in the past. We are now starting to go in that direction. We are now giving guidance to the services in terms of
planning for rapid increase of surge in a peacetime environment
such as, for example, Herman Kahn's talk about a mobilization
war environment—that sort of thing even in peacetime.[40]

Elsewhere, Gansler has urged the need "to institutionalize the concept that the defense industrial base is a national resource."[41]

Indeed, Gansler's arguments have now become commonplace in
public justifications for new arms programs. In making the case
for acquiring the XM-1 Main Battle Tank and its associated
family of weapons systems—the Infantry Fighting Vehicle, ground-
attack aircraft, improved artillery, etc.—Percy A. Pierre, Assistant
Secretary of the Army for Research, Development and Acquisition,
and Lieutenant General Donald R. Keith, Deputy Chief of Staff
for Research, Development and Acquisition, argued:

> Our defense industrial base is not in good shape. Facilitizing
> for and maintaining a warm production base for our most essen-
> tial equipment insures a responsiveness that we believe this
> nation must have.
>
> If we produce all the weapons systems we have developed,
> we will be creating a modern production capacity for very highly
> leveraged weaponry, a capacity that could be expanded rapidly
> in case of war or threat of war. If we were to shelve some of
> these weapons so as to produce larger quantities of the others,
> we would in effect be eliminating them from our arsenal. Ad-
> vanced attack helicopters and air defense missile plants do not
> spring up overnight; the tooling is too complex and specialized
> and the talent pool too difficult to round up and train. . . .[42]

The recession in the arms industry of the early 1970s was, of
course, part of a wider world economic recession and a sense of
political instability not experienced since World War II. In 1971,

the United States experienced its first balance-of-trade deficit and
the dollar was devalued. 1973 was the year of the oil crisis. Europeans and Japanese were displaying an unusual independence.
Defeat in Vietnam and the coup in Portugal sharply reduced the
U.S. sphere of influence. And, domestically, the postwar consensus
about U.S. foreign and domestic policies was seriously questioned
for the first time.

The symbolic response to these problems was not long in coming. The Nixon Administration introduced a number of new major
aerospace projects, including the B–1 bomber, the space shuttle,
the F–14 and F–15 fighters, and what was to become AWACS, the
airborne look-down radar system. Under Deputy Assistant Secretary of Defense David Packard, reforms in the weapons-acquisition
process were introduced; their main effect was to make the abuses
less visible. Packard's "high-low" mix, whereby low-cost weapons
systems were to be built alongside expensive, sophisticated systems,
helped to spread contracts around but did little to alter the direction of military technical change. The "low," as we shall see,
showed disturbing tendencies to approach the "high." The Nixon
Administration also encouraged the export of arms. As these projects approached fruition under the Carter Administration, military
spending began to rise again.

Thus, since 1945 the arms industry has developed its own
momentum, that increased the American rate of armament. There
have been three periods when major jumps occurred in postwar
military spending: the early 1950s, when the follow-on system
came into being with the first postwar generation of aircraft; the
mid-1960s, when the second generation of postwar weapons systems were produced and when the automobile and shipbuilding
industries were incorporated into the follow-on system and infected
by baroque technology; and the late 1970s, when the third generation of postwar weapons systems came to fruition. Each jump occurred in an atmosphere of international tension and, to some
extent, economic insecurity, and the first two at least were associated with a shift in military strategy. Nevertheless, the fact that the

response to these external factors took the form that it did and occurred at the time that it did is much more easily explained in terms of the logic of the follow-on than in terms of the logic of the world political and military situation.

Consequences

The tendency to design and produce more weapon per weapon has parallels in the defence-related sectors—automobiles, commercial aircraft, and merchant ships. Alfred Sloan, the president of General Motors, who is regarded as the creator of planned obsolescence for cars in the 1930s, told *Fortune* magazine in 1953:

> In the postwar sellers' market, [the auto industry] has found itself selling more car per car—more accessories, luxuries, improvements and innovations. Now it has to plan it that way. . . . The widening spread between unit demand and purchasing power will create a powerful drive to sell still more car per unit.[43]

Planned obsolescence consists of product rather than process improvement. Product improvement is characteristic of the early and late stages of an industry. In contrast, process improvement, which results in lowering the costs of a product, is a characteristic of the middle and successful stage of industrial development.

In the early increasing returns phase of a technology, manufacturers experiment with the product and each new version may represent an enormous improvement on the earlier version. As the design of a product stabilises, as its market is tested and proved, manufacturers turn to the production process; they introduce new machinery and ways of organising labour to undercut rivals. In the later stages of technical development, when a mass market and a mechanical production process is established, manufacturers often revert to product improvement, to the attempt to attract customers through the extra gimmick or a new fashion, so that enormous expense may be expended in a relatively minor "improvement."[44] In peacetime, as we have seen, the emphasis of military technology is on such product improvement. Process improvement, by lowering the cost of weapons, could result in an overall financial reduction in the size of the military market. The government is the only customer and has to be persuaded to buy more weapon per weapon, not cheaper weapons.

Planned obsolescence could be said to be a sign of technological stagnation, a sign that the technologies of car making, aircraft manufacture, and shipbuilding, at least in the United States, have reached a point, which all technologies reach sooner or later, of diminishing returns, where new investments yield ever smaller improvements in productivity and hence competitiveness, where quality becomes more important than quantity, because new markets cannot be captured and old markets can only be preserved through apparent qualitative improvements. This is a characteristic of industries during the declining phase of a long wave. Baroque military technology could be seen as an extreme form of planned obsolescence. Because the consumer is the government, tastes can be more easily imposed, and there is almost no external discipline, as there is in a commercial market, on the so-called improvements which can be offered.

Since the automobile and aircraft industries dominate the U.S. economy, the consequences of baroque technology, this manifestation of technological stagnation, are pervasive. After World War II, the dynamism of the early twentieth century was never regained. To be sure, the 1950s and 1960s were a boom period. Military spending may have contributed to the boom, stimulating demand and providing technological spin-off, especially in the electronics industry. But the signs of economic decline could already be detected. From 1950, productivity growth lagged well behind Europe and Japan, and investment as a share of GNP was lower than any other advanced industrial country. (Japan had the fastest productivity growth and the highest rate of investment as a share of GNP and the lowest rate of military spending as a share of GNP.) America continued to be the highest spender on research and development (R&D), but a large share of this spending was devoted to military purposes. In the late 1960s, Germany and Japan overtook the United States in the share of GNP devoted to civilian research and development. Furthermore, most of the German and Japanese R&D went to the fast-growing sectors of chemicals and electronics and was undertaken by private corporations, whereas in the United States the bulk of civil R&D went to aerospace and was financed by the government.[45]

Military spending, as we have seen, was partly a response to the problems of the defence-related sectors. And these, in turn, were the dominant industries. High military spending could thus be viewed as a consequence of economic decline. But the causal connection need not be only one-way. If military spending played a role akin to overseas investment in the cumulative process of Britain's decline, might not the same be true for the United States? It has been widely argued that U.S. overseas investment is both a cause and a consequence of the slowdown in the American rate of growth. The same might also be true of military spending.

In her study of the automobile industry, Emma Rothschild argues that the auto business

> like all dominant industries—and like the British railroad industry in the nineteenth century— . . . depended for its early glorious growth on the sustenance of social and institutional partiality. Such support provided roads, a favorable tax structure, a dispersal of cities and jobs. It encouraged the decay of alternative modes of transportation, and suspended rational calculation of the costs of auto development and auto waste: it made possible the great and sustained power of American demand for automobiles.[46]

This "partiality," which was once such an asset, could be said to become a liability as the limits of auto-industrial development are reached. For it preserves and promotes the auto-industrial structure; it entails a kind of technological overdevelopment, which fetters the growth of new sectors and new technologies. Military spending, it can be argued, is one aspect of the "social and institutional partiality." Just as British war production depended primarily on the dominant engineering and shipbuilding industries, so American war production depended on the automobile and aircraft industries. In both cases, military spending became a central part of the industrial culture.

The industrial culture of the United States was based, first and foremost, on the automobile. By the late 1920s, the only innovations which had still to come were the all-steel body, the infinitely variable automatic transmission, and the "drop frame" construction. By the Great Depression, the American automobile industry was already fully developed. By 1930, there was one car for every five-and-a-half Americans, a degree of auto saturation that was not reached by Britain until 1966 and by Holland until 1970. At that time, the industry had also settled down to its characteristic market structure, dominated by the three giants, GM, Ford, and Chrysler. Such increases in auto sales as occurred in the late 1930s were due primarily to Alfred Sloan's styling changes, the new doctrine of planned obsolescence. The Depression was a signal, if ever there was one, of the necessity for change. Yet change was postponed by World War II. The war entrenched the position of the big three,[47] expanded industrial capacity, and suppressed consumer demand, making both necessary and possible the postwar auto boom. It thus allowed for a renewal, albeit temporary, of prewar expansion and confirmed the direction of industrial change. Except during Korea, the military market was never again so important for the automobile industry, although for most of the period the big three were among the top twenty-five prime military contractors, and during Vietnam their defense sales increased somewhat. When the domestic postwar boom came to an end, overseas investment proved a much more important outlet—with much the same consequences. Military spending, it could be said, contributed indirectly to overseas investment, although this is outside the scope of the present argument, by helping to create the kind of political conditions abroad favourable to overseas investment. The continued emphasis of the American auto industry on big cars, on stylish

extras and minute but fashionable variations, has ironically under-
mined the effectiveness of those same Fordist techniques which
created the American auto industry and underlay the triumph of
World War II. The modern equivalents of the Model T are the
Toyotas and VWs, which have captured a significant share of the
American market.

The aircraft industry was much younger than the auto industry
when war broke out. The major innovations had been made. The
DC–2, which was introduced in 1934, and its successor, the DC–3,
which carried 95 percent of U.S. civilian air traffic by 1938, introduced the all-metal body, wing flaps, the variable pitch propeller,
cantilever design, and significant improvements in power plants,
and was not so very different from a modern airliner. The only
major innovation introduced after the war was the jet engine.
But the aircraft industry before World War II had not reached
the stage of mass production. There was a sense, on the eve of
World War II, that future innovations in the aircraft industry
would be process improvements, the introduction of mechanization to reduce costs and thus increase the volume of the market.
Most of the aircraft manufacturers in the late 1930s were installing
expensive facilities in anticipation of assembly-line operations for
civil aircraft production. The engine maker, Pratt and Whitney,
which, in its history, had run the whole gamut of mass production
from firearms to sewing machines, bicycles, and automobiles, was
among the first to establish a mass-production facility. In 1937, the
president of Curtiss-Wright said that it had become "apparent that
aviation was embarking upon an era when quantity production was
at a greater premium than at any time in the industry except during the hectic days of the World War."[48]

The war and the subsequent dependence on the military market
can be said to have stunted the development of the aircraft industry, to have shifted the industry from the design emphasis
characteristic of the early phases of an industry, which involved
increasing returns as each new investment yielded important inno-

vations, to the design emphasis characteristic of the later stages of an industry, more aircraft per aircraft, without ever going through the stage of production engineering. In the postwar period, only Boeing managed to make a profit on commercial aircraft, and that was not until after the introduction of the Boeing 727 in the 1960s and after Boeing had failed to win two major contracts for bombers —the B–70 and the TFX—so that designers were forced to focus on commercial aircraft and concluded, in the words of one, that the "more an airliner resembles a bomber the less successful it will be."[49]

The military market froze the structure of the aircraft industry— a deliberate decision that stemmed from the conclusions of the Finletter Commission—so that it was very difficult for any individual company to obtain an adequate volume of orders. More importantly, the dominance of military thinking infected the approach to civilian design and marketing. The massive engineering teams which proliferate ideas, problems of technical coordination, undetected mistakes, cost and complexity, and the constant striving for periodic improvements in performance were all applied to commercial aircraft. For example, over a thousand people designed the Boeing 727. According to Ronald Miller and David Sawers:

> Military development methods appear to be so ingrained into the consciousness of the industry that it cannot change, even where it is free of close supervision of the design and cutting costs is vital to its prosperity. . . . Having established the habit of mass design and created the teams to employ it, manufacturers seem to find themselves trapped; it almost appears as if they are unable to control their teams, which is not surprising when they have become so vast.[50]

If the American aircraft industry, despite its lack of profitability, still dominates the world market, it is only because of the strength of the "social and institutional partiality," the network of airports, the volume of American commercial air traffic (which might be much greater were commercial aircraft designed more efficiently), the indirect financial support from military and space expenditures, and a successful commercial past.

The American shipbuilding industry was stunted from the very beginning. It never had a commercial past. The United States had a flourishing wooden shipbuilding industry in the mid-nineteenth century. But the introduction of iron ships was largely a naval invention. The shipyards which were constructed in the late nineteenth century to participate in the pre-1914 naval arms race were largely the same as those in operation today. They are almost entirely dependent on the Navy and on the Maritime Administration, which subsidises the construction of ships for the U.S. Merchant Marine. The main problems of U.S. shipbuilding are said to be the "small number, great variety and high unit cost of units produced." This is ascribed to the high standards of U.S. design, the performance rather than cost orientation of the designer, the custom-built approach, much of which is a consequence of "government dominance."[51] It is said that

> past [naval] procurement practices, whose stated purpose was to preserve our mobilization base by spreading orders, have had exactly the opposite effect. World War II shipyards were preserved but not improved. The building of one or two ships at a time only preserved the capability to build large numbers of such ships.[52]

The same applies both to warships and to merchant ships.

The counter example is the electronics industry.[53] Few would deny the proposition that the military market has been of critical importance in the technical revolution which created the electronics industry and the dominant position of U.S. firms. Closer inspection, however, may reveal that electronics is the exception that proves the rule. Electronics companies are, by and large, subcontractors to the aerospace and automobile primes. The potential of military electronics has hardly begun to be realised. Many com-

mentators believe, as we shall see in a later chapter, that the various
technical changes associated with developments in electronics have
rendered obsolete the modern weapons system and that it is the
structure of the armed forces—and, by implication, the defence
industry—that explains the continuing attachment to aircraft and
tanks and thus hinders the full development of military electronics.
This discrimination or reverse partiality may well turn out to exist
in the civilian sphere as well. That is to say, precisely because of
the entrenched position of the automobile and aircraft industries
and the existence of a whole industrial culture which influences
patterns of consumption, production processes, and ideas about
design, a larger share of consumer and investment expenditure
is spent on the products of those industries than is the case in
other less arms-intensive economies. Consequently, a smaller proportion of consumer and investment expenditure is available for
the electronics industry than is the case in Japan, say, or even
some European countries, and consumers and investors may be
less receptive to new electronic technologies than in these other
countries.

The electronics industry can be roughly divided into four: electronic components, e.g., semiconductors, microprocessors etc;
consumer-end items, e.g., audio-visual equipment, calculators, digi-
tal watches, etc.; electronic applications to industrial products,
e.g., numerically controlled machine tools; and military end-items,
e.g., command and control equipment, precision guided munitions,
etc. The United States lead in electronics is based on its role in
electronic componentry. The Japanese are the leading manufacturers of consumer-end items. They now account for approximately
half the U.S. market. The Europeans, particularly the Germans,
together with the Japanese, are at the forefront of electronic applications to industrial products.

The United States lead in electronic componentry is based on its
virtual monopoly over innovation. Since the war, there have been
three revolutionary innovations in electronic componentry: the

transistor, the integrated circuit, and the microprocessor. Each innovation has caused an upheaval in the market and has utterly changed the composition of the industry. New companies have entered the market with new devices or new production processes and have achieved a leading position within a few years. The transistor was invented by the Bell Laboratories of Western Electric in 1948. The integrated circuit was invented by Texas Instruments in 1959 and perfected by Fairchild. The microprocessor was invented by Intel. All these inventions were financed by private funds. Although military research and development has accounted for a significant share of total R&D expenditure, it appears to have yielded few commercial applications. A survey by the Department of Defense in 1960 showed that very few patents arose from government-funded R&D, and very few of these were used commercially. Likewise, Texas Instruments reported that between 1949 and 1959, only 5 of 112 patents awarded to the company were developed under government contract, although the government funded two-fifths of R&D spending. Further, only 2 of the 5 patents were used commercially.[54] (These figures may, of course, be distorted by the fact that companies like to finance commercially profitable inventions independently.)

Nevertheless, the military market played an important role in promoting the inventions of, at least, the transistor and the integrated circuit. In the case of the integrated circuit, the U.S. Air Force had a contract for the development of molecular electronics with Westinghouse at the time; this was somewhat similar to what eventually resulted in the integrated circuit. More important, military procurement provided an initial outlet for new devices at a time when the unit cost was too high for the industrial and consumer markets, i.e., during the increasing returns phase of the industry. As experience was gained through military production, unit costs fell and it became possible to apply the innovation in the commercial market. Thus the major contribution of the government was the creation of a

conducive climate. . . . The various government agencies, by
their insistent demand for electronic components that were more
reliable and smaller, continually maintained a pressure on the
industry to move toward these goals. The military services and
NASA created an atmosphere of urgency which carried a double meaning. For those firms who could develop the desired
devices, the government would be a very obvious first customer;
for those who did not generate improved components, the government might not be a customer at all. . . . This "carrot and
stick" theme had its effects both on the components and systems
houses and especially upon those companies that greatly relied
upon military procurement for their livelihood. For a firm less
dependent upon the military and NASA as a company, it saw a
first customer willing to pay the higher initial price—assuming
the right product could be developed—that would facilitate the
offering of a product line to a non-military, non-space clientele.[55]

In the case of the microprocessor, the invention was a direct
response to a request from a Japanese calculator company, Busi-
com, for a sophisticated custom integrated circuit. But it is probably
fair to say that the innovative activity at Intel, which was a spin-off
from Fairchild, could trace its historic roots to the climate fostered
by the military market in the war and in the 1950s.

This is not a surprising conclusion when one compares the history of other major technologies. Mass-production methods were
pioneered in the U.S. firearms industry in the early part of the
nineteenth century. The initial European lead in the manufacture
of automobiles and aircraft was the consequence of military support. In the early stages of technical development, as in the late
stages, when the product is not sufficiently cheap or efficient to
meet commercial standards, government support may prove highly
significant. The question is whether such support also promotes
the diffusion to commercial markets in the long run, whether it
is beneficial at the middle stages. And here the evidence is much

less clear. It was the United States, unfettered by the military partialities of another technological epoch, that reaped the commercial benefits of the automobile and the aircraft. And it may prove to be Japan and perhaps Western Europe that reap the full benefits of the American innovations in electronics technology.

John Tilton, in a study undertaken for the Brookings Institution, argued that the rate of diffusion of new innovations in electronic components was dependent on market opportunities and not on the availability of technology.[56] Because of a liberal licensing and patent policy and the mobility of engineers and scientists, no innovation can be monopolised for long. Initially, the diffusion of American innovations to Japanese and European firms lagged several years behind domestic American firms, because the military market is much smaller in these countries. As the cost of a device fell sufficiently to compete in the commercial market, the innovation was diffused abroad and the United States' comparative advantage declined. The favourable trade balance in electronic componentry was thus due to continued American product innovation and the dominance of the military market.

As the military share of the market for electronic end items has declined and as design emphasis in the industry has shifted from product improvement to process improvement, this favourable trade balance is being whittled away. Already, the Japanese have captured over 50 percent of the U.S. market for the 16K RAM memory chips, which is middle to established technology, and are rapidly gaining in the markets for 64K, 128K, and 150K chips. Patents taken out by Japanese subsidiaries in the United States increased by 32 percent every year between 1963 and 1977. There is now growing pressure from U.S. companies for the introduction of tariffs. And the main reason for the loss of American leadership is said to be the preoccupation with product technology that stems from experience in the design of the baroque weapons system, from the lack of interest in process technology which would reduce costs and increase the competitiveness of civilian products. The big innovating manufacturers have increasingly moved out of the military market and

> have sought high volume, non-military users which they consider more accessible and less encumbered by constraints imposed, for instance, by the temperature and high-reliability demands typical of military applications.[57]

Small companies which produce custom-built high price and performance componentry, and aerospace contractors with electronics capabilities like Rockwell, have remained in the military business.

In November 1978, the Pentagon announced a new program which would spend $150 million on a new generation of ultra-high-speed, high-density integrated circuits—VHSI (Very High Speed Integrated Circuits). The successful electronics companies were not interested. According to one executive: "We could all benefit from submicron line widths and bigger memories. But those incredibly complex VHSI circuits the military wants don't seem to have their use elsewhere."[58] Intel publicly announced that it would not take part in the program. *Business Week* reported that Intel executives were worried that

> a big infusion of government money will disrupt the VLSI (Very Large Scale Integrated circuits—currently the focus of commercial technology) effort, because the industry currently is hard pressed to find enough technicians and engineers to keep up with the soaring demand for its high technology devices.[59]

It is significant that the three major non-military microprocessor companies have ties with Japanese end users. This fact, combined with the more rapid growth of the Japanese electronics consumer market and the rapid international penetration of Japanese consumer-end products and Japanese and European NC machine tools, suggests that as innovation slows down and as more emphasis is accorded to production, to new end uses for electronic devices and to the cheapening of devices, the leading position of U.S.-based manufacturers will continue to be eroded.

This suggests a paradoxical result. American preeminence in aircraft and electronics is due, in part, to the sheer volume of military resources. And yet the military orientation of these industries—and indeed the military market as a whole—impedes current and future commercial developments which provide the economic basis for military spending.

The result can be generalised. American military power has been based on the strength and dynamism of American industry. It is probably true that, in the postwar world, American military power was needed to underwrite the Western economic system and the spectacular long boom. But the form and cost of American military power cannot be so directly related to the international economy and geopolitics. The ritualistic replay of World War II in the acquisition of ever more sophisticated aircraft and tanks and in the imaginary extension of strategic air missions as the nuclear armoury grew more grotesque was peculiarly an outcome of the American industrial structure. It has served to preserve this structure, and to extend it, ironically, in ways that were probably quite alien to its original creators. World War II marked the beginning of a kind of self-consciousness about American achievements that prevented their ever being repeated.

American economic growth in the early part of the century, as we have seen, had been centred on the automobile and the techniques of mass production. The Depression was the depression of the automobile. It marked a turning point in industrial history— the saturation of the automobile market, the slowdown in automotive innovation, the end of the heyday of mass production. Like the depression of the 1880s, it was a signal, not necessarily recognised at the time, for new technologies and new directions in industrial change. Instead, the war confirmed the importance of the automobile industry and interrupted the full development of the commercial aircraft industry. It entrenched the "social and institutional partiality" for the automobile and the aircraft. And, as a

consequence, continued military spending after the war inhibited
commercially-oriented innovation in the defence-related sectors
and eventually constrained the development of new sectors. Military spending absorbed resources that might otherwise have been
used for domestic investment or public consumption and attracted
industrial energies that might have been deployed elsewhere. It
recruited the best scientists and engineers, and infected ideas and
methods of innovation. "Through the advent of R&D," writes
Robert Solo,

> those who were or might have been restless, probing industrial-
> ists, innovating entrepreneurs, or inventors tinkering in the shops
> became, instead, engineers on project teams, heads of research
> divisions, scientists in laboratories, or subcontractors with the
> task of developing a component for a complex weapon system.[60]

It consolidated the corporate giants and created tier upon tier of
management and tier upon tier of smaller dependent companies,
and thus suppressed the very creativity that had been so central
to its early development. (And this was even true of electronics,
where military R&D spending tended to concentrate on the older
receiving tube firms like Western Electric, General Electric, and
Raytheon.) It institutionalised planned obsolescence, which persuaded the customer to buy more as a consequence of marginal
design improvements (so that there was less to spend on other
things). It was a concept utterly out of keeping with the concepts
of simplicity and cheapness, of egalitarian consumption, that had
prompted American industrial success and underlay the very victory
of World War II to which soldiers and industrialists harked.

The cyclical process that we have observed in late-nineteenth-
century Britain was repeated in America, although it was obscured
perhaps by the abruptness of war. After World War II, technological stagnation and hence periodic recession led to increased
military spending—a reassertion of American predominance with
the symbols of military power which were also the products of
the depressed sectors. And increased military spending further

channelled technical change in what might be called decadent directions, reinforcing stagnation and establishing the conditions for worse recessions in the future.

It is not a cycle that can continue indefinitely. Decadent technical change in the civilian sphere undermines the economic basis of military spending. Decadent technical change in the military sphere can be challenged in war, as it was in Vietnam. The impending fragility of the weapons system and its associated military and industrial constituencies represents the potential for change. Before we can explore this potential properly, however, we need some understanding of the consequences of the weapons system elsewhere.

4

Soviet Conservatism

From the moment that the Bolsheviks achieved power, Soviet leaders and thinkers were preoccupied with Russia's backwardness, with survival in a world where Western capitalist countries enjoyed industrial and technological dominance. "Those who fall behind," said Stalin, in a speech in 1931,

> get beaten . . . the history of old Russia was the continual beatings she suffered for falling behind. She was beaten by the Turkish beys. She was beaten by the Polish and Lithuanian gentry. She was beaten by the British and French capitalists. She was beaten by the Japanese barons. All beat her—for her backwardness; for cultural backwardness, for political backwardness, for industrial backwardness. . . . Such is the jungle law of capitalism. You are backward, you are weak—therefore, you are wrong; hence, you can be beaten and enslaved. You are mighty—therefore, you are right; hence, we must be wary of you. That is why we must no longer lag behind.[1]

The policies of rapid industrialisation and military build-up initiated by Stalin in the late 1920s were aimed at "catching up" with the West. Behind these notions of "backwardness," "falling behind," and "catching up" lay a linear view of progress—an idea that there is only one way of achieving economic and political strength and that Soviet society would have to move, albeit faster and more efficiently, along directions already charted by the "advanced" capitalist countries. It was this idea that dominated Soviet armaments policy both before and after World War II. In effect, it served to endorse Western military doctrine and Western criteria of what constitutes military power and, by the late 1970s, to establish the Soviet Union as the second superpower, on the basis of those criteria. This fact—Soviet acceptance and, indeed, participation in the Western "weapons systems culture"—was to have immense significance for the rest of the world. It was also not without its effects on the economic and social development of the Soviet Union as a whole.

Any attempt to describe Soviet armaments policy and its role in the Soviet socio-economic system is severely constrained by lack of information, owing to the secrecy that prevails in the U.S.S.R.* There is, however, a small group of academic specialists in Soviet military affairs who painstakingly piece together information from official literature, newspapers, memoirs, Western intelligence services, and Soviet émigrés, and who publish their conclusions in English. This chapter is heavily dependent on their work.

Soviet Armaments Policy

Probably no one knows the true size of Soviet military expenditure. Official figures provided by the Soviet government cannot be relied upon because they are very low and have hardly changed in the last ten years. There is considerable debate about how to detect military spending in other portions of the Soviet budget and about alternative ways to calculate the resources devoted to defence. The resulting estimates vary widely, from 17 million roubles to over 80 million annually (the highest figure being quoted in *Peking Review*), and it is doubtful whether the Soviet government could identify the correct estimate—so blurred is the distinction between military and civilian production and so distorted is the Soviet price system. Nevertheless, most estimates

---

* A State Department economist has described research on Soviet military production as "an exercise in meta-intelligence. Analysts engage in the exegesis of obscure texts, guess at unexplained residues, hunt after analogues and indulge in assumptions."[2]

show similar trends, and these trends suggest that changes in Soviet armaments policy were largely a reaction to United States policy.

In the immediate postwar period, Soviet military spending fell drastically and many military production facilities were converted to civilian purposes. Military spending rose after the American intervention in Korea and fell again after 1954. A slow but steady increase began again in the early 1960s, largely, it appears, in response to the Polaris and Minuteman programs, as well as the new American emphasis on conventional weapons. This increase has apparently been maintained up to the present period, although some estimates[3] suggest that a stabilisation of military spending occurred in the mid-1970s. The reactive nature of Soviet military spending was also suggested in a study, done at Birkbeck College, London, which applied the alternative estimates of Soviet military spending in an action-reaction model of the East-West conflict. The results did seem to show that United States military expenditure had a greater effect on Soviet military expenditure than the other way round.[4] This conclusion seems to be supported by what we know about Soviet military doctrine and the content of military spending.

The military thinking that guides and rationalises Soviet armaments policy largely derives from doctrines developed during the 1930s. These doctrines accompanied the military build-up of the 1930s and the development of a self-sufficient defence industrial base which was such a central feature of the first three five-year plans. They were based on Bolshevik experience during the Civil War and on the new theories of tank and aerial warfare that were emerging in Britain, Italy, and Germany. Essentially, they emphasised the importance of mass "in both the maintenance of large forces-in-being and in the practice of applying large numbers of men and equipment in combat"[5] and the importance of mobility, the offensive, and a balanced combination of weapons and services. After the catastrophic losses in the early part of World War II, these doctrines were applied and their utility was confirmed by the Soviet victory. As was the case for the United States, it was numbers that won the war. The Soviet Union produced 140,000 aircraft and nearly 70,000 tanks during the war. And it was their massive combined offensive that proved decisive. Military leaders continue to emphasise the significance of this experience. According to General Pavlovsky, Deputy Defence Minister, and Commander in Chief of the Land Forces:

> *Thirty years have elapsed since the final battles of the Second World War, in the course of which the Soviet Land Forces enriched themselves with experience in the theory and practice of battles and operations. . . . In spite of the qualitative postwar changes in weaponry and in the methods of their use, this rich experience has not lost its significance and is now an important source of knowledge for training and educating the troops. Scientifically generalized, this experience has found its expression in all manuals of the Soviet armed forces.[6]*

The idea that Soviet forces should be sufficiently large "to repel (or at least absorb) any attack and then to go on and win the war"[7] has continued to govern Soviet military thinking and it justifies the extent of the reaction to the U.S. military posture. It explains, for example, why Soviet nuclear doctrines focus on fighting and winning a nuclear war rather than deterring an unwinnable nuclear war, and this in turn justifies the quantitative build-up of nuclear weapons.

For the Soviet Union, the Second World War was largely a land battle. The Air Force was primarily viewed as an appendage of the ground forces—the "handmaiden" of artillery[8]—and strategic air power was considered unimportant. The Navy had played a marginal role, mostly confined to coastal defence. In the immediate postwar period, despite the dramatic reduction in armed forces, from 11.4 million to 2.9 million between 1945 and 1948, the emphasis on ground forces, designed for theatre operations in Europe, remained. In addition, two new elements were added to Soviet armaments policy, both in response to the postwar American emphasis on strategic air power: nuclear weapons and air defence. The Soviet nuclear-weapons programme was evidently influenced, if not determined, by the United States programme. According to David Holloway:

> The decision to embark on building the bomb was taken in 1942 only after reports had been received that the United States and Germany were already pursuing this goal. The dropping of the bombs on Hiroshima and Nagasaki demonstrated that the bomb could be built and that it was extremely powerful. Before 1945 many Soviet physicists had doubted that the bomb could be built; now the Soviet effort was intensified. Work on the fusion bomb was stepped up after the U.S. explosion of 1952.[9]

The Soviet Union did, during this period, embark on a ballistic-missile-development program, some five years before the United States, but as we shall see, this was in keeping with the Soviet view of nuclear weapons as an extension of artillery to be used against military targets rather than a new approach to strategic nuclear warfare. The importance of air defence, which was quite neglected during the war, was indicated by the decision to create an independent air defense service (PVO–S) in 1948. This was clearly a response to the perceived threat from American long-range bombers. Throughout the 1940s and 1950s, PVO–S received substantial resources, and it is estimated that throughout the period since World War II the U.S.S.R. spent roughly two and a half times what the U.S. spent on antiaircraft defence.[10]

After the outbreak of the Korean War, expenditure on all military branches was increased. The size of the armed forces rose to 4.6 million by 1952, and plans were laid for the construction of an oceangoing navy. After Stalin's death, military spending was curtailed and the ground forces and the surface navy were downgraded. The main priority during this period was the development of ballistic missiles, although again the intermediate- or medium-range ballistic missiles (I/MRBM) received much greater emphasis than intercontinental ballistic missiles (ICBMs). The Soviet Union tested its first ICBM a few months before the

United States, in August 1957, but the programme was plagued with technical difficulties, the missiles were said to be inferior to the American missiles, and only four of the first ICBMs were actually deployed. By 1962, the United States had deployed 294 ICBMs, compared with 75 for the Soviet Union, and by 1964, this number had increased to 834, compared with 190 for the Soviet Union. Further, the United States began, in the late 1950s, to deploy submarine-launched ballistic missiles (SLBMs), nearly ten years before the Soviet Union.

Emphasis on I/MRBMs was in keeping with the Soviet view of nuclear weapons as an extension of artillery, for the destruction of military targets in anticipation of and in association with a ground-based offensive. In December 1959, the Strategic Rocket Forces (SRF) were created as an independent service and its first commander in chief was the former Chief Marshal of Artillery, Nedelin, who also became Deputy Minister of Defence. The Dzerzhinsky Artillery Academy became the Dzerzhinsky Military Engineering Academy, whose curriculum is now said to be fully devoted to the study of missile systems. Stalin apparently always had a "special affection" for artillery.[11]

During this period, the ground forces, long-range aviation, and the surface navy were all reduced. Admiral Gorshkov, writing about this period in 1967, said:

> Unfortunately, we had some quite influential "authorities" who believed that the appearance of nuclear weapons meant that the Navy had completely lost its significance as a branch of the armed forces. In their opinion, all the basic tasks of a future war could be resolved without participation of the Navy at all. . . . Not infrequently, it was claimed that land-based missiles alone would suffice for the destruction of surface strike forces and even of submarines.[12]

The "authorities" presumably included Khrushchev, although he was a patron of Admiral Gorshkov, who never concealed his views, even during visits to the West, on the obsolescence of aircraft, surface ships, and tanks.

In January 1960, Khrushchev announced a radically new force posture and military doctrine to the Supreme Soviet:

> The U.S.S.R. Council of Ministers is submitting for your examination and approval a proposal to reduce our armed forces by another 1,200,000 men. If this proposal is adopted by the Supreme Soviet, our Army and Navy will number 2,423,000.
>
> Our state has a powerful rocket technology. Given the present development of military technology, military aviation and the Navy have lost their former importance. Military aviation is being almost entirely replaced by missiles. We have now sharply reduced and probably will further reduce and even halt production of bombers and obsolete equipment. In the Navy, the submarine fleet is assuming greater importance and surface ships can no longer play the role they played in the past.
>
> In our time, a country's defense capacity is determined not by the number of soldiers it has under arms, the number of men in uniform. Aside from the general political and economic factors of which I have spoken, a country's defense capacity depends to a decisive extent upon the firepower and means of delivery it has.[13]

Khrushchev's announcement sparked off a debate about the idea of minimum deterrence. Khrushchev seems to have been supported by representatives of the strategic rocket forces and the PVO–S, as well as some leading military philosophers, including General Talensky. Khrushchev pointed out in May 1960 that "missiles are not cucumbers, one cannot eat them and one does not require more than a certain number in order to ward off an attack."[14] But he was resisted by the conventional services and traditional military thinkers like Lieutenant Colonel E. Rybkin, who stressed the importance of war-fighting as opposed to war-deterring military doctrine:

> To assert that victory is not at all possible in a nuclear war
> would not only be wrong on theoretical grounds but dangerous
> as well from the political point of view. . . . Any a priori rejec-
> tion of the possibility of victory is harmful because it leads to
> moral disarmament, to a disbelief in victory, and to fatalism and
> passivity.[15]

It was also argued that improved firepower *increased* rather than
decreased the need for quantitative superiority.

Khrushchev's "new look" was undermined by the Berlin crisis of
1961, the growing Sino-Soviet split, and, above all, by the Cuban
missile crisis, which seemed to suggest a massive American nuclear
superiority. The Kennedy Administration, which came to power
in January 1961, announced a number of defence decisions, including the acceleration of the Polaris and Minuteman programs
and an increase in conventional military strength. "Equally important in terms of Soviet threat perceptions," writes one analyst,

> was the crusading rhetoric of the new administration, with its
> willingness to go any place, pay any price, and the detached
> logic of the tough-minded academic strategists who were think-
> ing the unthinkable, and developing theories of limited nuclear
> war.[16]

A new Soviet military build-up appears to date from this period.
In the 1962 edition of *Military Strategy*, edited by General
Sokolovsky, a new synthesis was presented, which

> combined a greatly increased emphasis on strategic missiles and
> nuclear weapons with a determined defense of the continuing
> need to prepare for massive ground-based operations which re-
> mained absolutely essential for the achievement of victory. The
> compromise character of this authoritative treatise almost cer-
> tainly reflected a unified position hammered out within the
> Ministry of Defense to protect the interests of the services
> against Khrushchev's "radical" initiative.[17]

Khrushchev apparently continued to cling to his "radical" views. In his memoirs, he describes his failure to reach agreement with the Americans and his continued belief that "we should go ahead and sharply reduce our own expenditures unilaterally."[18] And in September 1964, shortly before his removal from power, he was reported in *Pravda* as saying:

> When I went out into the training field and saw the tanks attacking and how the anti-tank artillery hit these tanks, I became ill. After all, we are spending a lot of money to build tanks. And if—God forbid, as they say—a war breaks out, these tanks will burn before they reach the line indicated by the command.[19]

All branches of the armed forces seem to have benefitted, to a greater or lesser degree, from the increase in military spending that appears to have begun in the early 1960s. The novel elements of this increased expenditure were the build-up of ICBMs and SLBMs and the forward deployment of the Navy. Western observers differ in their interpretation of these developments. But the view put forward by Michael MccGwire, a former British naval commander, that they were a response to the United States strategic threat does seem the most convincing.[20] MccGwire bases his argument on the war-fighting as opposed to the war-deterring doctrines of the Soviet military establishment and demonstrates the way in which ICBMs were designed to destroy military targets in the United States, while the SLBMs and forward deployment of the Navy, including missile-firing surface ships and the new vertical take-off aircraft carriers, were a response to the increased U.S. strategic threat from the sea with the build-up of Polaris submarines and the increased range of manned bombers operating aboard U.S. carriers. The alternative view, that these developments represent a new offensive Soviet capability, is less easy to support. The idea that emphasis on war-fighting capabilities reflects an intention to use nuclear warfare as an instrument of policy is contradicted by numerous Soviet statements, as well as by the emphasis, accorded by Soviet leaders, on the disastrous consequences of nuclear war.* Many of the very same spokesmen who have opposed the adoption of Western concepts of deterrence have made it clear that the

> *contemporary revolution in means of conducting war . . . has led to a situation where both combatants cannot only destroy each other, but can also considerably undermine the conditions for the existence of mankind.*[21]

Likewise, the view that the forward deployment of the Soviet Navy is aimed at political intervention seems unlikely, in the light of the size of the Soviet surface navy, the overstretched nature of forward deployment, in particular the shortage of support vessels and the political instability of overseas bases, and the inadequacy of naval aviation and naval infantry.[22] Undoubtedly, the Soviet Navy now undertakes certain peacetime roles, for example, the support of third parties like Egypt in local conflicts. But, as yet, Soviet naval capabilities are not sufficient for a major interventionist role.[23]

The overall consequence of the growth of Soviet military spending during the past fifteen years is, nevertheless, to widen the range of military capabilities as perceived by Western military planners. By the mid-1970s, the Soviet Union had reacted to and was competing with the United States in most kinds of weapons technology.

---

* MccGwire himself has pointed out:

> The Soviets are not looking to be attacked and obviously hope that their defense capability will be sufficient to discourage or hold back an aggressor, which is of course deterrence in its traditional sense. But the crucial distinction between this and "nuclear deterrence" theory is implicit in the Western comment that "if the deterrent is used it will have failed." The Soviets do not entertain such ideas, while they would much prefer to avoid general war, should war come their defense will only have failed if their armed forces are unable to recover and go on to victory.[20]

According to Mikhail Agursky, a Soviet émigré who worked in the Soviet defence industry,

It is precisely in the field of new concepts and ideas where Soviet military designers can and do "borrow" extensively from the West. . . .

This process of "borrowing" Western military technology is well known in the U.S.S.R., particularly from the time of the development of nuclear weapons and missiles, where information obtained by Soviet intelligence plays a major role in arms production. It seems that no fundamentally new conceptual ideas have emerged in the Soviet Union since the Second World War, the pace and direction of military technological innovation being set primarily in the Western countries, notably the United States.[24]

Nearly all commentators agree that, by Western criteria, the Soviet Union "lags behind" the United States technologically. In 1972, a Pentagon study showed that the Soviet Union had technological superiority over the United States in eleven deployed weapons systems, approximate parity with the United States in four systems, and lagged behind the United States in seventeen systems. A Pentagon study in 1973 looked at 167 "areas" of weapons technology and found that the United States and the Soviet Union were equal in knowledge in seventy-two "areas" and in application of fifty-seven "areas"; the United States was ahead in knowledge of sixty-seven "areas" and in application in seventy-three "areas," and the Soviet Union was ahead in knowledge in twenty-eight "areas" and in application in thirty-seven.[25] In 1977, Admiral Stansfield Turner, Director of the CIA, concluded that "Soviet weapons technology generally lags behind that of the United States."

The Soviets trail the U.S. by 3 to 14 years in the introduction of certain electronic technologies. [Security deletion] The technology and fabrication techniques of Soviet computers and elec-

tronics are no better than those of the U.S. five years ago.
[Security deletion] While the Soviets may match the U.S. in
military laser design, they may have difficulty in fielding the
equipment as widely. [Security deletion] The design and manufacturing technology incorporated in Soviet aircraft and missiles
also lags behind that of the U.S.[26]

According to H. General Eugene Tighe, Director of the U.S.
Defense Intelligence Agency:

> Their [the Soviet Union's] principal lag, in my judgment, is in
> microminiaturization in computers, the ability to package a lot
> of complex command and control apparatus in their equipment.
> They use a great deal of their throw-weight capability today in
> rather, as I would describe it, very rigid 1960's technology.[27]

The difficulty with these government studies is that the methodology is not publicly accessible. But some careful studies, available in the open literature, undertaken at the Rand Corporation,
on aircraft turbine technology,[28] and by David Holloway on tanks
and ICBMs do confirm the finding of so-called technological backwardness.[29] Indeed, the studies by David Holloway suggest that
the gap may be widening, owing primarily to Soviet backwardness
in electronics technology. The MiG–25, for example, one of the
latest and most advanced Soviet fighters, uses vacuum-tube technology.

But if Soviet armaments policy appears to follow, at a little
distance, the U.S. technological lead, it has not proved entirely
imitative. Indeed, some of the apparent gaps in technology may
have been deliberately chosen, because the technology in question does not accord with the design precepts of Soviet weapons
technology. There have been major differences in the style of
armament, and as we shall see, these reflect differences in the
organisation of defence. Alexander has characterised the prevailing
design practises as simplicity, commonality, and inheritance:

These terms describe concepts that are interrelated, though basically different from each other. Simplicity here means un- complicated, unadorned, unburdened, the performing only of what is required and no more. Examples of simplicity are the absence of powered controls on large passenger jets, the use of common materials, and the lack of detailed finishing on parts where it is not required. Commonality means the use of stand- ardized parts, assemblies, and subsystems wherever possible, as well as the sharing of design features among different weapons. The same guns, radars, and pumps are found on a wide variety of aircraft. The Su–7 (ground attack and tactical air cover) and the Su–9 (all-weather interceptor) had common fuselages, tails, and (originally) engines, whereas the wings, armament, and equipment were chosen for their different roles. Design inheri- tance is similar to commonality but it is inter- rather than intra- generational. We find this in the long series of models and modifications of the MiG–21 (first designed in the mid-1950s) which have incorporated new versions of engines, armaments, radar, and aerodynamics as they have become known and avail- able.[30]

These design precepts were strongly emphasised by Stalin, who condemned the "epidemic of improvements"[31] and issued stern penalties "for groundless and frivolous changes in the design of military technology."[32] They are in keeping with the emphasis on quantity, both for production and use, and, *pari passu*, the high level of redundancy. Apparently, the cost of Soviet weapons sys- tems has risen more slowly than the cost of Western systems, and the number of different types of weapons systems has declined much less rapidly.

If Western military technical change can be characterised as baroque, then Soviet military technical change might be termed "conservative." Baroque technical changes combine conservatism, with respect to performance characteristics, with technological

dynamism, with respect to hardware, so that immensely sophisticated technology may be incorporated into a weapons system that
represents a minor improvement in military effectiveness. Conservative technical change is conservative—or evolutionary or incremental—with respect *both* to performance characteristics *and*
to hardware. With diminishing marginal returns, the gap in military effectiveness, as opposed to technology, between baroque and
conservative weapons systems must necessarily narrow. Indeed,
some commentators have gone so far as to suggest that the conservative approach is actually *more* effective than the baroque,
implying negative marginal returns to baroque technical change.[33]

Nevertheless, the conservative does seem to be infected by the
baroque. Soviet weapons systems do seem to be becoming more
costly and more complex, and the quantities are declining. A
Soviet writer has observed a

> direct link between the constant replacement of generations of
> armaments and the huge increase in economic expenditure on
> their production. The competition in military might between
> states places ever-new demands on the tactical-technical char-
> acteristics of this or that type of weapon. Meeting these demands
> leads to the creation of improved systems of combat equipment
> but also dearer systems.[34]

Hence, despite the differences in style, Soviet and American
armament policies do seem to be merging into a joint acceptance
of the dominance of the modern weapons system and, in particular,
to a joint affirmation of the overwhelming importance of nuclear
weapons. This concurrence underlies recent arms-control agree-
ments, particularly SALT, which have the paradoxical effect of
institutionalising the military competition between the superpowers. Soviet armaments policy has, in effect, confirmed the military dominance of the United States and placed itself, the Soviet
Union, in second place or even in an equivalent position. This
confirmation has considerable significance for power relationships,

not only with the rest of the world, but also within the respective blocs. Just as, in NATO, the U.S. monopoly over nuclear weapons and its dominance in the supply of sophisticated weapons has proved an important instrument for cohesion, so in the East, the dependence of smaller socialist states on Soviet military technology, especially nuclear weapons, "serves to unify the Warsaw Treaty Organisation around the Soviet Union."*

It could have been different. Khrushchev proposed one alternative that might have de-escalated the armament process. More recently, the Vietnam War has implied the possibility of other alternatives for socialist states. That it was not different, or not so very different, has to be explained in terms of the nature of Soviet military institutions, which were, after all, formed in the same historical circumstances, namely, World War II, as were American military institutions, and their role in Soviet society as a whole. Both the similarities and the differences may also help to illuminate what happens in the West.

The Soviet Arms Economy

Oscar Lange has described the Soviet economy as a "war economy" in the sense that the centralisation of economic management resembles that of a capitalist economy in wartime.[36] David Hollo-

---

* Christopher D. Jones writes: "According to Soviet texts, the WTO members agree (1) that the only possible military defense for small socialist countries in Europe threatened by the NATO imperialists armed with nuclear weapons is to form a socialist military coalition led by the Soviet Union to hold the NATO aggressors at bay; (2) that in order for the Warsaw Pact states to coordinate their joint military defense they must have a complete 'unity of views' on the question of military doctrine, military science and military art; (3) that Soviet military doctrine, Soviet military science and Soviet military art must be the basis for the 'unity of views' in the WTO because the Soviet armed forces have resolved the problems of conducting a nuclear war; (4) that each WTO army must thoroughly study and master Soviet military doctrine and the 'leading experience' of the Soviet armed forces."[35]

way, in an important forthcoming study,[37] has gone further and suggested that the priority given to defence is a critical attribute of the war economy, for this provides the justification and *raison d'être* for such a concentration of economic power. Certainly it was the dangers of the international situation, the frailty of the Soviet regime in the event of a future war, that underlay the policy of rapid industrialisation that was associated with the first five-year plan, which began in 1928. And it would not be exaggerating to say that it was this policy that enabled the Soviet Union to turn back the German invasion of 1941 and to determine the outcome of the Second World War.

We have seen how, in the West, the war sector has tended to stagnate, caught, as it were, in some dominant experience of the past. And we have seen also how that stagnation has tended to pervade the whole economy. In the Soviet Union, where the characteristics of the war sector are much more widely shared, the consequences of the dominant experience which led up to World War II are likely to have been even more pervasive.

The Soviet system, which was primarily established during the first five-year plan, was one in which central, directed planning was substituted for the market mechanism and the profit motive. It is a technique which has proved remarkably efficient for carrying out certain ambitious specified tasks, such as raising the level of industrialisation within a predetermined framework or mobilising resources for war. But it entails certain long-term economic and social costs. At factory levels, traditional economic incentives are replaced by direct instruction, relating to the fulfilment of the plan. Managers and workers are encouraged to obey these orders through the promise of material and political rewards and the threat of social, and even physical, penalties. The difficulty is that the indicators for plan fulfilment cannot, a priori, take into account the nature of local circumstances. The centre cannot possibly collect sufficient information to make correct estimates for appropriate output and input, especially since the smallest units have an interest in misinformation in order to preserve some de-

gree of autonomy, to exaggerate success, and to downplay failure.*
The consequence is immense wastage from overestimation and
recurrent bottlenecks from underestimation. The endemic tendency for overinvestment,† for duplication, and for redundancy—
in the sense of preserving obsolete machines and production
processes—has been widely observed. Likewise, the process dis-
courages technical progress because emphasis on quality or innovative change might disturb the quantitative fulfilment of the
plan indicators, disrupt established supply lines, and face new
supply constraints, and might incur unacceptable risks of failure.
These problems, says Nove, are not

> mistakes; they are not instances of individual stupidity. Given
> the institutional structure, given the objectives . . . given that
> the plan can never be completed or fully balanced in time, given
> that prices (and therefore profitability) are not related to scarcity
> or need, given finally that the basis of the Soviet model requires
> that the centre tells the production management what needs to
> be done, the complexities and distortions follow as night fol-
> lows day.[40]

These problems, moreover, are not only manifest at the factory
levels. In the absence of market rule, of democracy where priorities
might be directly related to social need, or of some overriding external necessity like war, priorities and targets for the plan tend
to reflect the internal political balance. This has the effect, as
Nove points out,

* According to Antonio Carlo, it was estimated in the 1960s that "if planning were continued in the same fashion, a million computers with a speed
of 30,000 operations per second would have to calculate for several years
uninterruptedly in order to elaborate a gigantic mathematical model with a
million equations."[38]

† An interesting parallel can be noted with the Western defence sector. One
of the reasons for overinvestment is persistent underestimation of costs. One
Soviet economist has said that "if we showed the full cost at that stage, the
project might not be approved."[39]

of making investment allocations in some degree a function of
the relative influence of the various sectors and groups. This
introduces a rigidity into the system: by definition, anything
that is new and ought to be rapidly growing is not yet big and
powerful.

This same trend is reinforced by what could be called "input-
output conservatism." The planners, themselves divided into
departments, work with material balances tables, or input-output
coefficients, which inevitably reflect the past.[41]

Thus, if in the West the defence sector serves to uphold declining
sectors and to inhibit the emergence of new dynamic sectors,
then in the Soviet Union the same tendency results from the
operation of the planning system as a whole. For example,

throughout the period from 1950 to 1973, Soviet production of
crude steel per capita expanded much more rapidly than in the
United States and the United Kingdom, and the output of cotton yarn per capita steadily expanded although it fell in other
major countries. . . . This reflects a more conservative pattern
of industrial production in the Soviet Union: plastics and artificial or synthetic fibers have replaced steel and cotton much
more slowly than elsewhere.[42]

It is in the newest industries, like chemicals, computers, and numerically controlled machine tools, that the Soviet Union appears
to lag behind most. Moreover, technical progress is slow *both* in
declining industries and in dynamic industries as traditional techniques continue to be used long after the introduction of new
ones and as new techniques come up against socio-economic
barriers.

The Armament Sector

The defence sector is often said to be the most important of the
pressure groups.[43] Observers point to the fact that so-called defence-
industry alumni are powerfully represented on economic and

political decision-making bodies. Both Ustinov, the Defence Minister, and Brezhnev gained their formative experiences in the defence-industrial sector. Military representation on state and Party organs is relatively high, although not at the topmost levels. Military spokesmen have always been the most consistent advocates for traditional heavy industry, which is regarded as the "foundation of the entire economy . . . (and) the basis of the military power of the State."[44] It is widely considered that military-industrial opposition to Khrushchev's *economic* reforms, which included decentralisation and a new emphasis on consumer industries, as well as his reforms for defence, determined their demise.[45] Khrushchev in 1963 complained about Ustinov and his "metal eaters"[46] and in his memoirs he has criticised the role of military leaders:

> *I know from experience that the leaders of the armed forces can be very persistent in claiming their share when it comes time to allocate funds. Every commander has all sorts of convincing arguments why he should get more than anyone else. Unfortunately, there's a tendency for people who run the armed forces to be greedy and self-seeking. They're always ready to throw in your face the slogan "if you try to economize, you'll pay in blood when war breaks out tomorrow." I'm not denying that these men have a huge responsibility but the fact remains that the living standard of the country suffers when the budget is overloaded with allocations to unproductive branches of consumption. And today as yesterday, the most unproductive expenditures of all are those made by the armed forces. That's why I think that military leaders can't be reminded too often that it is the government which allocates funds and it is the government which must decide how much the armed forces can spend.[47]*

But the interest-group argument does not explain why some groups become more powerful than others. Nor does it account for fundamental requirements of the system. From time to time, the Soviet regime does need to carry out certain functions, and in order to overcome the "routine and inertia" of the system, the political leadership imposes a kind of "shock treatment." This was evident in the Stalin years and, to a lesser extent, under Khrushchev. The military sector has, perhaps, been the most important beneficiary of this kind of shock treatment. And this is the consequence of the military requirements of the Soviet system. Egbert Jahn[48] describes the Soviet system as a "militarised" society. The role of force is much more important, both at home and abroad, than it is in the West. The absence of democracy and of legal and economic mechanisms to cope with inequality, the contradiction between the theory and practise of a people's state, the use of technologies, e.g., Taylorism, which reproduce the hierarchical relations of production that are found in the West, the unequal distribution of material benefits, are all factors which explain the prevalence of physical repression. Internationally, the Soviet state has been isolated and has faced threats, first from Germany, then from the United States; it has also attempted to impose unity in the socialist camp.

The external requirement for armaments and the armed forces is not entirely unrelated to domestic considerations. First, the military have played an important role in offsetting the power of the domestic security organs; witness Khrushchev's dramatic description of the military role in the downfall of Beria. Second, and more important, the link between domestic vulnerability and external threats has always been recognised. The Bolsheviks, after all, achieved power in the chaos created by the First World War. And Soviet military writers have been much preoccupied with what they call the "reverse effects" of war on society.

Citing Lenin's assessments of the relationships between military defeats and domestic disorders in Tsarist Russia and citing similar experiences of several Western states (particularly that of the United States during the war in Vietnam) Soviet military writers declare that military setbacks often exacerbate tensions in domestic politics and undermine the legitimacy of the government in power. Such "reverse effects" of war on politics in turn affect the ability of a government to recover from its military defeats; further deterioration of the military situation further aggravates domestic tensions. Colonel Rybkin, a leading Soviet military analyst, declares in no uncertain terms that a ruling Communist Party must base its decision on whether to wage a war according to the likely influence of war on its own society.[49]

The dual nature of the defence sector, as one rather powerful interest group, on the one hand, and as a priority sector for fulfilling urgent military requirements, on the other hand, is reflected both in its internal institutional characteristics and in its effects on the rest of the economy. In some respects, the defence sector exhibits all the tendencies to conservatism that are so prominent in Soviet society as a whole. In the West, military technology represents a combination of conservatism and technological dynamism reflecting at once the stability and continuity of the main defence institutions, the armed forces and their prime contractors, *and* the competitive nature of the private enterprise system and the arms industries, in particular. In the Soviet Union, the main defence institutions exhibit even more stability and continuity than in the West. Apart from the creation of two new services, PVO–S and SRF, which were, in effect, added on to the existing force structure, the organization of the armed forces and the corresponding doctrinal concepts have hardly changed since World War II. Indeed, the present structure of the defence industry, probably organised into nine defence industry ministries, was more or less established by the late 1940s.*

Unlike in the West, research institutes, design bureaus, and production plants are organised as separate entities. The research institutes are attached to the central ministry. The design bureaus

---

* These are Aviation, Defence Industry, Shipbuilding, General Machinery, Medium Machinery, Radio, Electronics, Communications, Machine Building.

enjoy varying degrees of autonomy, depending on the level of technology. Thus, for "low technology" items, e.g., tanks, artillery, and ships, the design bureaus are attached to the production plants. In aviation, the design bureaus are relatively independent. And in the Ministry of General Machinery, which makes ballistic missiles, the design bureaus are apparently attached to the research institute. It is likely that, as in the West, strong informal links exist between these supply organisations and the technical administrations of the armed forces, which specify military requirements.

The continuity of the individual supply entities is guaranteed by the system of planning and budgetting. Unlike in the West, where competition, the pressure for technical advance, the winning or losing of contracts may lead to the amalgamation of design teams and prime contractors and to massive shifts in the composition of subcontractors, the various industrial organisations are assured of a steady flow of work. The budgets of the design bureaus and the research institutes are much more stable than in the West; only 25 percent of R&D is nominally subject to production-biassed fluctuations.[50] This has allowed R&D institutions to pursue their specialties, in effect, to institutionalise the follow-on. This is reflected in the larger number of prototypes and in the maintenance of several different types of weapons. In the West, as we have seen, the growth of cost and complexity, reflecting the amalgamation of design teams and associated production plants, had led to sharp reductions in the variety of weapons. In the United States, fourteen fighter and attack aircraft entered service in the years 1945–49, compared with eleven in the Soviet Union. In the years 1965–69, only two fighter and attack aircraft entered service in the United States, compared with five in the Soviet Union. Likewise, the number of bombers entering service in the Soviet Union between 1945–49 and 1960–64 remained constant, while in the United States the number declined from six to one.[51]

This is not to say that there is no internal institutional pressure for technical innovation. Competition among design bureaus is an important feature of the Soviet weapons-acquisition process. Successful designs lead to production contracts, follow-on assignments, more manpower, prestige, state prizes, and substantial monetary rewards. The heads of design bureaus are chief designers, like Mikoyan, Yakovlev, and Tupolev, who can achieve great fame. The personal status of the chief designer may often determine the future of the design bureau. In his memoirs, Yakovlev tells how he used his personal influence to change a decision by Stalin to prohibit further design work on fighter aircraft and to concentrate instead upon modernising the MiG–15: "I was very worried about the situation. You see behind me stood 100 people, who might lose faith in me as the leader of the design collective."[52]

Nevertheless, the degree to which design bureaus might be tempted to propose a radical innovation in order to win a design competition is severely constrained by, on the one hand, the doctrinal emphasis on simplicity, commonality, and inheritance, and, on the other hand, the imperatives of production which these doctrinal precepts largely reflect.

Like the R&D institutions, the production plants enjoy much greater stability of output and employment than their counterparts in the West. They do not need to compete for production contracts, because excess capacity, if it exists, is a deliberate or mistaken consequence of planning. All the defence enterprises are responsible for substantial civilian production as a matter of policy. Brezhnev, in an often-quoted statement, said that 42 percent of the output of defence enterprises is intended for civilian purposes. Civilian production serves as a buffer between defence contracts and increases the flexibility of production, the ease of convertibility from peace to war, and vice versa. Many enterprises in the civilian ministries also produce defence goods. Indeed, according to one estimate, two-thirds of all Soviet enterprises are producing for defence.[53]

There is a tendency for supply autarchy among the defence-industry ministries as there is with civilian ministries. Because of the unreliability of the planning process, there is a tendency to keep as much of the manufacturing process as possible within the ministry in order to avoid supply bottlenecks. Most ministries are said to have their own metallurgical bases and machine-tool manufacturing facilities. The Electronics Ministry has to produce many materials and components, e.g., electrovacuum glass and ceramics, organic film for condensers, cast permanent magnets, etc., because it cannot rely on other ministries to meet quality requirements. According to Alexander:

> Of the thousands of components going into aircraft, 90 to 95 percent are produced in the aviation industry itself. The Ministry of Aviation Industry includes metallurgical plants that roll aluminum and magnesium alloys, stamping and extruding facilities, and plants that manufacture rubber and plastic goods. The prime assembly plant of the 84-passenger, four-turbo-prop, 1L-18 manufactured all components except the engines, radio equipment, accessories, propellers, and wheels. It produced in-house, the landing gear and shock absorbers, hydraulic system accessories, seats, cast parts, nuts and bolts.[54]

The consequence is continuity, not just of prime contractors, as in the United States, but of subcontractors as well. This helps to explain the emphasis on commonality and inheritance, as well as the inhibition against major design changes, for any other practice might involve a change of suppliers, of going outside the ministry to obtain new materials and components.

The emphasis on simplicity can be explained by the interests of the production plants. Like all enterprises in the Soviet Union, production plants tend to resist complexity as well as design changes because they disrupt production and interfere with the fulfilment of quantitative plan indicators. There is also some evidence that low prices for defence products also encourage an emphasis on long series production.[55] Hence, the production arrangements serve to reinforce the doctrinal inclinations of the armed forces for conservatism in weapons technology.

In addition to these horizontal relationships, there are vertical relationships, which, as is usual in the Soviet Union, tend to be dominant.

> The activity of the R&D establishments is planned and directed by the ministries, whose work is in turn co-ordinated by the Military-Industrial Commission. On the military side, the technical administrations work very closely with the commands and staffs of their own branch or arm of service, whose plans and activities are in turn co-ordinated and directed by the General Staff.[56]

Final decisions are taken by the Defence Council, which is subordinate to the Praesidium of the Supreme Soviet, or by the Politbureau.

> In other words, cooperation between customer and supplier is organized on the basis of decisions taken at the top and transmitted down through the military and industrial hierarchies.[57]

Insofar as the defence sector is simply another, albeit powerful, interest group, then the decisions of the leadership are likely to reflect the dominant conservative bias within the defence institutions, no more or less pronounced than in any other set of Soviet institutions. But insofar as military strength is an important attribute of state power, then the priority given to the defence sector, the insistence on consumer requirements, and the episodic shock treatment is unique. By all accounts, defence is a privileged sector in the Soviet Union. It receives the best machinery and parts, it can commandeer scarce materials and parts, defence employees earn higher incomes and obtain better non-monetary benefits like housing or medical care; requests and orders from the administration tend to be dealt with more quickly. Likewise, many commentators have remarked on the unusual degree of consumer sovereignty in the defence sector—the ability of the consumer to ensure that specifications are met and to overcome resistance to demand induced changes. Military representatives, known as Voyenpreds, are located at production plants to prevent bottle-

necks, police pricing, and ensure quality standards. Finally, the
need for shock treatment to overcome the inertia of the system
has been explicitly recognised in the defence sector. Indeed, a
Russian textbook warns that

> *dogmatic utilization of this method (of design inheritance) can
> result in slowing down the rate of technological progress. . . .
> Upon reaching a certain state in the development of a given
> type of aviation design, it is necessary to forgo the design in-
> heritance method and to look for new solutions with the purpose
> of substantial improvements.*[58]

The political leadership has initiated major new programmes; for
example, jet-engine technology, nuclear weapons, the missile program, helicopters, swept wing, and V/STOL technology. Antonov,
the famous designer of transport aircraft, asks:

> *Have you not noticed that the Party has several times rolled up
> its sleeves, gone after one industry or another, and, dragging it
> out of the morass of gradualism, given it a powerful push in
> the direction the country required?*[59]

As we have seen, the impulses behind this kind of shock treatment
are largely imported from abroad; they are a response to technical
development in the West, and consequently perhaps, they provide
an important mechanism for adapting these developments to
Soviet conditions.

ARMS AND THE ECONOMY

From the very beginning of the first five-year plan, defence played
a central role in Soviet industrialisation. At the XV Party Congress in 1927, Voroshilov, who replaced Trotsky and Frunze as
Commissar for Army and Navy Affairs, said:

> *We have taken as our main goal and fundamental content of
> the five-year plan the raising of the technical strength of the
> Red Army to the level of first-class contemporary armies.*[60]

And Stalin said that the aim of the plan for heavy industry was "to create in the country all the necessary technical and economic pre-requisites for increasing to the utmost the power of defence in this country."[61]

During the 1930s, defence obtained a major share of budgetary allocations for industry, rising to between 40 and 50 percent in the period 1938–41.[62] The defence sector accounted for between one-fifth and one-sixth of machine tools, one-fifth of the output of steel, 10 percent of all chemical industry equipment. It is said to have exerted a "decisive influence" on the development of quality iron and steel products, non-ferrous metals and alloys, fuel, rubber, and chemicals. Many civilian enterprises were constructed with the objective of convertibility for war in mind. This was particularly true for tractor building, which was important for tanks; the clock and watch industry, which was later to play an important role in making fuses; and the bicycle and motorcycle industry. Nearly all civilian enterprises had special shops which were responsible for preparing production processes to be adopted in the event of war. These shops had the right to reorganise equipment and disrupt normal work. Because the military techniques adopted by the Red Army during this period made use of many of the most advanced industrial techniques available in the West, this massive effort undoubtedly had important consequences in mobilising resources and accelerating the development of certain branches of production. But from the point of view of overall economic efficiency, this strategy was not without cost. The demand for special materials may have slowed down the provision of basic materials for the civilian sectors. For example, investment in non-ferrous metals may have been responsible for a slowdown in investment in iron and steel in the late 1930s. The heavy demand for fuel for aircraft and military vehicles resulted in the inefficient use of gas-generator equipment for agricultural tractors. The need for special materials and machine tools also entailed a heavy dependence on imports, which actually increased before and during World War II. The convertibility requirement

also led to inefficiency in the organisation of factories. According
to Lowry, an American who acted as munitions consultant to the
U.S.S.R. during the 1930s:

> Stalingrad and Chelyabinsk, two of the world's largest tractor
> factories produce only half of what factories in the United States
> of equal capacity can produce, the latter having much less area
> and half the labor force. But these giant Soviet factories could
> be turned over to small tank production, almost at the wink of
> an eye. Efficiency in these cases is partially sacrificed for the
> future protection of the country.[63]

By the end of the 1930s, moreover, the massive absorption of resources by the defence sector diverted badly needed resources from
civilian uses:

> There is no doubt that the rapid build-up of defense produc-
> tion had a serious negative impact on the consumer-goods sector,
> and an even greater impact on living standards, insofar as an
> increasing share of consumer goods output must have been
> diverted for military use.[64]

Military production was, of course, hugely expanded during the
war, and by 1942, it amounted to 63.9 percent of total output.

The 1930s was perhaps the most dynamic period of Soviet economic development, and it established an industrial structure
which still shapes the direction of economic growth because of the
rigidities of the planning system. In recent years, there has been
much concern about the slowdown in the rate of growth of the
Soviet economy. As the rate of growth of the labour supply slows
down, it becomes more and more difficult to achieve economic
growth through incremental additions to existing sectors. Yet
precisely because of the inflexibility of the industrial structure and
because investment is more likely to be directed toward those
sectors which are best established and therefore most liable to
diminishing returns, it becomes more and more difficult to achieve

productivity increases. In 1950, it was estimated that an increase in the capital stock of 10 percent led to an increase in the output of goods and services of 9 percent. In 1970, a similar increase in the capital stock only yielded a 4 percent increase in the output of goods and services.[65] The rate of economic growth declined from 5.8 percent a year in the period 1951–60 to 3.7 percent a year in the period 1971–76, according to CIA estimates, and productivity growth declined from 1.2 percent to −0.6 percent over the same period. (The CIA attributes the negative productivity growth to consumer discontent.) In a sense, the planning system as a whole has had much the same consequence for the Soviet economy as the defence sector has had in Britain and America.

The defence sector remains deeply embedded in the Soviet industrial structure. Estimates of the share of GNP devoted to defence vary from 8 to 14 percent, nearly double the American defence burden.[66] One Soviet economist has estimated that between 30 and 40 percent of the national work force is engaged in defence production.[67] Another estimate suggests that military production accounts for 25 percent of industrial production. Aspaturian says that 50 percent of durable output is used for defence, leaving 40 percent for investment and 10 percent for consumption.[68] According to the U.S. Defense Intelligence Agency, the nine defence ministries increased their share of machinery GVO (Gross Value of Output) from 54 percent in 1965 to 61 percent in 1978, and their share of total industrial GVO from 9 percent in 1965 to 16 percent in 1978.[69] Finally, the CIA estimates that defence absorbs a third of the output of the machine-building and metal-working sector (a comparable figure for the United States is 10 percent), one-fifth of metallurgy, one-sixth of chemicals, and one-sixth of energy.

Even these measurements tend to understate the impact on the Soviet economy because they fail to take into account qualitative considerations. Most importantly, defense takes the lion's

share of the high-grade scientific, technical and management
talent that exists in the Soviet Union. It similarly draws heavily
on the output of scarce and high-quality materials, components
and equipment that are produced in the West.[70]

It is sometimes argued, however, that these negative effects
of military spending are offset by the positive, mobilising effects
of defence. Precisely because conservatism in the defence sector
is tempered by the priority system, by consumer sovereignty, and
by the shock treatment now known as programme planning, it is
more dynamic than other sectors of the Soviet economy, and can
and does transmit some of its more modern techniques to boost
lagging productivity in the civilian sector.

After the Second World War, civilian industry, in contrast to
the major military-technological effort then underway, was recon-
structed on the basis of prewar plants. From the mid-1950s, it
became clear to Party leaders that it was necessary to stimulate
civilian industry, if only to provide an advanced technological
base for the military sector. New institutions were set up, headed
by men with military-industrial experience. There is some evidence that military programmes placed demands on civilian industry which resulted in modernisation. This pattern continued
into the 1960s and 1970s. In particular, organizational and management techniques drawn from the Western experience of major-
weapons-acquisition programmes, for example, the systems concept,
quality control, and reliability assurance (sic!) were adopted in
civilian industry.[71] Brezhnev's call for a "contemporary scientific
and technological revolution"[72] in the early 1970s was explicitly
related to his experience in the military sector. At the XXIV
Party Congress in 1971, he said:

> Taking into account the high scientific-technical level of de-
> fense industry, the transmission of its experience, inventions and
> discoveries to all spheres of the economy acquires the highest
> importance.[73]

Thus, despite the secrecy that prevails in the military sector, there do seem to be significant spin-offs.* Indeed, much of the dynamism of Soviet technology as a whole could be said to come from the arms race. Yet the consequences of such spin-offs for future Soviet development are likely to be paradoxical. For the technology that is transmitted from the West through the medium of military competition is, as we have seen, a decadent form of technology, advancing along in directions that actually hamper the progress of civilian technology designed for more socially useful ends. It is a technology shaped by those very same organizational structures that Soviet leaders seem so anxious to spread throughout Soviet industry. Hence, in the effort to catch up with the West militarily and economically, the Soviet system, insofar as it departs from traditional conservatism, is likely to be led technologically astray.

* Mikhail Agursky argues that spin-off is extremely limited because of the secrecy that prevails in the defence sector. This secrecy leads to inefficiency; hence the relatively slow introduction of NC machines in the defence sector compared with the civil sector. Insofar as new Western techniques have been introduced both in military and civil sectors, this is because both scan the Western literature and have better communication with the West than with each other.[74]

5

The World Military Order

Military institutions have their time and place. Every society has its characteristic military style; feudalism discovered the stirrup; capitalism emerged with the gun. Armies could perhaps be treated as proxies for society as a whole, weapons as a symbol of technical advance, military traditions as an aspect of wider social relationships, and wars, therefore, as a struggle between different forms of social organisation. "A history of militarism," wrote Karl Liebknecht, "in the deepest sense discloses the very essence of human development and of its motive force."[1] And, until recently, different types of armed forces coexisted side by side in different societies.*

Perhaps the most striking feature of the modern epoch is the sameness of military institutions. Historically, Western ascendency was based on advances in military technique; in particular, the development of gunpowder and the construction of large ocean-going sailing vessels.[3] Subsequently, the colonial powers depended on their near-monopoly of firepower. Today, with the independence of Third World countries, the weapons system and its associated military organisation, which originated in the West, has spread throughout the world. All types of armies have merged into what some Third World scholars now call the "global armament culture."[4] Even the armies of North Vietnam, China, and Israel,

---

* Jack Goody has shown how different military systems characterised different societies in pre-colonial Africa, although production systems were not so different; hence, the gun was the weapon of the slave-based coastal societies, the horse of the aristocratic societies of the savannah regions, and the bow and arrow were used by the various acephalous peoples.[2]

which appear to be different, are gradually losing their special identities.

If, indeed, military institutions are a reflection of society, then this pervasiveness of the weapons system, this drawing together of all military systems, must surely have deep-seated implications for broader social relations between nation and nation.

The Spread of the Weapons System

The United States first extended large quantities of military assistance during the Second World War under the Lend-Lease Program. Then, after the war, starting with the Truman Doctrine in 1947, which provided military aid to Greece and Turkey, the United States began to build a global collective-security system. This comprised a series of individual mutual-defense treaties with particular countries and a chain of regional alliances—SEATO in Southeast Asia (now dissolved), ANZUS with Australia and New Zealand, CENTO, formerly the Baghdad Pact (of which the United States was not formally a member), NATO, and the Rio Treaty in Latin America—shored up by military assistance. An official United States report in 1959 concluded that

> the military assistance program has provided the mortar, giving cohesion, strength and credibility to our collective-security arrangements. It is the foundation on which our forward strategy is built.[5]

Over the thirty years 1946–77, the United States provided $78,718 million in loans and grants for military purposes, and this does not include commercial sales of military equipment and services, which have greatly increased in recent years.[6]

Through the various forms of military assistance, currently known as Security Assistance, the United States was able to fashion foreign armies in its own image. As late as 1970, the President's Task Force on International Development reported that the United States played the determining role in shaping the force structure and military equipment of receiving countries.[7] Despite its recommendations for fostering a form of military self-reliance, and despite the decline in military loans and grants as opposed to commercial sales, the various mechanisms through which this influence was exercised are hardly less powerful today.

First of all, those countries which were members of military alliances enjoyed various forms of joint command and joint exercises, as did certain individual nations, such as Korea. NATO, for example, has an integrated command structure, headed by an American Supreme Commander, which comes into effect in times of crisis. This implies that NATO countries must agree on a common strategy, and cooperate in tactical planning, and encourage the interoperability and standardization of weaponry. Joint exercises are carried out to assess the adequacy of common capabilities. In the annual REFORGER exercise, for example, American ground troops are airlifted to central Europe and engage in manoeuvres with other NATO forces. Similar exercises are carried out with United States allies in Southern Europe and the Far East. In the annual UNITAS exercise, U.S. ships circle South America and engage in anti-submarine warfare (ASW) and other exercises with the navies of various Latin American states. This kind of activity helps to link foreign military forces into what might be described as a single but diverse multinational force structure.

Second, the United States has exported thousands of aircraft, tanks, ships, and missiles.[8] In the five years 1973–77, U.S. weapons deliveries included approximately 5,000 tanks, 3,500 artillery pieces, 7,000 armoured personnel carriers and armoured cars, 200 naval vessels, 1,000 supersonic combat aircraft, 1,500 other types of aircraft, 1,200 helicopters, and 4,500 surface-to-air missiles.[9] Deliveries of major weapons systems, as opposed to small arms, support equipment, and services of various kinds, have accounted for roughly two-thirds of the total value of military hardware deliveries.[10] In the early postwar years, Third World countries tended to receive matériel that was being phased out of the U.S.

inventory. Today, like the European nations, several Third World recipients have acquired weapons systems as advanced as anything possessed by the U.S. armed forces. Iran, before the revolution, ordered the F–14 naval fighter and the AWACS (Airborne Warning and Control System) look-down radar flying platform. Saudi Arabia and Israel have the U.S. Air Force's latest fighter, the F–15.

There has also been a shift in the direction of United States weapons supplies, from the so-called forward defence areas bordering the Soviet Union and usually tied to the United States through some form of bilateral or multilateral treaty, to the less committed nations of the Middle East—oil-rich countries like Iran and Saudi Arabia, and the participants in the Arab-Israeli conflict.

The acquisition of one weapons system begets the acquisition of another. Once Iran decided to buy the F–14, the purchase of AWACS was inevitable, because the F–14 depends, for maximum combat performance, on radar support for target identification. On a less exalted plane, the acquisition of tanks is likely to be associated with a combination of armoured cars and artillery in order to form an armoured fighting unit. Weapons systems are likely to be linked to one another in Third World armies, in much the same hierarchical order as they are in the American or British armed forces.

In addition, these weapons require a certain amount of supporting equipment for repair, operation, and maintenance. When Egypt purchased the F–5 aircraft from the United States in 1978, a site survey conducted by the Department of Defense raised the cost of the F–5 package from $400 million to $700 million, to make up for underestimation of support requirements. The cost of a company of tanks in an underdeveloped country, including maintenance, spares, fuel back-up facilities, administration, and buildings was estimated, in 1975, at $12 million a year, *excluding* acquisition costs.

Weapons systems also have certain technical requirements for personnel. A squadron of F–14 aircraft, for example, typically has thirty-six officers (six pilots, sixteen radio intercept operators, three ground-maintenance officers and one intelligence officer) and 240 enlisted men. Some of these work in administration and security and may not, therefore, be technically necessary. Others form part of a service team, which does such things as refueling, lubrication, and replenishment of fluid for the hydraulic system and oxygen for the pilots between flights. Others are engine mechanics, ordnance specialists, metalsmiths, electricians, etc., who perform on-the-spot repairs. Forty are assigned to repair shops, along with forty from a sister squadron, and a similar number of permanent staff. Other weapons have similar, although less grandiose, organisational requirements.

These technical requirements, linking the organisation of men to the weapons systems and to each other need not necessarily impose a social command structure on receiving countries. The extent to which the *technical* division of labour is translated into a *social* division of labour similar to that which prevails in the United States also depends on other elements of military assistance—most notably the provision of advice and training. Under the bilateral mutual-defense treaties, MAAGs (Military Assistance Advisory Groups) and MLGRPs (Military Groups) under various names work jointly with their host countries to establish the kind of forces and training a country is thought to need. In the late 1960s, there were approximately 10,000 American training or advisory personnel stationed in Third World countries "in daily contact with those eighty-eight military establishments."[11] Although the role of MAAGs has been reduced as a result of the recommendations of various reports which were enshrined in the 1976 International Security Assistance and Arms Export Control Act, large numbers of American personnel are still touring the world in mobile technical and training teams. As of 1975, there were roughly 9,500 such people in 132 teams in thirty-four countries under contracts valued at $727 million.[12] In addition, many of these activities are now undertaken by private corporations—

for instance, the Vinnell Corporation of Los Angeles in helping
to modernise the Saudi National Guard. It is reasonable to suppose that, given the increase in U.S. arms sales during the 1970s,
the number of such "white collar mercenaries," as they are sometimes called is growing rapidly. The continued effectiveness of
military advice, despite nominal reductions in the permanent
military presence, was indicated by a recent report on fifteen
MAAGs by the U.S. General Accounting Office. The role of military advice in determining military organisation was explained in
a memorandum from the U.S. Embassy in South Korea:

> Our national security interest requires that we furnish a sub-
> stantial amount of advice to the ROK forces, particularly in
> the management area. The ROK forces are growing not so much
> in size as in the quantum leap from a force equipped with rela-
> tively simple weaponry to one reliant on modern military tech-
> nology and the much more difficult tactics and organization
> that go with it. The ROK military does not have the capability
> now to manage large complex systems effectively in an integrated
> fashion. They are not likely to develop such a capability in the
> foreseeable future without outside assistance. Such assistance,
> in practice, involves highly qualified people working directly with
> ROK counterparts to inculcate the skills necessary to the man-
> agement of major enterprises.[13]

The report also emphasized the important role of MAAGs in
"strengthening ties" with the host country's military, particularly
where, as in Morocco, the military represent "the country's primary source of power should anything happen to the king" or, as
in Panama and Brazil, the government "is controlled by the
military."[14]

The Carter Administration, as did previous administrations,
put considerable emphasis on training. Training has always been
considered particularly important for those Third World countries *not* militarily linked to the United States through alliances
and treaties. The International Security Assistance and Arms

Export Control Act established a separate chapter for International Military Education and Training (IMET) under the Foreign Assistance Act. Over the years since 1950, about 456,000 foreign personnel have been trained. Training includes formal instruction at schools in the United States and overseas (the Panama Canal zone, the Philippines, Libya [before 1970], Okinawa, Germany, and Thailand), mobile training teams, and various kinds of propaganda efforts including publications and so-called orientation tours. The Department of Defense

> feels that the training of foreign military personnel is of lasting value and provides a simple, direct, effective and relatively inexpensive contribution to the achievement of American foreign policy objectives. Participation in the program, it is hoped, will often create ties to the United States that endure long after the actual training experience is completed. Alumni of the program include many individuals who have become high-ranking military and government leaders in their countries today.[15]

To this end, many of the training programs include courses in politics and economics, and trainees are exposed as much as possible to "pro-Western thinking." In part, this is expected to be achieved through the "mere association with Western people"[16] and, in part, through orientation tours, which are organised as extracurricular activities, as well as for distinguished visitors. The orientation tours include "visits to military installations, important governmental centers, scenic areas and tourist attractions,"[17] as well as cultural presentations and contacts with industry. An Information Program memorandum from the Secretary of Defense in 1963 set out guidelines for such orientation tours. These included priority to "visits to stock brokerage firms and major corporations" and the instruction that when "visiting Washington, FMTs (foreign military trainees) should always be introduced to officials."[18] Senior naval officers taking a ten-month command course at the Naval War College enjoy a ten-day "Final Orientation Visit" at the end of their course. The purpose is "to acquire an increased appreciation of the industrial, economic and social structure of the United States."[19] The class of 1960, for example, visited ALCOA, Westinghouse Electric Corporation, J. J. Heinz Company, the University of Pittsburgh, and the Duquesne atomic power plant in Pittsburgh; the Chrysler Corporation, General Motors, and Ford plants in Detroit; International Harvester, the Chicago *Tribune*, and the Museum of Science and Industry in Chicago; the Fairless Works of the United States Steel Corporation and the Stock Exchange in New York.

Alumni of these training programs are encouraged to keep up the contacts they made during the program. The U.S. Army Command and General Staff College, Fort Leavenworth, has encouraged the creation of Leavenworth Clubs all over the world for graduates. The Naval War College publishes annual New Year's letters. A Brazilian officer believes that such an initiative serves "to join the great number of free countries through Naval Officers forming a FRIENDSHIP ALLIANCE and consolidating therefore, even more, the basis of the DEMOCRATIC BLOCK led by the UNITED STATES OF AMERICA." While a Korean officer writes:

> I really appreciate this wonderful idea and service of the Naval War College to be able to exchange our New Year's greetings and news through this "New Year's letter" with our dear friends of the Free World.[20]

In practise, personal ties and political indoctrination do not necessarily make a lasting impact on the foreign soldier. Trainees are often exposed to the less attractive undersides of the American "way of life"; there have been embarrassing incidents, for example, in which African soldiers have been subjected to racial discrimination. Graduates of such schools as Fort Gulick in the Panama Canal zone, familiarly known as the *"escuela de golpes,"* often turn out to be anti-American radicals in government. What is important, however, is the consequence of military assistance, in all its various forms, on the working environment of the soldier. The various military interconnections between the United States and foreign nations—hardware, people, planning, etc.—serve to create what might be described as subsidiaries of the military-industrial complex all over the world.

In this sense, in the sense of replicating the American military system, the spread of the armament culture has not fundamentally been affected by the entry of other arms suppliers into the world market. Today, the United States accounts for less than half the total arms trade. The Soviet Union, depending on how Soviet weapons are valued, accounts for around 30 percent of the market, while the remainder comes mostly from West European countries.* In the period since 1954, when Soviet arms exports began, the CIA has estimated that total Soviet military assistance amounted to $21 billion, which is considerably less than that of the United States.[22] Typically, Soviet military assistance has been focussed on a few important clients; in 1977, for example, Syria, Algeria, Ethiopia, India, and Libya accounted for 90 percent of Soviet arms sales.[23] In addition, training and advice have received much less emphasis than in the United States. There were only 10,000 Soviet and East European personnel in less-developed countries in 1977, compared with 12,400 American government and contract personnel in the Middle East alone. (There were, also according to the CIA, 21,850 Cuban personnel in the Third World.) Approximately 40,000 military personnel were trained in the Soviet Union between 1956 and 1977, compared with several hundred thousand trained by the United States. But there, for the most part, the differences end. Because Soviet military institutions were formed in World War II and developed in competition with the United States, the weapons-system-based force structure, as we have seen, is not so very different from that which is to be found

* According to the U.S. Arms Control and Disarmament Agency, total arms exports amounted to $17.6 billion in 1977, of which the United States accounted for $6.9 billion and the Soviet Union for $4.9 billion. These figures are based on Central Intelligence Agency figures, which value Soviet weapons at Western prices and hence tend to overestimate Soviet arms exports, from the point of view of either resource cost or military value.[21]

in the West. It is true that during the 1960s, Soviet advisors in Egypt supervised a reorganisation of the Egyptian Army from its British-style brigade pattern to Soviet-style divisions. But the organisation was still built around the tank and associated armoured vehicles, and after the break with the Soviet Union, it was possible to substitute Western types of weapons. Differences in Soviet-influenced military organisation could perhaps be treated as variations on a persistent underlying military theme.

The same is true of West European suppliers. Britain was always an important arms exporter; indeed, its role was eclipsed in the late 1950s by the United States and the Soviet Union. It reemerged, along with France and West Germany, and, to a lesser extent, Italy, Belgium, and Canada, in the heady commercial competition that accompanied the oil boom and the American shift from aid to sales in the 1970s. These suppliers are more commercially orientated than the United States and the Soviet Union and, consequently, place more emphasis on hardware than on training and advice. But precisely because European military organisation, weapons systems, and arms industry were developed within the framework of NATO—through the integrated command system and the postwar military assistance programs—European military transfers serve as an indirect mechanism for the spread of the American military system.

Finally, several Third World countries have become producers and exporters themselves. South Africa, Egypt, Iran, Israel, India, Spain, Yugoslavia, Argentina, Brazil, South Korea, Pakistan, the Philippines, and Taiwan all produce a wide range of military equipment. South Africa, Israel, Argentina, Brazil, and India also export weapons. Many other countries produce one or two categories of weaponry, particularly small arms and small naval vessels.[24] But such production is heavily dependent on producers in advanced industrial countries. First of all, many United States and European military corporations have subsidiaries in the Third World. Volkswagen owns a major share of Brazil's aircraft company EMBRAER, while Aerospatiale has a stake in Helibras, the

Brazilian helicopter company. In Argentina, Renault partly owns Industrias Kaisers, which manufactures tanks and armoured cars; Mercedes Benz and Fiat are also active in the Argentinian arms industry. ARMSCOR, the notable South African producer of ammunition and explosives, is jointly owned by ICI and the Anglo-American Corporation. U.S. military-industrial subsidiaries in Israel include Motorola, Astronautics Corporation, and Soltam. And so on.

Second, most Third World countries produce military equipment under licence from advanced industrial countries, and the licencer helps in the construction and management of the production plant. Aeromacchi, the Italian aircraft producer, has such arrangements with Argentina and South Africa. American F–104 fighters and F–5 fighters have been produced all over the world. India produces Soviet and British equipment largely under licence. Indeed, production often amounts to no more than assembly, so that the foreign-exchange cost of the parts may actually exceed the cost of importing a complete weapon. This was the case, for example, with the Indian MiG–21. Even where parts are produced domestically, dependence continues. A Vickers manager complained that the government-owned factory in Madras, where the Vijayanta, an Indian version of the Vickers Main Battle Tank, is produced, "call us in when they have to change the light bulb." Finally, even where, as in Israel or Brazil, weapons are indigenously designed, Third World producers are heavily dependent on advanced countries for know-how, special materials, and advanced components. German scientists and engineers toured the world after 1945 and played a critical role in the development of aircraft and rockets in Argentina, Egypt, and India, among others. British aircraft specialists play an important role in Israel. As one description of the Israeli arms industry puts it, "Even the advanced level of Israel's arms industry does not eliminate a total dependence on foreign imports of raw material and high technology components."[25]

In effect, domestic defence production in the Third World

merely adds an industrial dimension to the West's military subsidiaries in the Third World. Not only armies but armament
factories are reproduced abroad, so that the armament culture
draws both military and industrial organisations into a complex,
interconnected global system.

The elaborate military edifice created in Iran during the 1970s
provides an excellent example. It is said that, on his visit to Iran
in May 1972, President Nixon promised the Shah all the military
equipment he asked for, short of nuclear weapons. There followed
a meteoric rise in military spending, from $1.9 billion in 1970 to
$8.8 billion in 1976, a competitive drive to sell armaments on the
part of Western arms suppliers, and the construction of military
bases and arms production plants. Iran, as we have seen, acquired
the most advanced weapons in the United States inventory; so
much so that it was estimated that, if all the hardware ordered had
arrived, Iran would have possessed more weapons than Britain,
France, or Germany, a helicopter fleet that was second in size
only to the United States, and a hovercraft fleet that was the
largest in the world. "Iran in 1976," wrote one commentator,

> spent as much on defence as the People's Republic of China,
> but had only one tenth the number of men in the armed forces;
> per capita defence expenditure was 26 times higher in Iran
> ($314) than in China ($12).[26]

In support of all this equipment, numerous military missions
were stationed in Iran. In addition to ARMISH–MAAG (which
advised the armed forces), the General Accounting Office report
cited above lists no fewer than seventeen other "Department of
Defense elements" with names like TSARCOM (Troop Support
and Aviation Matériel Readiness Command) or PEACE LOG
(San Antonio Air Logistics Center) or Detachment 8 (1141st U.S.
Air Force Special Activity Squadron). In addition, there were
mobile training teams (MTT), technical assistance teams (TAT),
contract engineering technical services (CETS), contract management services (CMS), and technical-assistance field teams

(TAFT). Not to mention a secret mission to SAVAK (National Information and Security Organisation)—the secret police—and GENMISH, a police mission to the Iranian gendarmerie.

United States arms manufacturers also had an important role to play. In addition to selling weapons, they were deeply involved in establishing an arms production base. Northrop owned 49 percent of Iran's major aircraft industry, and provided operation and nearly all maintenance services for the Iranian armed forces. Bell helicopters and the Italian firm Agusta were involved in the licenced production of various subsystems and airframe components for helicopters. Grumman Iran Private Company Ltd. was established to maintain the F–14 fighters. Hughes Tool was contracted to construct a plant for missile-guidance systems; initially, it was to be used for maintenance and training purposes, but ultimately it was expected to fabricate complete components, subsystems, and systems. United States and British firms were involved in setting up an electronics industry. Other firms with an active role in Iran's arms industry included British Aircraft Corporation, Litton Corporation, and Vickers.[27]

Not only did United States military and industrial organisations spawn in Iran, but the relations between them were replicated, thus extending the dynamic of the American armament process. A study by the staff of the Senate Foreign Relations Committee reported that

> during this period, vociferous and often conflicting advice was being freely offered to the Iranian military establishment and the Shah by a host of U.S. actors, including the U.S. Navy, the U.S. Air Force, and U.S. weapons manufacturers, each of whom had a vested interest in selling Iran different weapons systems.[28]

This was why, for example, Iran ordered both the Air Force's F–16 fighter and the Navy's F–18 fighter, designed for identical roles, although, in the end, President Carter vetoed the sale of the F–18.

The creation of these military-industrial subsidiaries in the

Third World can be viewed from two perspectives. First of all, soldiers all over the world share a common military know-how. The joint possession of weapons systems and appropriate organisation creates agreement about what constitutes military power. American criteria for military strength are based on the number and sophistication of weapons systems where sophistication is assessed according to a set of given performance characteristics and a special importance is accorded to nuclear weapons. Because Third World military organisations are built around these same weapons systems, the criteria are almost everywhere accepted. Although these have, as we shall see, come into question in the test of war, as in Vietnam and the Middle East, the criteria are still based on a linear evolution from the Second World War, deriving their legitimacy from the "reputations forged or lost" in that war. The consequence is that the possession of weapons systems allows for an ordering of international military relations, conferring political influence, merely through perceptions about military power. This military order is dominated by the United States and the Soviet Union, with their monopoly of nuclear weapons and panoply of weapons systems. It is not surprising that, by their own criteria, they come out "top," so to speak.

In essence, the weapons system represents a form of international legitimacy for Third World governments and, at the same time, a tacit admission of their subordinate role. By accepting the ideology of the weapons system, Third World governments create the conditions for direct military intervention by advanced industrial countries, particularly the superpowers, as well as for the political use of military force, and this has been a central feature of postwar international relations. In addition to direct intervention in places like Lebanon, the Dominican Republic, and even Vietnam, the United States has frequently used "a show of force" to demonstrate support for a particular regime or a particular policy. A recent Brookings study lists 215 such incidents involving the United States since 1945, and most of these have taken place in the Third World.

The B–29 bomber, the Missouri Class battleship, the Midway-Class aircraft carrier were potent symbols of American power in the immediate post-war period. Successive generations of bombers, fighter aircraft, warships and ground combat equipment have helped to maintain the image of the United States as a nation in the forefront of military technology, an image that conditions the reactions of friends and foes alike to expressions of U.S. desires. The Soviet Union too has obtained political advantage by the development and display of advanced weapons systems.[29]

This kind of external support, whether explicit or not, provides backing for Third World governments, both in relation to rivals and domestically. Regional powers like Brazil, Iran, and India have been able to coerce other Third World governments lower down the perceived military hierarchy. Equally, regional shows of force, like Iranian adventures in the Gulf* or the Indian atomic explosion, reinforce the state's claim to be the legitimate guarantor of the nation. The effectiveness of such activity, it should be stressed, is entirely derived from the common acceptance of a set of perceptions about the nature of military power which are generated by the spread of the weapons system. The Third World state thus

contains a double movement: both independent and with an exclusive claim to political loyalty within a given territory; and yet dependent on international recognition and resources, in some cases for its very existence.[31]

The weapons system could be seen as a form of international recognition.

* According to a British official in Iran: "Advisors to the Iranian Government told us that the Shah did not want the islands [which he seized in the Gulf in 1971] for military or strategic reasons, despite his statement and much official propaganda to that effect. Rather he needed to take them in order to enhance his image as a forceful and decisive monarch."[30]

The Third World military organisation also becomes a part of
Western industrial culture in its broadest sense, including both
Russian and American varieties. This is the second aspect of the
spread of the weapons system. The Third World soldier becomes
Western industrial man; he has as much in common with his
counterpart in the West as he does with members of his own
society. "We are Europeans," wrote one of the group that sur-
rounded Kemal Ataturk, the military instigator of modern Turkey,
in 1929. "This phrase on our tongue is like the chorus of a very
stirring martial song. All of us, poor and rich, young and old,
have this phrase on our lips. . . . To be European is our ideal."[32]
The Shah of Iran described in his memoirs the views of his father,
a sergeant who had risen to power through a military coup:

> My father admired Persia's great past and he wanted to keep
> those of our ancient ways of living that were not incompatible
> with modern progress. But he was convinced that Persia's na-
> tional integrity, as well as the welfare of her people, demanded
> rapid modernisation. Although his travels abroad were so lim-
> ited, my father was always filled with visions of modern factories,
> power plants, dams, irrigation systems, railways, highways, cities
> and armies. Just how he did it I don't know, but he always
> seemed to know of the latest industrial, economic and military
> advances abroad.[33]

Modern American military sociologists, following the tradition
of Morris Janowitz, have made much of this idea—of the Army
as the spearhead of "modernisation" or "Westernisation." It is
not just the aspiration for industrialization that stems from
familiarity with modern industrial technique in the Army and
the vested interest in an industrial environment in which modern
military techniques can be utilised effectively. It is also the in-
culcation of essentially Western attitudes; in the words of one
American expert, "living and working by the clock . . . spending

and saving money; using transportation (bicycles, motorcycles, autos, buses, boats, planes, etc.); listening to radio,"[34] which are supposed to permeate society. The Third World Army, according to Lucien Pye, who pioneered the argument, is an "industrial-type" entity "typical of and peculiar to the most highly industrialized civilization yet known—instinct with the spirit of rapid technological development."[35]

Whether or not this Western military-industrial entity does have "modernising" influences, whether it is any more than a parasite on Third World society, must surely depend on wider social and economic developments. In the late nineteenth century, both China and Japan acquired Western weapons. Yet China was decisively defeated in the war with Japan. "In a deeper sense," writes one authority on the subject,

> China's defeat was rooted in a fundamental miscalculation. Self-strengthening [the acquisition of Western weapons] assumed that China could defend its traditional society against the West with Western weapons, that the West's military technology could be detached from Western culture as a whole. But could it? Some Chinese officials came to see, reluctantly, the unbreakable chain that led from firearms and ships to coal mines, iron foundries and railroads; from military technology to industrialization; from the weapons of the West to Westernization.[36]

To what extent, today, does the armament culture represent a harbinger of Western culture?

If Western culture was initially spread through force, through the superiority of Western military technology, might not the imitation of Western military ways have the same ultimate effect? In Western civilisation the criterion of advance, according to Lévi-Strauss, is the development of mechanical resources.[37] If this criterion is applied in the military sphere, does it necessarily infect other spheres of activity?

The Weapons System and Industrialisation

In fact, the spread of industry does appear to have accompanied the spread of the weapons system. "Development," in the sense that has been achieved by Third World countries since World War II, has essentially involved the creation of Western industrial enclaves in the Third World. Over these years, income per person has risen by about 3 percent a year in developing countries. But this growth has largely been achieved in the towns. Agricultural production has barely kept pace with the growth of population. Countries like South Korea, Brazil, India, and Egypt have embarked on programmes of industrialisation heavily dependent on imported Western know-how and capital goods, aimed at the manufacture of import substitutes or, in a limited but growing numbers of cases, of exports to other developing countries.

The Army and the nascent arms industries have been part of the industrial enclave. It is the more industrialised Third World nations that have imported the most advanced weapons systems, although the level of arms purchases varies enormously from country to country. Likewise, where domestic arms production is undertaken, the style of military industrialisation closely parallels the style of civil industrialisation. India undertakes state-owned manufacture of import substitutes, while some Southeast Asian countries are involved in a form of military offshore production. Singapore, for instance, exports fast patrol boats produced by a subsidiary of Vosper Thorneycroft. The Brazilian government has undertaken a number of joint ventures with multinational companies and is beginning to export armoured cars, artillery, and light aircraft to other Latin American countries. Egypt has created the Arab Military Organisation with European technology and now uncertain Arab finance.

But the connections between militarisation and industrialisation are not just a matter of style. Indeed, there is a growing body of evidence which suggests that arms production and the various services associated with the import of major weapons, such as the development of skills, roads, communications, repair depots, may represent the main impetus behind industrialisation, biassing industrial development in favour of the capital-intensive types of technology which are the basis of arms production in rich countries.

We have already seen how the acquisition of a weapons system creates a chain of supplementary demands for various kinds of support equipment. In countries where the industrial base is limited, such demands may account for a major portion of the budget. In Saudi Arabia, for example, 80 percent of the 1977 defence budget was spent on infrastructure; the money was used, according to *Newsweek*, "to put the bases together, give them roads, houses, schools and the trimmings."[38] These infrastructural projects create further demands. For example, the construction of the Khatami Air Force Base in Iran "brought to the surrounding area a highway, a commercial airport, running water, electricity, a bus system, and $15,000 a day in base-generated local business. Factories started to meet military needs have begun to supply civilians as well with goods such as ammunition, batteries, computers and digital clocks."[39] In Pakistan, one commentator has argued that the

> huge defence expenditure contributed enormously to the growth of West Pakistan's economy by way of establishing a variety of defence industries and an extensive network of transport and communications. This gave income and employment opportunities to her people. The persistent demand for a wide range of goods and services for military purposes gave rise to a large number of contractors, traders and manufacturers, which led to the growth of a vast number of ancillary activities.[40]

Similarly, in India, civilian production resulted from the establishment of arms factories. After the Department of Defence Production acquired the Magazon Docks Complex and Garden

Research Workshop in 1960, orders were received for two liners and for maintenance-and-repair services for civil shipping. "In addition, many small scale projects were undertaken, such as the construction of barges and tugs, and the resulting revenues allowed the workshops to diversify and to establish new units for the manufacture of diesel engines, compressors, cranes and pumps."[41] Military electronics establishments have also expanded into civil markets, supplying radio components, transmitting receivers, and navigational aids for shipping.

Often, civilian projects are part of a package deal to supply arms. France sold an air-traffic-control system worth $60 million to Brazil as part of a deal to supply Mirage fighter aircraft. The transfer of British steelmaking facilities to Brazil was part of a deal to build warships. And in Argentina, Renault established a car factory as part of a plan to build French tanks. Indeed, in both Brazil and Argentina, military industrialisation was viewed by the governing military establishments as an integral part of industrial development as a whole. A group of Latin American social scientists point out:

> Brazilian increasing capacity for arms production is a form of industrial capitalist dependent expansion, providing for the gathering of different industrial owners in the lucrative possibility of canalising investments into the arms business. Brazil has managed to gather around fifty of the biggest suppliers of vehicle parts of Brazil in a programme for producing and exporting a variety of aircraft parts and engines. . . . Thus regional involvement in international arms production amounts for the restructuring of productive orientation in arms producing countries.[42]

In Argentina, the military, from the beginning, "played an important role in the formation of heavy industry, national research and development centers, including nuclear research. The legacy of structures laid down after World War II as part of a strategy of latecomer industrialisation in the national context of a capitalist economy is still marking the level and diversification of domestic arms production in Argentina."[43]

But military industrialisation is not without cost. Arms production is capital-intensive and import-intensive. One estimate suggests that, in India, an investment of $13,500 is needed to generate one job in an ordnance factory, compared with $3,800 in industry generally, $90 in road construction, $80 in agriculture, and $9 in trade and commerce.[44] In civilian terms, such capital formation is often wasteful: "Super highways which can withstand the weight of army trucks are not necessary for oxcarts (and many of these roads have been built at the cost of farm and pasture lands). Digital clocks are not of much use when there is no electricity. . . ."[45]

The effect of heavy capital investment does not, moreover, eventually trickle into the civilian economy, because of the heavy import cost. For example, the import cost of a programme to install factories for the production of the American M–16 rifle in Taiwan, South Korea, and the Philippines, all of which have an incipient industrial base, varied between 53 percent and 80 percent of the total cost. These figures were calculated by the U.S. government to include installation and production over a period of five years. The foreign-exchange cost would be even higher for more sophisticated projects like the production of aircraft or tanks or in less advanced Third World countries. Israel paid an average of $20 million for each of its F–15 fighter aircraft purchased from the United States, while Saudi Arabia will pay more than twice this sum, over $40 million for each F–15. The difference indicates the difference in support costs. It has been calculated that arms imports alone, excluding the cost of associated equipment for repair, maintenance, and production of arms, absorbs between a fifth and a half of total machinery imports for the more advanced Third World countries.[46] Military projects thus often compete directly with civil projects. In Iran, when oil revenues fell in 1976, plans for three oil refineries and a nitrogen fertiliser plant were shelved, along with other projects, while military programs were hardly affected. In India, it has been said that the foreign-exchange cost of the 1965 and 1971 wars was a major factor in the slowdown of industrial growth from the mid-1960s.[47]

Arms imports and arms production also absorb other kinds of scarce factors of production, like skills and energy. In many countries, skilled personnel ranging from German scientists, Indian and Pakistani pilots and doctors, to Filipino or South Korean maintenance men, have to be imported. In Iran, before the revolution, there were seven thousand Americans undertaking defence-related tasks. A helicopter airframe technician was paid $17,000 a month, while a low-level American mechanic was paid $100,000 per annum. A five-year program to train two hundred Iranian Air Force personnel as naval flight officers and weapons system operators was expected to cost $128.7 million. Furthermore, these people, once trained, are generally overqualified and too specialised for civilian tasks.

The Hamburg Study Group on Armaments and Underdevelopment concludes:

> Generally speaking the evolution of the industrial pattern of developing countries tends to be dominated by the requirements of the arms industry whenever an ambitious program is launched. In the absence of sufficient economies of scale and lack of potential civilian applications for utilisation of established capacities a highly specialised and capital-intensive suboptimal industrial agglomeration evolves as a consequence of national strategies towards increased levels of self-sufficiency in the production of arms. The production of modern weapons systems imposes itself by backward and forward linkages on previous and subsequent production stages. The choices of techniques in large sectors of industry are pre-determined by the technological imperatives of arms production. Capital intensity, minimum scales of production, quality not otherwise warranted and too expensive for civilian production are determining industrial standards of incipient industries in these developing countries.[48]

Military industrialisation has to be financed in the same way as industrialisation in general. Some countries, like South Korea and Taiwan, were fortunate to receive large quantities of U.S. economic aid; one of the perks of joining a military alliance. Otherwise, the purchase of arms can be financed through foreign borrowing. This has been greatly facilitated by the growth of the Eurodollar market during the 1970s. But it results in an ever-increasing debt burden. In 1978, for example, debt servicing accounted for 12 percent of total exports of goods and services by all developing countries.[49] Or it can be done through the export of primary commodities. The size of military spending is often directly related to the size of international earnings. Robin Luckham talks about "rentier militarism" in relation to the heavy increases in military spending by oil-exporting countries during the 1970s. In Nigeria, for example, "the 1967–70 civil war was also a major factor in military spending; but . . . the increases in military spending during the war were less than those which occurred during the OPEC price rises *after* it had ended."[50]

In a study covering nine commodities (aluminum, cocoa, coffee, copper, cotton, steel, rice, rubber, and sugar), the price of commodities was shown to be significantly related to expenditure on arms imports by exporters of such commodities. Particularly important in this respect were cocoa and coffee, which, after petroleum, are the highest earners of foreign exchange in Third World countries.[51]

The need to increase the export of primary products to pay for militarisation and industrialisation and to feed the growing population in the towns has had a profound effect on the countryside. Rural producers have been drawn into the money economy, a phenomenon which results in a fictitious statistical increase in agricultural income, as more and more commodities are produced for urban and world markets instead of subsistence. Cheap labour is drawn into the towns, as poor farmers are squeezed out by the introduction of more efficient capitalist methods of production, or by worsening terms of trade between manufacturers and pri-

mary commodities, or by imports of cheap food from industrialised countries, notably the United States. The standard of
living of the rural poor has stagnated, and even in some cases
deteriorated, while the ranks of the urban unemployed swell as a
result of capital-intensive industrial investment. This uneven pattern of development within towns and between town and countryside is reproduced in the uneven development of regions. Industrial
regions can pass on the costs of industrialisation to agricultural
regions through the export of manufactures and the extraction of
a rural surplus. And this can occur on an international scale particularly where the creation of customs unions like the Andean
Pact or the East African Common Market sanctions interregional
trade in manufactures.

In this way, the spread of arms and industry emerges as a turbu-
lent process, throwing up rural resistance, urban riots, civil war,
and international rivalries. And these in turn create the need for
armaments.

This need is not a simple response to the occasions of organised
violence. Domestic repression in the form of surveillance, arbitrary arrest, and torture is widespread in the Third World, and
the instruments of repression are supplied by advanced industrial
countries.[52] Many armed forces and paramilitary forces have, with
outside help, prepared for and engaged in counter-insurgency
operations against guerrillas based in the countryside. And Third
World armies have fought each other, in the Middle East, India,
and Pakistan, or the Horn of Africa, or Southeast Asia more or
less according to the manoeuvres outlined by their military advisors from the North.

But equally important, the weapons system has a symbolic significance, linking military and industrial components of the global
order. The modern Third World soldier, as we have seen, has a
vested interest in membership in the international system and in
the widening of industrial society. The political backing of armed
forces and, in many cases, political action are essential to maintain regimes which can cope with the dissatisfaction engendered

by the process variously called "Westernisation," "modernisation," "industrialisation," or "development." Militarism in the Third World is the counterpart of the military-industrial complex in the advanced industrial nations.

There are, of course, wide variations in the political role of armies. The majority of military regimes have been "conservative," in the sense of favouring closer ties with the West and supporting liberal economic policies, such as minimum state intervention, increased foreign investment, and trade liberalisation. But there have also been many radical military regimes, as in Egypt, Syria, and Iraq during the 1950s, or in Argentina, Peru, and Ecuador during the 1960s. Such regimes have sometimes carried out land-reform programmes, nationalised foreign holdings, established economic and military ties with the Soviet Union, increased the level of state investment in development programmes, and so on. Indeed, the political continuum of military regimes is not so very different from the continuum of civilian regimes. It may not make sense even to distinguish between military and civilian regimes, since the military are only likely to intervene when, by their own standards, the civilian regime has failed.

Those standards are determined, as Robin Luckham puts it, by the "institutional and material interests" of the military.[53] And as we have seen, those interests are shaped by the weapons system and its associated form of military organisation. On the one hand, the military are dependent upon and part of the world military order. And, on the other hand, they aspire to national industrial development, in order to create the conditions in which they can operate effectively. The differences between conservatives and radicals can thus be viewed as differences in the way that they pursue these interests.

The differences are the product of a complex, interrelated set of factors that are always specific to every historical situation. Luckham has attempted to categorise these factors;[54] they include the level of underdevelopment, the style of industrialisation, the interplay of class forces, the interplay of international, regional, national, ethnic, and tribal forces, and the internal structure of the military itself. It is often the case that conservatives make allies among foreign economic interests and the local oligarchy, landowners and wealthy capitalists; while radicals seek political partners among the domestic middle classes—professionals, emergent enterpreneurs, white-collar workers, etc.—created in the process of industrialisation. But these alliances are necessarily the product of military self-interest, which may be variously defined according to institutional conflicts within the armed forces themselves. Often, conservatives and radicals divide along the lines of the military hierarchy; generals and admirals tend towards conservatism, and junior officers, particularly the growing numbers of technicians associated with the sophistication of the modern weapons system, tend toward radicalism. In Latin America, political attitudes have often divided along service lines—the more technically advanced branches of the armed forces, like the Air Force or the mechanised cavalry, tend towards radicalism. Political competition has tended to transform each service into a complete military force; most navies and armies have air arms, the Air Force of the Dominican Republic possesses tanks. The only pitched battles fought in South America since the Chaco war of the 1930s, have been between different military services in the same country. In Africa, social and institutional cleavages often reflect ethnic or tribal patterns. In a case study of the Nigerian military, it was shown that

> one of the most extreme examples of ethnic and regional fragmentation in the military could also be accounted for in terms of the army's organisational cleavages, the social relations of force. The distribution of power in the military hierarchy overlapped with regional and ethnic differences in such a way that ethnicity became a symbolic master key that unlocked the contradictions of both army and society at the same time. . . .[55]

However great the differences between conservatives and radicals (and the various political shades in between), a common interest is demonstrated in the fact that neither group has ever chosen to break with the international system or to abandon the goal of industrialisation in favour of more equitable policies. The differences in policy essentially have to do with the distribution of the benefits of industrialisation. The radicals could be said to have attempted to improve their bargaining power within the international system, to increase the share of the benefits which remain in national hands, and this has involved making use of the competition between advanced industrial nations, between the United States and the Soviet Union or the United States and Western Europe.

There is a growing body of research on the subject.[56] And one common conclusion seems to emerge: military regimes, whether radical or conservative, tend to pursue policies of industrialisation rather than welfare or equality, and few change significantly the relations of dependence. Thus, a statistical study by Tannahill, which compared the performance of civilian and military regimes in South America, concluded, as did Nordlinger,[57] that "military governments have been somewhat more successful than civilians in promoting industrialization." That this is because military regimes can afford to be less sensitive to public pressure is suggested by the fact that

> the major difference in the performance of military and civilian governments, however, is a political one. On every indicator of political responsiveness to demands for reform—government sanctions, social welfare spending, and direct taxes—the military as rulers opt for more conservative or more repressive policies than their civilian counterparts.[58]

Similar conclusions have been reached in case studies. Anouar Abdel Malek, for example, has explored the development strategy pursued by Nasser and his Free Officers in Egypt between 1952 and 1967. Throughout the period, the soldiers accorded primary importance to industrial investment, but their associated policies went through a series of different stages. The initial period,

1952–56, was characterised by an alliance with the peasantry, abolition of the monarchy and political parties, and agrarian reform aimed at weakening agrarian capital. After Suez came the Egyptianisation or nationalisation of foreign economic interests and an attempted coalition with the Egyptian bourgeoisie. Finally, after 1961, the military inaugurated a full-scale programme of nationalisation and created the Arab Socialist Union: the net result of this process, according to Malek, was a society based on economic planning, subject to the laws of the world market, moulded by the interests of a new managerial class, based on an American and German-influenced bureaucracy, and a new landowning class which emerged after the agrarian reform of the 1950s. Thus, the military achieved economic growth for the benefit of a domestic elite without improving the conditions of the poorest classes.[59]

John Samuel Fitch reaches similar conclusions in his study of the radical military regimes in Peru and Ecuador during the 1960s. Despite the fact that, in both countries, the regimes strongly condemned the "unjust distribution of wealth," in both countries the main beneficiaries of the various economic policies undertaken were the middle classes, while the rural population remained at close to subsistence levels.[60]

The evidence also seems to suggest that military regimes remain inextricably linked to the international system. Philippe Schmitter, in a survey of Latin American countries between 1950 and 1967, found that militarism, which he measures as frequency of domestic military intervention in politics, i.e., military coups, is closely associated with foreign dependence, and it is this which explains the tendency for high rates of growth and control of inflation and public spending.[61] Likewise, Fitch found that despite the commitment of the regimes in Peru and Ecuador to eliminate "all economic, political, social, cultural, military and ideological dependency on the great international centers of decision-making," neither country had *really broken the links of dependency which tied them to the larger structure of Western capitalism. Peru has done more to reduce the political and economic power of foreign firms . . . on the other hand, Peru has in one sense only shifted the terms of its dependency, from direct foreign investment to dependency on foreign financing . . . while both governments were undoubtedly more nationalist than the civilian regimes which preceded them, neither government has been very successful in redefining the relationship between the local economy and the larger world capitalist system.*[62]

The overarching interest of the armed forces in Western-type industrialisation has, in some countries, become institutionalised. In Burma, the Defence Services Institute, formerly concerned with the procurement of Army supplies, was expanded in 1961 "to include the Burma Economic Development Corporation. This entailed military responsibility for commercial enterprises such as steel production, shipping and also pharmaceuticals."[63] In Indonesia and Turkey, the armed forces actually control a large number of industrial enterprises, providing independent sources of finance for the military establishment. The military thus constitutes not just an institution interested in industrial development but a class that is actively involved in the process. This widening of the role of the military has been expressed in the development of coherent military ideologies in many Third World countries. In Latin America, this has become known as the National Security Doctrine:

National Security, as an official or semi-official doctrine, is said to be aimed at guaranteeing the state's existence and expansion. The material guarantee of this process is the permanent increment of national power, which is conceived of as embracing almost all spheres of national life. Thus, National Security should be seen as a system designed for the increasing of national power. Insofar as the military are professionals in security affairs, it should be them who control the process headed towards increasing national power.[64]

National power, both military and economic, is inextricably associated with the development of industry. Militarism is the guarantor of a form of industrialisation needed to provide an operational base for the modern weapons system. It is a form of industrialisation that is capital-intensive, import-intensive, energy-intensive, and skill-intensive, and it can be carried out only through authoritarianism and repression. But if this were a mechanism that could achieve long-term growth, and establish an industry which would eventually compete on world markets and expand to provide jobs and income for the poor who are squeezed out of their traditional rural occupations, it could be justified. After all, militarisation played much the same role in other "latecomer" nations; for example, Tsarist Russia or Meiji Japan.[65] The political and financial cost of this form of development might be the price of industrial breakthrough.

The tragedy, however, is that these costs are borne, by and large, for nothing. And this is because of the nature of the weapons system. The technology of the weapons system, as we have seen, is not "advanced" either in relation to the technologies that compete in world markets or in its potential for satisfying social need. The sophisticated weapons system represents decadent technology, the know-how of older industries elaborated beyond what is useful along a technological dead-end. It is this kind of technology which is transferred to Third World countries, condemning them to an industrial structure that is perpetually backward by the standards of the most advanced industrial nations.

Walt Rostow outlined the "stages" theory of development, in which he argued that underdeveloped countries would follow an industrial path already taken by advanced industrial countries; starting with textiles and footwear, then shipbuilding, engineering, iron and steel, and eventually automobiles, aircraft, and even chemicals and electronics.[66] The theory has been rightly criticised on the grounds that developing countries can never develop through imitation, that underdevelopment is not a historical stage but an ongoing consequence of the development of the world economy. The weapons system puts the stages theory into practice. It creates a dependent, backward form of industrialisation.

Recently, there has been much discussion about the newly industrialising countries—Third World nations that are beginning to export manufactures. It is noteworthy that, first, such exports are associated with and dependent upon increases in the import of capital goods and arms. Most of the NICs have experienced a rapid growth in indebtedness; their trade deficit with OECD countries rose from 4½ billion in 1973 to 17½ billion in 1976. Second, the NICs competed best in the less dynamic, more arms-intensive Western economies; namely, Britain and the United States. In contrast, it is Japan, at the forefront of the latest civil technologies, that has opposed protectionist moves by OECD countries against the NICs. Japan opposed an American plan to restrict exports of steelmaking facilities and technology to less-developed countries because, according to Japan's Ministry of International Trade: "If realized the American bid would have a serious impact on Japan's national policy to help in the industrialization efforts of developing countries."[67] Japan is not threatened by increased exports from the NICs; on the contrary, the growth industry in these countries merely serves to expand the market for Japan's ever-buoyant exports.

If the capital intensity of warfare, measured as military spending per man, is a rough indicator of the spread of the weapons system, then it is interesting to note that the two most successful NICs, South Korea and Taiwan, which are also recipients of Japanese aid, have the least capital-intensive defence establishments. These two countries spent $2,700 and $3,300 per soldier, respectively, in 1977, compared with an average of $5,600 for the NICs as a whole, $7,500 for the OPEC countries, and $31,800 for developed countries.[68] And these two, together with Hong Kong, which has no domestic military establishment, are the only NICs to have achieved a surplus in their balance of payments.

The implication of this argument is not that industrialisation is a mistaken strategy, or simply that militaristic industrialisation raises the costs—urban unemployment, rural poverty, political repression—of developing industry. It is rather that industrialisation induced by the weapons system is the wrong kind. It can never provide the basis for self-sustained development.

Breakdown

In his book *Race and History*, Claude Lévi-Strauss distinguishes between "stagnant" and "progressive" culture or "stationary" and "cumulative" history. He argues that the "progressive acquisitive type [of society] in which discoveries and inventions are accumulated to build up great civilisations . . . depends on the *number and diversity* of the other cultures with which it is working out, generally involuntarily, a common strategy."[69] As we have seen, the monolithic armament culture imposes a kind of stagnation on the industrial development of the dominant military powers. The spread of the weapons system draws Third World countries into this stagnant industrial structure and, at the same time, creates an interconnected world military order which can more or less cope with the dissatisfaction engendered by the process.

During the 1970s, the dominant military powers have experienced a major recession (probably as a result of competition from more "progressive" industrial nations[70]). And this, as we shall see, has been the main impetus behind the speeding up of military technology transfer—an arms boom unequalled in history. Between 1968 and 1977, the total value of arms imports rose more than three times, from $5,370 million to $17,600 million (or in constant 1977 dollars, from $8,670 million to $16,700 million). For underdeveloped countries, the increase was even greater; arms imports rose by a factor of nearly four, from $3,640 million to $13,680 million; while arms imports by oil-exporting countries rose fifteenfold. And yet, far from reinforcing the world military order, this spectacular accumulation of weapons in the Third World has merely contributed to growing fissures within the international system.

First of all, industrial growth increased income disparities both between and within countries. It was what the World Bank calls middle-income countries that enjoyed the benefits of industrial growth. The rate of growth per capita of advanced industrial countries and low-income countries actually declined during the 1970s. Rapid growth and militarisation of the NICs and OPEC countries amounted to the creation of what some have described as sub-imperial powers. Nor, with a few exceptions, notably South Korea, Taiwan, and Yugoslavia, were the benefits of industrialisation widely shared. Standards of living of the mass of the populations remained at subsistence levels and, in some cases, as in Brazil and Mexico, actually deteriorated. Developing countries which did not export oil or manufactures greatly increased their debt burden in order to pay for the influx of capital goods and arms from market-starved industrialised countries and for the higher price of food and fuel. The main effect of the short-lived commodity boom was to increase rural disparities, since it helped to improve the position of the more successful surplus farmers. Because of the capital intensity of industry, growth did not reduce the level of urban unemployment, and both rural and urban poor suffered from the effects of inflation. And the unevenness of economic development was often distributed along ethnic or tribal lines, channeling resentment along cultural lines. The consequence was increased political instability and/or the establishment of more repressive, authoritarian regimes; the reemergence of long-buried nationalist rivalries like that between Brazil and Argentina, Peru and Chile, Afghanistan and Pakistan; the explosion of regional irridentism as in the Horn of Africa; or the subimperial temptation to embark on local military adventures, as Iran did before the revolution.

Second, the World Military Order became less capable of containing the tensions thrown up by the development process. The American defeat in Vietnam, which is discussed in the next chapter, undermined the credibility of American military power—the belief in the American ability and inclination to intervene militarily in order to maintain world order—and, at the same time, increased domestic American resistance to such intervention. During the 1970s, as the Brookings study shows, the number of incidents in which the United States used force for political purposes declined sharply, as did, it seems, the effectiveness of such shows of force. Correspondingly, the ability of armies created in the Western image to act as Western proxies is likely to have weakened.

In actual conflicts, whether international war or so-called counter-insurgency operations, the sophisticated weapons system has proved less than useful. Its very complexity has been its undoing, entailing, as the Americans found to their cost in Vietnam, mammoth logistical operations in countries where transportation, storage facilities, communications are inadequate and the high level of skill that the complex equipment demands is often lacking. In guerrilla wars, as the Americans also found in Vietnam, the most suitable weapons are not those designed for a European war. And in international war, the more sophisticated weapons may actually prove a handicap. In the 1965 war between India and Pakistan, for example, the Pakistanis were unable to operate the automatic control needed to fire the guns of their Patton tanks, and their missile-equipped F–104 Starfighter was easily matched by the subsonic Indian Gnat.[71] In the fighting between Iran and Iraq that began in 1980, neither side appears to have been able to make use of the highly advanced systems which were acquired earlier from the United States and the Soviet Union.

The experience of war, particularly counter-insurgency war, has often had a decisive effect on armies. Middle- and junior-level officers, given a role in the war that is not commensurate with their rank, may often become frustrated by the ineffectiveness of

the war effort and demand alternative military strategies or new
economic strategies which could help to solve the underlying
socio-economic conflict and, at the same time, create the conditions for effective military operations. In some cases junior-level
officers and ordinary ranks may become disaffected and even join
with their civilian counterparts in resistance against political and
economic oppression. It was the experience of such wars that appears to have precipitated the coups in Brazil and Peru in the
mid-1960s[72] and in Portugal, the Movimento das Forcas Armadas
(MFA), which overthrew the old regime, was a direct product of
the colonial war. Disaffection with the overall command structure
appears to have been a major factor in all these cases. In Brazil,
for example, Alfred Stepan argues that counter-insurgency operations increased the military responsibilities of sergeants. Because
this was not associated with any increase in social and political
status, the sergeants began to ally themselves with trade unionists
and actually succeeded in preventing a coup against the radical
leader Goulart. This fact, combined with the fear that a revolutionary government might disband the armed forces and create a
militia (as in Cuba) led officers to redefine their role and their
attitude to government, and eventually brought about the 1964
coup, which set in process a heavily militaristic form of industrialisation.[73] In Portugal, it was the junior officers and other ranks
that precipitated the coup. According to Philippe Schmitter,

> The MFA's historical origins seem to have come primarily from
> the Guinea-Bissau theatre where the military structure was
> unique and where the strategic situation was most immediately
> hopeless—unlike Angola and Mozambique. In Guinea-Bissau,
> real military defeat seemed imminent and, owing to the theatre's
> small size and spatial confinement, interaction among junior
> officers was particularly intense.[74]

In the end, what persuaded the Army officers in late 1975 to divert
Portugal from its revolutionary course was fear of the consequences

of growing lack of discipline among the ranks. General Fabiao, Chief of Staff of the Portuguese armed forces, said of the rank-and-file organisation, Soldiers United Will Win (SUV): "The SUV has a certain strength. But I have reservations because it is a horizontal organisation and in the army we have a vertical organisation."[75]

Growing tension, the hollowness of the weapons system, cleavages within the armed forces were all elements of the Iranian situation. The massive military build-up was seen explicitly by the Shah as part of a drive for development known as the White Revolution, which included land reform and rapid industrialisation, and which was largely instigated by American advisors during the early 1960s. The land reform, which was in any case not very effective, primarily benefitted the middle-level peasants, the oxen owners. The industrialisation program created a new class of urban workers and technicians who were immensely frustrated by the waste, inefficiency, overcapacity, and periodic crises of industry. The urban population was also significantly non-Persian (Arab, Kurdish, Azerbaijani), and resented the Shah's emphasis on Persian culture. Above all, the mullahs, who are independently financed by religious taxes, lost their religious lands in the land reform and, at the same time, the mosques, which were insulated from state activity, became centres of political opposition. Eighty percent of the mullahs' funds were provided by the bazaar, and this, too, was threatened by the growing of banks and supermarkets and by the Shah's anti-profiteering campaign of 1975.

To uphold his position, the Shah relied heavily on the Army. Both he (in 1953) and his father (in 1922) owed their positions to military coups. The Shah bought splendid equipment for his Army. He set up secret police and intelligence organisations which carried out such activities as surveillance, torture, and arbitrary arrest, and were used to spy on each other and on the Army. He used the Army to promulgate an imperial Persian ideology of nationalist monarchism. He embarked on subimperial adventures, like intervention in the Oman war and the seizure of three islands in the Persian Gulf in 1971. He also used the Army directly to organise the development programme, creating Armies of Health and Literacy, which were sent out into the countryside.

But even before the 1978 revolution, there were problems in the Army. There was an immense shortage of skilled men. In 1975, U.S. Air Force personnel went on strike because they were being forced to pass ill-qualified pilots. And many soldiers resisted the implications of modern soldiering.

> Many Iranians who do have a familiarity with machinery have retained an active dislike for it; they find it ridiculous. Man is the supreme end of existence and should not have to submit himself to the tyranny of schedules, precision, etc., which machines require. "You [Americans] think we are careless, inefficient. But when we do what is wrong, we fail of our own free will . . . and is that not a kind of freedom?" said a student pilot.[76]

There was also immense wastage of equipment; U.S. officials estimate that 40 percent was being wasted. And when the pre-revolution armed forces were used, in Dhofar and Iraqi Kurdistan, the Iranians were dependent upon American personnel to advise and to fly planes. In Dhofar, observers noted the Iranians "were reluctant to engage directly with the guerrillas but relied on their heavy fire-power instead."[77]

When the revolution broke out in August 1978, the Army was inexperienced in fighting and found it impossible to crush the opposition. The expensive Chieftain tanks purchased from Britain were exploded by Molotov cocktails thrown into the rear exhaust. Army conscripts from rural religious backgrounds were influenced by the masses on the streets. Senior and junior officers were divided on how to deal with the situation. The Americans were unable to intervene and, in January 1979, through the NATO envoy, General Huizer, advised against a coup. Then, in February 1979, the Army collapsed and the troops began to fight each other.

And, according to Fred Halliday: "it was this, rather than a straight civilian-military conflict, which detonated the final explosion."[78]

The Iranian unheaval was not an isolated phenomenon. It was, however, the most important in a series of crises that ranged from Ethiopia to Yemen to Afghanistan. Nor was the situation in Iran unique. Saudi Arabia, Kuwait, Nigeria, and to a lesser extent, Argentina, Brazil, and Egypt, among others, are all creating monstrous military-industrial edifices on fragile social foundations. The tremors of Iran still shake the arms industries and politico-military institutions in Western countries. They are, like the tremors of Third World crises still to come, merely occasions when the problems, contradictions, and weaknesses of the head office of the military-industrial complex become apparent.

6
Military-Industrial Crisis

In July 1969, a young American officer, Brian Jenkins, gave a talk at the Rand Corporation on his return from his third trip to Vietnam. He had been a captain in the Special Forces from December 1966 to December 1967 and a member of the Long Range Planning Task Group at MACV Headquarters in Saigon from October 1968 to July 1969. His talk was a passionate plea for change in Vietnam. He believed that the war could have been won and that it "could have been done with less violence and at less cost to ourselves."[1] He believed that the Army was

> prevented by its own doctrinal and organizational rigidity from understanding the nature of this war and from making the necessary modifications to apply its power more intelligently, more economically, and, above all, more relevantly.[2]

Senior officers, he went on, believe that Vietnam is irrelevant, an "aberration." "The higher military echelons," he said,

> tend to be dominated by men of World War II European theater experience whose concept of the future war, for which the Army must be prepared, is a European style general war. The Army's doctrine, its tactics, its organization, its weapons . . . its entire repertoire of warfare . . . was designed for conventional war in Europe. In Vietnam, the Army simply performed its repertoire.[3]

Yet Vietnam may have been more like a future European war than we suppose. A future European war will probably not be a guerrilla war (although new technology may lead to guerrilla-type tactics), and it will not be fought in a jungle. But many of the reasons for the American failure in Vietnam—the complex, capital-intensive technology, the high rates of destruction, the economic cost, the logistical problems, the disintegration of Army discipline—could apply in Europe. Vietnam was the logical outcome of twenty years of baroque technical change. The interplay of the armed services and the armourers which underly the trend towards diminishing military effectiveness and growing industrial cost culminated in a war which could not be won and could not be paid for. A war which, in a wider sense, undermined American military power and marked the beginning of America's economic decline. Vietnam was the start of a crisis which not only affected every military-industrial institution but which also had profound, and as yet unknown, consequences for American society and for the wider international system. In what follows I shall try to describe the various aspects of that crisis as it relates to the users and producers of the weapons system.

Diminishing Military Effectiveness

Vietnam spurred the development of new technologies which, paradoxically, have served to speed up the degeneration of the weapons system. Unlike the predominant existing technologies, which are based on the industries which developed in the first half of the twentieth century—aircraft and automobiles—the new technologies are drawn from the new industrial sectors which led the postwar boom—electronics and synthetic materials. The new technologies have led to new forms of sensing or "seeing," using radar, sonar, infrared waves, microwaves, lasers, or map matching, a new form of control or "brains" based on miniaturized computers, and greatly increased destructiveness, as a result of new materials, improved aerodynamic design, etc. According to one expert:

The combination of sensing in the electromagnetic spectrum and control through solid state electronic devices has both captured the popular imagination and stimulated fears, which are expressed in discussion of the electronic battlefield and smart weapons, of war machines out of control.[4]

The new technologies have been or can be incorporated into all kinds of munitions—missiles, bombs, artillery, and mines. Mines, for instance, can now be designed so that they are "capable of being directed remotely and of carrying internal logic . . . [and] can be emplaced rapidly and remotely, and are capable of self-sterilization or self-destruction on command."[5] The new Copperhead artillery shell

in flight will suddenly sprout wings and home in on a moving tank illuminated by a beam of laser light. Later in the decade a forward observer will no longer be required to expose himself to enemy fire while keeping the laser beam focussed on the tank; the small artillery shell will contain its own microwave or infrared sensor, a memory bank to compare what it sees with known types of enemy targets and a microcomputer to perform the calculations necessary to assure a direct hit.[6]

Certain weapons, such as cruise missiles or remotely piloted vehicles, which have lain fallow for many years, have come to prominence as a result of the new technologies. Terminally guided cruise missiles, for example, are now widely used for naval purposes, for they allow "a patrol craft to pack the punch of a battleship."[7]

The new munitions, which are generally known as Precision Guided Munitions (PGMs), have, together with increases in destructive capabilities, vastly increased the vulnerability of all targets and the lethality of warfare (both conventional and nuclear). Although the new technologies had been around for some time, their use in the 1973 Middle East War was a shock to many people.* For the duration of the war, one aircraft was shot down, on average, every hour, and one tank on average was destroyed every fifteen minutes. On the Israeli side, the war consumed $2.5 billion worth of U.S. equipment and it took four years for the United States to rebuild its depleted stocks. Even today, the carcasses of expensive fighting vehicles are lying around in the Sinai Peninsula. Yet as James Digby, a Rand Corporation analyst who is one of the best-known exponents of PGM technology, has pointed out, the Middle East war was just "a glimpse" of the material (and presumably human) losses of a future war; "a war in Europe could dwarf those consumption rates."[9]

The advent of PGMs has been widely hailed as a revolution in warfare, affecting both nuclear and conventional weapons, comparable to the advent of the machine gun or the tank. Proponents of PGMs argue that their effective use requires a total change in tactics and organisation. Because of the increased vulnerability of all targets, big complex weapons systems, which are difficult to hide and expensive to replace, have, it is said, become obsolete. Because of unacceptably high attrition rates, many of the tasks currently undertaken by tanks, aircraft, and surface ships could be undertaken, in future, by unmanned vehicles, including ballistic or cruise missiles based on land or underwater, remotely piloted vehicles (RPVs), and even long-range guided artillery. Certain military roles, like long-range bombing, would become foolhardy in the hostile environment of contemporary warfare. And certain performance characteristics, routinely requested by the military since World War II, like aircraft speed or altitude, have become irrelevant. Only the submarine, because of the current limitations

* Sceptics argue that missiles, which are usually what people mean when they talk about PGMs, were responsible for only a small proportion of the "kills" in the Yom Kippur War. Leaving aside the fact that missiles were used only in limited areas and that where they were used by Egypt and Syria they forced a complete change in Israeli tactics, the point is that the destructiveness of war was greatly increased as a result of improvements in munitions of all kinds.[8]

of underwater sensors, will continue to operate in much the same mode as at present.

In contrast to the baroque weapons system, PGMs could be cheaply mass-produced in great quantities and operated by relatively unskilled soldiers. Manned vehicles, used for launching PGMs and transporting soldiers, could be small, agile, and easy to conceal. Instead of the cumbersome weapons-system-based organisation, with its complex and vulnerable support systems and its oversophisticated and vulnerable centralized command system, armed forces could be organized in small dispersed mobile units, on the basis of decentralized authority. This is the essence of the so-called chequer-board strategy devised for NATO by Stephen Canby,[10] another Rand analyst, and the target-oriented military forces proposed by James Digby, in which,

> for example, the job of attacking air bases might be handled by PGMs launched from the land or the sea as well as the air, and it might be institutionally efficient to allocate funds for these systems from a common task-oriented budget.[11]

Such strategies would, it is said, favour the defence over the offence, in much the same way as did the machine gun and heavy artillery before the invention of the tank.

These views are not universally accepted. Indeed, it is widely argued that the proponents of PGMs have greatly exaggerated their capabilities.[12] For some time to come, PGMs will be able to operate only in clear daylight; in Europe, this represents only a small proportion of the time. There are various countermeasures, such as smoke, artillery-barrage fire, electronic jamming, or fog. And weapons systems will still be needed for offence, since defence always needs to be able to counterattack. Indeed, say the critics, the new technologies merely imply the need for bigger, *more* complex, *more* expensive weapons systems in order to increase protection. Armour will have to be stronger and heavier (the latest American and German tanks, for example, have new nylon-titanium Chobham armour), engines will have to be bigger in order to achieve more powerful thrust-weight ratios and thus maintain the advantage of speed, and all weapons systems will require grander, more elaborate electronic systems for target location and identification, weapon guidance, and jamming and counter-jamming. And the growth of any one weapons system, of course, infects whole families of weapons.

Without the test of war (if we discount the Middle East experience), the pros and cons of an alternative PGM-based strategy can never be decisively proved. The ways in which the new technologies are and will be incorporated into preparation for war, in the end, turn out to be the outcome of institutional choice rather than of rational argument. PGMs threaten to undermine the organisation of the Army, based as it is on the weapons system, and to shift the present hierarchy of command towards more decentralised authority. PGMs also threaten the present industrial structure. PGMs are, in a sense, a form of process technology— they reduce the cost of armaments. Arms manufacturers have always emphasized product improvement—process improvement could reduce the size of their single-customer market. Where price competition is *not* a significant feature of the market, it makes much better sense to offer bigger, more complex and costly products than those that are small, cheap, and simple. In fact, if PGMs were procured in large quantities, the total market might remain the same, but it would involve a significant shift in the composition of the arms industry. In contrast to the weapons system, PGMs are based almost entirely on electronics technology. In the United States, electronics companies act as prime contractors only in a few instances; Raytheon makes ground-to-air and air-to-air missiles, Texas Instruments makes an anti-radar missile. So long as the weapons system predominates, the electronics companies will continue to act as subcontractors to the manufacturers of weapons platforms—the aircraft, shipbuilding, and automobile companies. A PGM-based strategy would vitiate the role of the present prime contractors.

The prime contractors are presently sustained by their relationships with the different branches and services of the armed forces. The persistent and powerful alliance between individual defence companies and military units has ensured the survival of the weapons system. New technologies have been, as it were, grafted onto existing systems, embraced by the baroque. Those new weapons which cannot be absorbed, like the remotely piloted vehicle (RPV), get squeezed out in order to make room for the bigger traditional systems.[13] In the absence of some drastic stimulus to organisational change, such as a major war, new technologies which "rarely fit into the old patterns . . . are made to fit, like the odd-shaped piece in a child's puzzle, or they simply fall between the cracks."[14]

Yet it is becoming apparent that continued "improvement" of the weapons system has become self-defeating. Even assuming that it makes sense to continue to carry out traditional missions and to make incremental improvements to a given set of performance characteristics, growing cost and complexity is defeating the weapons system on its own terms. There is a plethora of evidence now which, when put together, calls into question the ability of modern armed forces to fight wars. A small segment of this evidence is summarized below.

The motto of the U.S. Air Force's First Tactical Fighter Wing is "Readiness is our profession." And yet, in June 1980, the wing failed a test given by the Air Force's Tactical Command to see if it was ready to mobilize for a war in the Middle East. Only twenty-three of the sixty-six F–15s were "mission capable."[15] One of the main advantages of the F–15 when it was first built was said to be its ease of maintenance. It was designed and built around the concept of "black boxes," modular components that could be easily moved and replaced in case of a parts failure. Yet this advantage has been swamped by other difficulties: drastic shortages of parts, including an insufficient number of "black boxes," so that "war readiness supply kits" have had to be cannibalized;

shortages of experienced engineers; engine failures; lack of durability of the engines and parts because of poor design, poor materials, and "harder" flying than expected.[16]

These problems are not unique to the F–15. On the contrary,
in one form or another, they plague nearly every weapons system
in the United States and most Western inventories.

RELIABILITY

Three out of the eight United States helicopters that were sent to
rescue the American hostages in Iran broke down. This caused
many people, in Congress and the media, to wonder about the
reliability of American military equipment. There were mutterings
about accidental spraying, seawater, and sand, but this did not
allay the concern. In fact, the failure rate of the helicopters, 37.5
percent, was relatively low. The RH–53D helicopters, which were
used in Iran, have a mean time between failures that is less than
the time it took to fly the helicopters from the *Nimitz* aircraft
carrier in the Persian Gulf to the landing site in Iran. In their
normal occupation, which is minesweeping, 55 percent of the
RH–53D fleet is not capable of performing its mission at any
given time. For every flight the RH–53D requires forty hours of
maintenance.[17]

Other aircraft have even higher maintenance requirements and
even lower mean time between failures than the RH–53D. A
consolidated guidance report sent to the Air Force and Navy by
Secretary of Defense Harold Brown in the spring of 1980 showed
that two-thirds of the F–111D bombers are grounded at any one
time and that the F–14A is not ready to perform its mission
nearly half the time. The time between failures varies from
twelve minutes for the F–111D to eighteen minutes for the F–14A
and F–45 fighters, and to seventy-two minutes (easily the longest)
for the A–10 ground-attack aircraft. Maintenance hours per flight
vary from ninety-eight hours for the F–111D bomber and the
F–14A fighter, to eighty-three hours for the F–4J, to thirty-four

hours for the F–15, and eighteen hours (easily the lowest) for the A–10.

Complex military equipment tends to be unreliable. The more parts there are, the greater the chances that one will fail and the greater the likelihood that the system as a whole will break down. "For instance," writes one of McNamara's former systems analysts,

> destroyers fifteen years old and older experience one fifth as many major combat systems failures as destroyers less than five years old (despite the traditional annual testimony on the decrepit condition of the superannuated destroyer fleet).[18]

In the fiscal year 1981 statement on the defence budget, we find the U.S. Air Force reporting "increases in accident rates," problems of reliability with Navy sensor systems and with telephone systems in Europe.[19]

Among the latest weapons systems there have been some dramatic examples of unreliability. The TF–30 engine, which powers the F–14 Navy fighter, and the F–100 engine, which powers the F–15 and F–16 Air Force fighters, have had persistent operational failures. The operational problems of the TF–30 have caused several crashes of the F–14. The F–100 engines have a high rate of stalling or choking, which rapidly increases the engine temperature and forces the pilot to shut down and restart.[20] This is particularly nerve-racking for pilots of the F–16, which has only one engine; the F–15 has two engines.

The F–14 has had several crashes due to other causes also. In addition to the problems with the engine—$200 million has already been spent to correct a "malfunctioning" of the fan blades— there has been a failure of the hydraulic system; a problem of "water intrusion," which means basically that the F–14 leaks when it rains and this causes various "malfunctions," such as "data freeze," or loss of control of the spoilers, which, in turn, control the surfaces on the wings rather like the wing flaps; and a mysterious electronic fault which nobody has been able to locate. It has been suggested that the cause of this last problem is "electron overload," resulting from the close proximity of numerous electrical circuits with different functions; "the difficulty of achieving perfect insulation means that one circuit could be activated by the charge from another."[21] To cope with this, the company has installed voltage monitors, so that when a malfunction occurs, the voltage drops and the monitor will automatically switch off the electronic flight controls so that the pilot can use the alternative mechanical system. Installing the monitors takes some time; meanwhile, the Navy imposed flight restrictions on all F–14s.

According to an industry executive:

> You have a plane [the F–14] that has to fly slow to land on a carrier, fly fast to intercept the latest MiGs, be agile enough to dogfight but big enough and have the complicated electronics required to handle the Phoenix missile. When you wrap metal around all those requirements you come up with an extremely sophisticated and complex airplane subject to all kinds of bugs.[22]

It is said that, given time and money, the bugs will be ironed out. But an F–14 pilot said:

> Some of my friends are dead. What grieves me is that the plane is so complex and so screwed up that it won't ever really get fixed. It will just trundle along with its inadequacies and Band-Aids, Band-Aids, Band-Aids.[23]

Similar problems are likely to beset the XM–1 tank, which was put into production in March 1980. In April 1979, J. H. Stolarow, the Director of Procurement and Systems Acquisition at the U.S. General Accounting Office, wrote to the Secretary of Defense asking that production be delayed because of critical problems of reliability and durability.

> In operational testing, the XM–1 demonstrated a cumulative 104.3 mean miles between failure (MMBF) compared to the testing goal of 272 MMBF. The demonstrated performance

was subsequently adjusted to 145 MMBF by Army officials as a result of their refining of test data [sic]. Nevertheless the tank still falls short of achieving the test goal of 272 MMBF. The design goal is 320 MMBF.[24]

There were problems with the new gas turbine engine; with the turret which did not turn properly and has been described as "a maintenance nightmare";[25] with the aluminum tracks which are "not durable enough to meet XM–1 performance standards,"[26] i.e., they come off on certain terrains; and with the transmission and the fuel system. The fuel consumption is about twice that of XM–1's predecessor, the M–60A1. The haste to put XM–1 into production was due to the contract between Chrysler and the Army since delay would increase the price of the tank; reportedly, there was considerable pressure from Chrysler, then, as is often the case, facing severe financial problems. In his letter, Stolarow points out that the problems of XM–1 are not unique.

We are also concerned that there is already deployed in Europe a number of systems whose availability for combat has been considerably reduced because of design problems. Had they been identified and corrected during system development the combat readiness of U.S. forces would be enhanced. To rush the tank into production may run the risk of adding still another critical weapons system to this list.[27]

The same point was made more forcefully by Representative Stratton of New York, a member of the Armed Services Committee who investigated the tank: "All I know for sure is that we've got a high risk item on our hands and if we aren't careful we could end up sending another piece of junk to our troops in Europe."[28]

DURABILITY

Closely related to reliability is durability, the rate at which parts and whole systems wear out. As weapons systems reach the limits

of technology, as they are required to meet exacting and often
conflicting requirements, the physical strain on the hardware
greatly lowers durability. "In many respects," explains one expert,

> the fighter plane combines the performance features of a race
> car in regard to speed and handling equipment with the mainte-
> nance problems of a vehicle driven in heavy traffic in terms of
> wear and tear on the engine.[29]

The classic example of the trade-off between performance and
durability was the C–5A, a plane designed to be capable of de-
livering two main battle tanks to NATO on an unrefuelled mission of 2,800 miles.[30] In order to reconcile the design specifications
for take-off distance, gross weight, and fixed empty weight, about
14,000 pounds had to be removed from the airframe structure,
mostly the wing.

> Subsequently, the Air Force concluded that the main structure
> had been so greatly weakened in the process that service life
> expectancy had been unacceptably reduced. If present plans
> (1979) are carried out and a "new" wing is retrofitted to all
> C–5A aircraft, the deleted 14,000 will be restored. The cost is
> likely to exceed $1.3 billion (1977 dollars); and unless perform-
> ance compensations can somehow be provided, the modified
> aircraft will be unable to perform the mission for which it was
> designed.[31]

SPARE PARTS, FUEL, AMMUNITION, ETC.
A major preoccupation of military men is logistics. This is not
surprising, given the complexity of the modern weapons system,
the quantity of fuel and ammunition they consume, and the high
rates of attrition that can be expected in a future war. A typical
American manoeuvre battalion in Europe, for example, carries between 500 and 1,500 basic spare parts—such things as bulbs, fuses,
batteries, track shoes, tyres, etc. Each battalion has a back-up

Direct Support Unit (DSU), which may carry as many as 10,000 spare parts. Then there are supply depots, which have a through-put of around 60,000 different parts a year in order to support different types of equipment—tanks, trucks, bulldozers, weapons, radios, etc. Each item has a federal stock number, which is fed into a computer in order to help the relevant unit to identify, pack, and ship the particular item required. The system itself is enormously complex and makes many mistakes. As it becomes more complex, the mistakes increase.

In Vietnam, despite the largest logistical operation ever mounted, there were perennial shortages. It took, on average, thirty days to repair minor battle damage to aircraft in Vietnam, primarily because of shortages of spares. Currently, shortages of spares and ammunition plague the operation of many weapons systems in the United States inventory, particularly the F–15.

An additional problem is the transport of spares, etc., by air-craft or ships which themselves consume fuel and spares. During the airlift to Israel in 1973, a ton of jet fuel was taken out of Israel for every ton of cargo delivered. The C–5s consumed more fuel than did the entire Israeli Air Force. "The success of the operation hinged on the fact that . . . [Israel's] adversaries could not or did not disrupt the fuel-storage facilities."[32]

MANPOWER

Modern military equipment requires highly skilled personnel for operation and maintenance. As complexity grows, so do the re-quirements. And as cost grows, it becomes more difficult to find the funds to hire suitable technicians. Despite growing unem-ployment, the armed services in the United States, Britain, and France have all experienced growing manpower shortages, and this has been a major reason for lack of operational readiness. In 1980, the U.S. Navy reported a shortfall of some 20,000 mid-grade petty officers, especially in electronics, propulsion, and nuclear-trained senior petty officers. Similar shortages were reported among line officers, particularly pilots and nuclear-trained officers. The

U.S. Air Force was short of about 1,200 officers in the engineering field. There was considerable concern about the impact of these shortages on training both in schools and on the job, and the effect this would have on future numbers. "In short," Admiral R. Baldwin told Congress, "we are losing our most critically needed and most experienced personnel."[33] And these shortages will continue as long as the weapons system continues to be "improved." There is a particular problem in finding suitable people for combat or "teeth" roles because modern weapons systems absorb such a high number of supporting or "tail" personnel.

Those that are found, moreover, lack operational training and practice. This is not just because of the lack of experienced teachers. It is also because of the high cost per operational hour, the mass of "safety rules" designed to limit loss or damage to expensive hardware and which in practise inhibit "realistic" training, and the shortage of spares, munitions, and fuel. Many soldiers, sailors, and airmen are familiar with the problem of being allowed only one live firing of their principal weapon per year.

Finally, the operation of a complex weapons system imposes incredible stress on the operator. Here are two descriptions of the kind of job a typical operator is expected to be able to perform: On the F-14, the Radio Intercept Officer

> is responsible for running the on-board computer, which can tell him (if he is skilled enough to use it) the longitude, latitude, altitude, and air speed of up to 24 objects within its range of more than 100 miles. It can indicate the course to intercept for either the M 61A1 Vulcan 20 mm cannon, the AIM-7E/F Sparrow, or the SIM-9G Sidewinder missiles, while guiding simultaneously up to six Phoenix missiles to separate targets 50 miles away or more. The RIO must be able to keep track of many things at once—his position, direction and air speed, those of several other aircraft, communications with the ground and with the rest of the squadron, navigation, weather, of any missiles directed at him, any evasive maneuvers that may be necessary

to suggest to the pilot, etc. Thus, as one former pilot put it, he is "busier than a one-armed man trying to hang wallpaper."[34]

The pilot of the F–15 is not so fortunate as the pilot of the F–14. He has to do all these jobs himself. The F–15 is designed to fly at 2½ times the speed of sound, at altitudes of over 60,000 feet, on an unrefuelled mission of 1,200 miles. The pilot "flies the plane and directs its two missiles, one for targets out of sight, another for those within sight, and fires its Gatling gun at targets nearby"[35] and, presumably, he also has to maintain communications, etc.

The British RAF recently reported that 40 percent of crashes are due to pilot error. Sir Christopher Foxley-Norris, Air Chief Marshal and former Commander in Chief of RAF Germany, said of the pilot error which allegedly caused the crash of a Tornado prototype:

> We have had it already with the Phantom, the F–4 (the less complex predecessor to F–44), which is a multi role aircraft. The strain on the pilot in trying to make him fully expert in all the roles is intolerable.[36]

All these problems—unreliability, lack of durability, shortages of spares and munitions, shortages of manpower, lack of training, pilot strain (the list could go on)—contribute to what people call the lack of "readiness." And because of the interdependence of hierarchies of weapons systems with their associated manpower and support systems, unreadiness is contagious and spreads through all the intricate connections of modern armed forces. Coordination of weapons systems, with each other, with support systems, and with the centralized command is dependent on so-called C^3 (communications, command, and control) systems. The cost and complexity of C^3 systems grows along with the weapons system. They break down, wear out, and need huge numbers of spares and skilled personnel. They make mistakes; there have been several false nuclear alerts in recent years. They are overburdened; in the 1973 Middle East War, there were several command and control failures, including the shooting down of friendly aircraft, because of overcrowding on certain frequencies.[37] And, in war, they could easily be disrupted, not only by direct attack, but by the side effects of weapons. A one-megaton nuclear explosion, for example, could disrupt high-frequency transmissions in a radius of up to 1,500 miles and even farther, and the blackout could persist for several hours. Further, electronic and electrical components are sensitive to electromagnetic pulse (EMP):

> a short intense electrical burst generated in the region of a nuclear detonation. The EMP effects of explosions at high altitudes can disrupt electronic systems at distances of a thousand miles, with computers, power supplies, antennae, radio stations and some telephone equipment being particularly vulnerable if not specifically hardened.[38]

These effects were experienced in atmospheric nuclear tests carried out before the Partial Test Ban Treaty of 1963.

In the 1978 Defense Authorization Act, the U.S. Congress has called upon the Administration to prepare an annual "Matériel Readiness Report."[39] And the U.S. General Accounting Office has commented on the "deteriorating combat readiness situation" of United States forces around the world.[40] It is often argued that these problems are a result of funding shortages. With more money, bugs could be ironed out, design could be improved, more spares and munitions could be purchased, engineers could be attracted away from civilian jobs. More money—a lot more—could perhaps in the short run reduce the huge backlog of aircraft and ships waiting for overhaul and maintenance, improve current systems, hire more people, give them more training, buy more spares and munitions. But in the long run, the problems would recur. More money would also buy even more "advanced" weapons systems. More money would re-create the problems in a grosser form at some future date, for it would speed up the pace of baroque technical change. In the end, the budget can never keep up with the demands of baroque technology.

There have, of course, in the past, been many advocates of the "austere alternative" to cost and complexity. In the 1960s, some of McNamara's systems analysts undertook design studies which showed that

> savings of factors of from three to ten are available in the great majority of tactical weapons systems when emphasis is placed on minimum complexity for achieving a single well-defined combat mission capability. In all these cases, these austere alternatives will achieve greatly improved reliability; in many cases, significantly improved performance and combat effectiveness also will result.[41]

The F–16 and F–18 fighters, the A–10 ground-support aircraft, and the XM–1 tank were all initiated on the basis of this kind of thinking. None of them, except possibly the A–10, can be said to have remained within their original guidelines. The F–16, for example, expensively transformed itself into a ground-attack plane, so that it could be sold in Western Europe. The XM–1, which was originally envisaged as "a moderately priced tank with improved performance over the M–60 but with few gold-plated extras,"[42] is now, with its gas-turbine engine and its turret, which is capable of taking two different-sized guns in order to accommodate a German gun, *more* expensive in real terms than was its predecessor, the MBT–70, which was cancelled by Congress because it had too many "gold-plated extras."

The latest weapons systems are positively rococo in their elaborate and frivolous features. In an earlier chapter I described the obese Trident, America's new underwater nuclear-weapons system (soon to be purchased by Britain). The second leg of America's strategic triad in the late 1980s is to be equally grotesque. The MX missile will replace the current land-based intercontinental ballistic missile, Minuteman III, at a cost which is estimated in 1980 to be $33 billion. The MX missile will be much bigger than Minuteman III and more than twice as heavy. Minuteman III carried three warheads capable of hitting their targets with an accuracy of within one nautical mile. MX will carry ten warheads capable of hitting their targets with an accuracy of half a nautical mile.

These advantages could theoretically enable the United States to destroy the Soviet ICBM force. This capability is only of value if the United States is aiming to achieve so-called disarming first-strike capability—something which would be highly destabilizing, since it would provide a future President with an incentive to start a nuclear war. However, so long as submarines remain undetected, the Soviet Union (and the United States) will retain a retaliatory capacity. In these circumstances, it is arguable whether the United States needs potentially vulnerable ICBMs at all, let alone improved versions.

The Carter Administration claimed that the MX was needed because of the possible vulnerability of Minuteman, currently emplaced in hardened sites, in the late 1970s. But like all weapons systems, because the MX missile is bigger than its predecessor, it is even more vulnerable. To get around the problem of vulnerability, the ingenuity and inventiveness of the weapon's designers were given full rein. They came up with all sorts of exotic ideas. The MX would be buried in underground tunnels or trenches; it would be carried by wide-bodied transport aircraft; it would be moved around by road or rail, across fields and open country, along canals, over lakes or pools, in vertical or horizontal transporters made especially for the purpose. Eventually, the U.S. Administration chose the race-track system—a system which could surely win an award for warped and labyrinthine imagination:

> Each MX is to be carried on board a transporter-erector-launcher (TEL) vehicle within a closed loop which consists of 23 shelters spaced about 7,000 feet apart on spurs along a road some 10–15 miles in length. The number of loops per complex ranges from 3 to 7 or 8 depending on the surrounding terrain, making for about 40 MX missile complexes.[43]

The TEL is a 6-axle, 24-wheel vehicle, weighing 670,000 pounds, which will carry the missile, which weighs 190,000 pounds, and a "modesty shield," weighing 140,000 pounds, designed to prevent satellite observation of the missile and its deportment to any particular shelter.

> A number of peculiar operational features have been adopted to enhance Soviet technical means of monitoring U.S. compliance with the SALT agreements. The MX cannister is loaded on to the TEL in a special missile assembly area, in full view of Soviet satellite surveillance. The TEL then enters the closed-loop road through a "choke point," which is immediately closed, and proceeds to visit each of the 23 shelters in turn. While the "modesty shield" prevents the Soviet determination of the particular shelter at which the MX is unloaded (if indeed, the decision is not to keep the missile aboard the TEL vehicle!) the Soviet Union can assure that there is only one missile within each loop. The shelter roofs each have four "SALT verification removable closures" or "plugs" which are opened periodically or on challenge to verify that only one of the shelters actually contains a missile.[44]

When warning of a Soviet missile launch is given, the TEL will "dash" from shelter to shelter, at a speed of 15–20 mph, "giving the system some residual survivability in the eventuality that the Soviet Union determines the location of the missiles in the shelter complexes."[45]

The shelters will probably be located in Nevada and southern Utah. Their construction would be the biggest construction project in the history of the United States (and probably the world), bigger than the Panama Canal and bigger than the Alaskan pipeline. Construction and operation over twenty years have been estimated to require some 10,000 miles of heavy-duty roadway, plus an additional 5,000 miles of road and some 172 billion gallons of water in a region where water is scarce.

In the spring of 1980, the race-track system was replaced by the grid system. The grid system consists of parallel roads, in the shape of a two-thirds-filled hexagon, instead of the so-called closed-loop railway. Instead of the "modesty shield," each shelter is to be equipped with

> two long concrete cylinders to simulate the presence of the
> missiles. Their weight would be the same as that of the missile
> (plus its erector-launcher) and they would be equipped with
> special devices to simulate the heat output of the missile. After
> depositing the missile in a shelter, the transporter would with-
> draw the simulators and would thereby display both the mass
> and infrared radiation pattern that it had when carrying the
> missile.[46]

The number of "SALT verification ports" are also to be reduced from four to two per shelter. The new system means that shelters can be somewhat smaller, somewhat less space will be needed, and presumably estimated costs can, in theory, be reduced. Nevertheless, the scale of the project is still vast. In addition to the shelter system, the MX will require 193 maintenance cluster facilities, 77 security-alert facilities, 7 deployment area support centres, where Strategic Air Command maintenance alert areas and security teams will be quartered, storage facilities for maintenance equipment, and operating test and training sites. Each of these support bases is expected to occupy around 3,500 acres.[47]

Ironically, it can be argued that the shelters may, in the end, fail to protect the MX missile. It will be easy enough to dream up a worst-case analysis to justify a follow-on to MX. If SALT II is not verified, the Soviet Union could acquire enough warheads to destroy all the warheads. The Soviet Union might also develop MaRV (manoeuvrable re-entry vehicle) technology, already possessed by the United States, which could enable Soviet missiles to attack the MX as it "dashes" around from shelter to shelter on its transporter.[48] This possibility offers the designers, the arms manufacturers, and the Air Force delightful opportunities for new extravaganzas: more shelters, ABM systems, perhaps amphibious flying TELS.

The biggest European project of the decade is the variable geometry (i.e., movable wings) multi-role combat aircraft or Tornado, jointly developed and produced by Britain, Germany, and Italy. It is expected to cost the British taxpayer something of the order of £10,000 million. MRCA has been described by Helmut Schmidt as "the greatest technological project since the birth of Christ,"[49] and, more mundanely, by the 1978 Aircraft Annual, as

a *splendid machine, the very ultimate of what can be achieved with today's technology. . . . From stern to stern, it is almost totally uncompromised. . . . Most of the engine is of radically new construction. . . . It is probably fair to claim that no other combat aircraft in history has ever had such a remarkable array of flight controls and high-lift devices.*[50]

This "splendid machine" is, in fact, an expensive compromise between the differing requirements of national armed forces and the differing capabilities of national arms manufacturers. The RAF wanted Tornado for long-range strike and strategic air defence (defence against bombers), the Germans wanted a plane for battlefield support, and the Italians wanted a plane for air superiority. None of these roles is easy to reconcile. To achieve the manoeuvrability (a fast rate of climb and powerful acceleration) needed for air superiority, the aircraft needs a small, light airframe and a second engine. Yet low weight, combined with the fuel requirements of the second engine, limit the range and payload needed for long-range strikes. The plane also needs to be large for stable flight at speed at low level when penetrating radar defences. Battlefield support requires yet another set of characteristics, a short take-off and landing capability, ruggedness, and cheapness. No wonder that it got the name "the milk-giving, wool-growing, egg-laying sow."[51] In the end, Tornado cannot satisfactorily fulfill any of its roles, except perhaps the long-range nuclear mission, which does not require a heavy payload. For battlefield support and air superiority, roles in which the plane can expect to suffer a high rate of loss, it is simply too expensive. Britain has designed yet another version of Tornado for air defence. Yet the Ministry of Defence has admitted that as an aircraft, the Tornado air defence version will not be much better than the Phantom (F–4) aircraft it was designed to replace, although "the weapon system is a complete step ahead."[52] Even in its nuclear strike role, Tornado will have many "wasted characteristics," like its STOL capability.

MRCA was not only a compromise between requirements; each national specification reflected a national manufacturing capability. A complicated system of work sharing was created which reflected the investment in the project made by each participating government. The British company BAC undertook the prime responsibility for the nose and fuselage. The German company Messerschmidt-Bolkoew-Blohm (MBB) undertook prime responsibility for the centre fuselage, even though it lacked any experience in variable geometry technology. The Italian firm Aeritalia undertook prime responsibility for the wings. Similar arrangements were established for the engine, the electronics, and each component part. Thus, the auxiliary power unit was designed by Kloeckner-Humboldt-Deutz, Mirotechnica, and Lucas Aerospace; the oxygen system by Normalair Carriett, Draegerwerk and Oleodinamica Magnaghi; and so on through the various subsystems that compose the aircraft.[53] The MRCA is thus a plane built upon competition and compromise. And like all such weapons systems, it is expensive and elaborate.

MRCA has not yet entered operational service. So far, there have been three prototype crashes. There have been problems with the engine and the stores management system, the central computer that controls the weapons, etc. We know that it is a plane stretched to the limits of technology and that the role of the pilot is unbelievably demanding, so that it is likely to experience all the operational problems that are typical of modern weapons systems. Yet the participants are merrily planning MRCA's successor. Already, elaborate follow-on schemes are being touted. This is the project known as TCA (tactical combat aircraft). It is proposed that this multirole air superiority/ground-attack plane should fly at supersonic speed, enjoy high manoeuvrability, a large weapons payload, a vertical take-off and landing capability, and so on.[54]

MX and MRCA have a dreamlike quality that is perhaps reassuring. It seems as though such weapons could never actually be used. But in Vietnam we caught a glimmering of what could happen if these crazy weapons were used. The weapons were clumsy, chaotic, and ineffective. But they were also immensely destructive. In a future European war, those characteristics of Vietnam could well be reproduced by several orders of magnitude.

Growing Industrial Costs

Vietnam also marked the beginning of America's economic decline. The absorption of scientists and engineers, the rigidities introduced into the American industrial structure as a result of twenty years of perfecting the weapons system, contributed, as described in Chapter 3, to the slowdown in productivity growth that began in 1965. American industry was no longer adept at competing with the newer, more dynamic industries of Germany and Japan. In the 1940s and 1950s, overseas expenditure had always returned to the United States through purchases of American goods, adding to America's balance-of-payments surplus and helping to underwrite the international role of the dollar. By the 1960s, this was no longer true. The Vietnam War drained the American economy and marked the fall of the dollar.

Vietnam interrupted the follow-on imperative. The running costs of the war led to the postponement of certain major procurement programs. The straitened economic circumstances of the early 1970s, combined with popular sentiment, led, for the first time, to major constraints on the American defence budget. Space expenditures also dropped sharply after the completion of the

Apollo program—the passing of a glorious moment of baroque civil technology. Shipments to the government by defence-oriented industries fell from $41 million in 1969 to $30 million in 1973.[55] This coincided with a downturn in civilian production. Consequently, the defence industry experienced the worst recession since the end of World War II.

Between 1968 and 1976, defence-related employment fell from 3.2 million to 1.7 million; nearly half the total industry manpower lost their jobs.[56] In certain companies, the situation was even worse. At General Dynamics' Fort Worth plant in Texas, employment fell from 30,000 to 7,000 over the same period.[57] Many engineers left the industry never to return.

Over the same period, thousands of subcontractors went bankrupt. Between 1968 and 1975, the number of active aerospace industry subcontractors decreased from 6,000 to under 4,000. And this does not include the parts suppliers. The foundry industry experienced a *net* of 280 closings. Many of these were sole source suppliers, and their disappearance created severe problems when defence production began to expand again in the late 1970s.[58]

The problems of the subcontractors stemmed directly from the problems of the prime contractors, who "pull back" subcontracting work during times of recession. All the main defence contractors experienced substantial problems of excess capacity. A study undertaken by the Department of Defense of seventeen major aircraft companies showed that, on the average, they used 55 percent of nominal one-shift capacity, 45 percent of peak-output capacity based on the experience of the past ten years (1.4 shift on a 40-hour week) and 20 percent of mobilisation capacity (using current floor space on an all-out three-shift basis).[59] (The results were the same whether capacity was measured in terms of employment, sales output, or physical output.) It is normally considered good economic practise to operate at between 85 percent and 95 percent of capacity, on an approximately 1.3 shift basis, with critical machinery used on multiple shifts.

The problem of excess capacity was reflected in the financial problems of the prime contractors. At the peak of the Vietnam War, many contractors borrowed heavily, only to find their markets shrink. For eight major aerospace companies, debt as a proportion of working capital rose from 30 percent in 1960 to over 80 percent in 1970.[60] For the aerospace industry as a whole, debt as a proportion of working capital stood at 80 percent in 1975 compared with an average of 35 percent for the years 1960–65, although increases in defence spending, combined with an upturn in commercial transportation, have reduced this to 60 percent.[61] At least two major aerospace companies, Lockheed and Grumman, were threatened with bankruptcy and had to be "bailed out" by the U.S. and Iranian governments respectively. Chrysler and several shipyards came close to ruin. A survey undertaken in 1976 by the conference board of thirty-four banking and financial institutions concluded that defence contractors were a bad risk. Among the reasons were:

1. *Profits are too low for the risks faced and their long-term viability compared with the profits of industries oriented to commercial markets.*

2. *Uncertainty is the principal risk perceived by the survey participants—uncertainty both as to the fulfillment of present contracts and winning of future contracts.*

3. *Other "negatives" seen include limited product line and over-reliance on a single customer, poor management practices and the propensity to "buy-in" programs; certain Defense Department policies, tactics and administrative practices such as excessive management and policy changes, a propensity to alter specifications in mid-contract, and adoption of an adversary posture toward suppliers.*[62]

The problems experienced by the American defence industry in the 1970s have been experienced for years in Europe. Excess capacity is, as we have seen, endemic to the defence business. As the cost of individual weapons systems rises, so more labour, plant, equipment, and materials are required for development and production within a given time period. Because of budget limitations, fewer types of weapons system and fewer numbers of any individual type are purchased, so that orders are distributed unevenly. Some firms manage to win the lucrative contracts; others face bankruptcy. As the competition to win contracts intensifies, "improvements" are offered which eventually find their expression in runaway costs. The hair-raising risks of managing an uncontrollable programme are almost as great as the risks of not having a programme to manage. Because orders are not spread evenly, although there is some sharing, and because delivery schedules have not grown nearly as fast as costs, it is the cost of the individual weapons system that largely determines the capacity of the prime contractor and his team of subcontractors. If a defence budget cannot keep up with increases in the cost of individual weapons systems, excess capacity is the inevitable result. Falling employment in some areas and sectors, the bankruptcy of subcontractors, and growing indebtedness are all aspects of the same problem. Vietnam did not create the problem; it merely hastened the inevitable consequences.

As in Europe, a number of solutions were attempted; none was more than ameliorative.

DIVERSIFICATION

During the 1960s and 1970s, many American defence companies attempted to move into civilian markets. There were two approaches. One was merger or acquisition. The other was the attempt to find alternative products to offer to the government.

During this period, many companies acquired civilian subsidiaries. United Technologies acquired Otis Elevator; Raytheon acquired Amana. Rockwell, which makes truck axles, merged with North American. Marietta merged with Martin. Also, many large conglomerates bought their way into the defence market; Litton, Ingalls, and Tenneco, for example, all bought shipyards.

Merger and acquisition undoubtedly increased the financial

stability of defence contractors. But, in general, defence divisions were operated as separate divisions and the same old problems reemerged. Indeed, some conglomerates, like Litton, found themselves trapped in a heavy and unexpected structure of debt.

Diversification, for a while, seemed promising. But the new civilian products developed into what might be called quasi-weapons systems. Space products were the first and most obvious example. But in the early 1970s many defence contractors started what they called "environmental" divisions in response to popular concern about energy, transport, housing, medical care, and so on. Products included urban transport systems (like the San Francisco BART system, or the Washington metro), artificial hearts or limbs, solar energy equipment, prefabricated housing, pollution surveillance and control, etc. General Electric, for example, was making prefabricated houses out of a honeycomb-structured plastic which had been developed for the space program. The houses came in several styles, mock Tudor, colonial, and red-brick, and could be assembled in twenty minutes by thirteen men.

Many companies, including Grumman, Alcoa, PPG Industries, General Motors, and General Electric have moved into the solar energy field. This offers some wonderful opportunities for baroque technology. The Sunsat Energy Council, which includes Lockheed, General Electric, IBM, Westinghouse, Boeing, Rockwell, and Grumman, is proposing to build a solar satellite power station (SSPS), a 36-mile grid of photo voltaic cells orbiting the earth, beaming microwaves to an earth station, where the microwaves would be converted back to electricity. The council has already received initial funding for the project, which is currently expected to cost $80 billion per satellite. It has been estimated that the same investment in flat-plate solar heating would create over twice as much energy. A scientist has compared the beam to "a giant microwave oven cooking all people, plants and animals caught by the wandering beam."[63]

A similar quasi-weapons system, on a far less ambitious scale, is the Concorde supersonic airliner, jointly developed and produced by Britain and France, at a cost of well over a billion pounds to Britain alone.

The evolution of these products has been viewed by some as a sign of the emerging social-industrial complex.[64] All the characteristics that are presently typical of the armament sector would imbue energy or the environment: capital intensity, centralized control, growing cost and complexity, periodic crisis. We have already seen something of this in the field of nuclear energy. Sinister as this sounds, a case might be made for the social-industrial complex on the grounds that it could act as a kind of lightning conductor, diverting pressures for increased military spending, channelling the technological dynamic of the armourers into, at least, less harmful pursuits. For the present, however, environmental spending cannot, in an era of economic weakness, command the same urgency among congressmen and the like as the Red Menace.

FOREIGN MILITARY SALES

The role of arms sales in supplementing the defence budget has long been recognized in European countries. In Britain and France, exports have for many years amounted to between 20 and 30 percent of total military production. Indeed, exports have come to mean the difference between having and not having an independent arms industry. In both countries, government salesmen actively promote the sale of armaments overseas.

Between 1965 and 1975, U.S. military exports increased four-fold, from 9 to 15 percent of total military production.[65] For some companies, and in some categories of equipment, military exports were even more important. In 1976, the Army Missile Command bought 76 percent of its procurement for foreign military sales. The same year, more military aircraft were procured for foreign governments than for domestic military use.

Moreover, the substance of military exports changed. Previously, secondhand or earlier-generation military equipment had been supplied to foreign countries, often gratis, under military-assistance programs. Now first-line equipment was being sold on commercial terms.

In theory, the surge in arms exports was part of the Nixon Doctrine of encouraging self-reliance. Third World countries should fight and pay for their own wars. Vietnamization was, of course, the model for the doctrine. In practise, the Nixon Doctrine, and the lack of restraint over arms sales with which it was associated, not only helped to employ the excess capacity created by the Vietnam War, but it may actually have saved some prime contractors from bankruptcy. Grumman is the well-known example, publicly saved by a $200-million loan from the Shah of Iran in order to maintain a production line for F–14 fighters ordered by Iran. It is also said that exports "saved" Northrop, General Dynamics, and Vought.

U.S. government spokesmen have stressed the importance of arms exports in maintaining capacity in much the same way as, in the late 1940s, they had stressed the need for increased procurement. The Department of Defense provided evidence to the Congressional Budget Office on the costs savings on thirty-five weapons systems as a result of foreign military sales. On twelve of these systems, the benefit of keeping production lines open was considered a component of the total savings.[66] Apart from saving on overhead costs, which is part of the same problem, other forms of saving, such as recovery of R&D and lower production costs resulting from long production runs, were much less significant. In evidence to Congress, foreign military sales were said to have played an important role in keeping open production runs on the M–113 armoured personnel carrier, the Lance Missile System, and the F–4E combat aircraft.[67] A Treasury report which accompanied President Carter's Report to the Congress on Arms Transfer Policy emphasized the immeasurable benefit of what amounts to keeping all the prime contractors in business:

Production for exports helps to maintain a warm mobilization
base by reducing the extent to which industrial capacity is idle
or underutilized, and to keep total output potential above peacetime domestic requirements, thereby providing reserve capacity
for emergency use. Production for exports makes it possible to
avoid the dispersal of skilled and experienced labor teams, and
by keeping some production lines active forestalls the necessity
to incur large start-up costs and to expand production of specific
items rapidly during an emergency.[68]

But as Britain and France have already discovered, foreign military sales cannot provide a long-term solution. First of all, such
a solution has distinct political disadvantages. An arms-sales policy,
as opposed to a military-assistance policy, implies a loss of political
control and leverage. Except in special circumstances, as with
Israel, it is almost impossible to maintain a monopoly position.
As the Carter Administration appears to have learned, it is much
more difficult to restrain arms exports in an atmosphere of commercial competition. Yet monopoly and restraint are important
ingredients of political control and leverage.[69] Further, many
strategic analysts are concerned about the strategic implications,
particularly for an interventionist policy, of the acquisition of
sophisticated armaments by Third World countries.[70] Rightly or
wrongly, it is argued that the growth of regional military powers
has been a major factor in reducing the ability of the United
States to intervene militarily in the Third World.*

Second, foreign military sales are not dependable. There is no
a priori reason why arms sales should coincide with interruptions
in the follow-on imperative. Indeed, there were many complaints,
both in Britain and the United States, about the way in which

* In the previous chapter it was argued that the acquisition of major weapons
systems merely legitimised a subordinate role in the international hierarchy.
It is the challenge to the modern weapons system displayed in Vietnam that
has been more important in reducing the frequency of intervention and the
effectiveness of shows of force.

production for Iran received priority over production for domestic armed forces. This was the case, for example, with the British improved Chieftain tank and improved Rapier missile, and the American F–14. In Europe, it has sometimes been the case that interruptions in exports may have actually been the cause of increased domestic procurement. This may have happened in Britain in the late 1950s, when a crisis in the defence industry was partly caused by a rapid fall in exports.[71] Foreign governments may be overturned and they may seek new suppliers. The fall of the Shah in Iran provided a dramatic example of the risks of dependence on foreign military sales. Britain may have lost up to $4.5 billion in orders for defence equipment from Iran, and the United States is said to have lost $8 billion. Among those companies badly affected were General Dynamics (producer of the F–16), Grumman, Swan Hunter and Yarrow (now British Shipbuilders), and Vickers. In Germany, six submarines ordered by Iran were said to be "critical" to the health of the shipyard Howaldswerke-Deutsche Werft.[72]

Finally, arms sales, except in a few instances, do not finance the capacity to develop as well as produce weapons. The necessity to develop new weapons systems, if only to continue to compete in the international market, re-creates the domestic follow-on imperative. Indeed, foreign specifications are sometimes built into the specifications for a new weapons system—a practise, which, if it became widespread, could superimpose yet more frills on the ever-elaborate weapons system. To date, most such instances have led to simplification. President Carter's new intermediate FX fighter, designed especially for the Third World, is one such example.[73] More ominous is the expensive way in which the XM–1 turret was adapted to take the German 120 mm. gun, allegedly as a quid pro quo for the German purchase of AWACs, or the evolution of the F–16 from a single-purpose plane to an expensive, complex, multirole system in order to satisfy European requirements.

INTERNATIONAL COLLABORATION

The alternative to expanding markets is to stem the expansion of industrial capacity. This can be done by developing and producing fewer types of weapons systems. Different branches of the armed services are persuaded to use the same system and firms are persuaded to collaborate in development and production, which mitigates the uneven impact of a reduction of different types of weapons system. This was the case, for example, with the General Dynamics/Grumman F–111 variable geometry fighter/bomber. If, however, the different branches of the armed services continue to insist on a particular set of military specifications, which in turn reflect the manufacturing capabilities of their industrial allies, the outcome, as with the F–111, is the complex and costly compromise of doing everything, but nothing very well.

In Europe, where defence budgets are much smaller, governments have had to break up long-standing procurement relationships. Governments have played an active role in the process of industrial reorganisation. Today, no single European country can claim more than two major airframe companies, and the only large aeroengine companies are Rolls Royce in Britain and Snecma in France. Several of the major defence contractors have been nationalised.

The process of domestic concentration, however, has reached national limits. Practically no European country can now afford to go it alone in the development and production of a major combat aircraft. France is planning to collaborate with Britain and Germany on Mirage 2000, the latest of the famous Mirage series. In Sweden, the cost of a successor to Viggen, Sweden's combat aircraft of the 1970s, is such that Swedes are seriously beginning to ask whether Sweden can afford an aircraft industry. To narrow the range of military production further, most European countries have adopted the policy of international collaboration in the development and production of major weapons systems. International collaboration now accounts for 80 percent of Germany's annual equipment budget and 20 percent of Britain's.[74]

The case for international collaboration is often made on strategic grounds. It is widely believed that lack of standardization in NATO is a serious disadvantage. The Senate Armed Services Committee has argued that failure to maximise standardization has cost NATO between $10 and $15 billion a year. The case of NATO's elite seven-nation force, Allied Command Europe (ACE) Mobile Force (AMF), which is supposed to demonstrate the cohesion of the alliance, is often cited as an example. AMF is armed with six different recoil-less rifles, four different antitank missiles, three different mortars and machine guns. Air support is provided by seven different types of combat aircraft. One commander apparently believes that standardization would permit him "to cut by half his unit's deployment time, airlift requirements, and logistics personnel."[75]

There have been two forms of international collaboration. One has consisted of a series of American projects—the F–104G fighter, the Hawk surface-to-air missile, the Bullpup air-to-surface missile, the Sea Sparrow missile, and the F–16 fighter produced under licence by several countries in Europe. Participants have generally been small European countries or those with relatively undeveloped arms industries, like Germany in the 1950s and early 1960s. The other has consisted of joint development and production of complete weapons systems, like MRCA, the Anglo-French Jaguar, the Anglo-French helicopters, the Franco-German missiles, and so on, generally without American participation. These two forms have been gradually institutionalized in what is known as the "Two-Way Street" and IEPG (Independent European Program Group) respectively.

The "Two-Way Street," an American initiative, is an attempt to liberalize the arms trade between Europe and America. Since 1975, the United States has progressively waived the Buy American Act; under the Act, the U.S. Administration used to impose the equivalent of a 50 percent tariff on defence products for European NATO countries. It is widely argued that the "Two-Way Street" is an attempt to increase American exports, since the

United States sells roughly ten times more military equipment to Europe than Europe sells to the United States. According to Roy Mason, when he was British Defence Secretary, the arms trade between Europe and America can be likened to "a few solitary pedestrians walking down the sidewalk one way and a mighty motorcade ten times larger going the other way."[76]

IEPG was formed in 1976, on the fringes of NATO, in order to include France. Its aims are

> to make more effective use of the resources that European countries make available for research and development; to increase standardisation and interoperability of equipment; to maintain a healthy European defence industry and technological base; and to strengthen the European factor in the relationship with America.[77]

Everyone agrees that international collaboration increases the cost of individual weapons systems, owing to waste, duplication, and high overheads, such as frequent air travel. Estimates vary from 5 percent to 50 percent; the extra costs are, however, thought to be offset by the benefits of spreading the burden of development cost. The F–16, for example, is said to cost 18 percent more than if it had been produced wholly in the United States, and the XM–1 is said to cost 15 percent more.[78] A study undertaken in October 1977 suggested that co-production of the F–16 cost an additional $142 million, excluding some of the avionics, and that this was offset by a saving of $369 million from recouping U.S. R&D and overheads, increasing employment in the United States and hence increasing income tax.[79]

But this kind of calculation does not take into account the increase in complexity which results from the need to take different national specifications into account. In order to satisfy the European partners in the F–16 project, the F–16 was provided with, as we have seen, an entirely new set of capabilities at great cost. The adaptation of the XM–1 turret is another example, while the complexities of MRCA are reminiscent of the problems encountered in the F–111 project. In other words, international collaboration merely speeds up the process of baroque technical change. Seen from this perspective, General Lissarague's estimate of the cost of collaboration appears to be more realistic than the estimates quoted above:

> It could be said that if N is the number of partners, the price of an aeroplane produced collaboratively is equal to the price of the same aircraft built in one country, multiplied by N (in reality it is sometimes more).[80]

International collaboration could only result in real savings through genuine military and industrial rationalization. This could come about only through a massive reassertion of the American Command System in NATO *or* through the creation of a European Procurement Agency, much like the one proposed by the European Community, with legal powers and budgetary control.[81] Only multinational institutions of this kind could break down national military-industrial alliances.

International collaboration does not provide a solution to industrial problems, nor can it be said to have contributed to standardization in NATO. General James Polk, who was Commander in Chief of the U.S. Army Europe and the Seventh Army until his retirement in 1971, has argued forcefully that, from this point of view, co-production is not worth the effort. First, many co-produced items are not, in fact, interchangeable, because of differing production standards, including different machine tools, different systems of measurement, different standards for quality, hardness, and strength of materials. The U.S.-built Hawks are not interchangeable with the European-built Hawk. The U.S. Roland missile, originally developed by a Franco-German consortium, will have only slight comparability with the European version—it will have an entirely different chassis of American design. Second, a standardized compromise system satisfies none of the individual national armed services and thus reduces overall tactical efficiency. Third, logistical systems are complicated and

mistake-prone enough already without adding the further compli-
cation of multinationalism. It is more efficient for each national
unit to be self-sufficient in spares, in which case the use of different
types of equipment does not matter. Indeed, some have suggested
that diversity of weapons systems might be a positive advantage,
forcing the Soviet Union "to adapt to different tactics, techniques,
and technology."[82] General Polk believes that the

> whole effort of standardization or interoperability or, better yet,
> cross-servicing, should, in fact, be concentrated exclusively in
> the area of petroleum products and ammunition. . . . We do not
> need an international supply system or dual production under
> license or common spare parts or identical engines or the rest.
> Quite simply, we only need to help each other in battle. We
> need to do this quickly and confidently by assisting with the
> essential expendables of ammunition, fuel, food, and medical
> supplies and by giving other help. The rest is just window dress-
> ing. It is not worth the time, trouble and money required.[83]

International collaboration, like diversification or arms exports,
has its own inherent shortcomings. All could temporarily fill the
gap between the growing cost of the weapons system and the
limitations on military spending; but all, in their different ways,
contribute to further problems in the future. Diversification tends
to create baroque civil technology. The arms trade creates new
pressures for "improvements" in order to compete in world
markets. International collaboration ends up in new multinational
forms of baroque weapons systems. All these attempts to solve the
problem of excess industrial capacity are not so much solutions as
manifestations of the growing industrial crisis. They do not deal
with the causes of the crisis, the institutional interests of the
armed services and the arms manufacturers, and they cannot, in
the long run, provide substitutes for new domestic military orders.
They modify but do not remove the follow-on imperative.

So it was that at the depth of the post-Vietnam recession in the early 1970s, a number of new projects were initiated—Trident, the B–1 bomber (later cancelled by the Carter Administration), the new family of fighter aircraft, the XM–1 battle tank, a nuclear-powered aircraft carrier, etc. And these emerged a few years later to ignite the defence budget. Indeed, already by 1975, it was clear that the new generation of weapons systems was immensely expensive. According to Senator Stennis of the Armed Services Committee:

> *The purchase cost of modern weapons systems has increased by many times even within the last few years. It was to be expected that a new fighter aircraft for the mid-1970s would cost considerably more than the fighters of World War II vintage. It is striking, however, that fighter aircraft now being developed for procurement in the mid-1970s will cost five or six times more than comparable aircraft at the beginning of the 1960s. The cost of tanks is increasing over fourfold during the 1967–75 decade. A burst of 50-caliber machine-gun fire, our primary air-to-air munition until the end of the Korean War, cost about $20; we are now developing tactical air-to-air munitions costing several hundred thousand dollars per round—an increase by a factor of tens of thousands. The avionics package in some types of new military aircraft will alone weigh two or more tons and cost several hundred million dollars. At over $1,000 per pound this is about twice as costly as gold. The foregoing tendencies are deeply troubling. If the geometric cost increase for weapons systems is not sharply reversed, then even significant increases in the defense budget may not insure the force levels required for our national security.*[84]

By the late 1970s, the atmosphere of alarmism about the Soviet threat had led to "significant increases" in the defence budget. But it was still not enough. The General Accounting Office reported, in 1979:

The cost problem facing the U.S. military is getting worse, and no relief is in sight. The so-called bowwave of future procurement costs is growing beyond the point of reasonableness. Current procurement programs are estimated to total about $725 billion. If these costs are spread over the next ten years (a conservative projection) the annual average of $72.5 billion will be more than twice current funding levels. Clearly most of the programs will have to be cut back or eliminated.[85]

This, then, is the essence of the industrial crisis. "Improvements" in the weapons system, fuelled by industrial competition, lead to accelerating increases in cost. The costs of individual weapons systems, as they reach the limits of technology, always rise faster than the total defence budget. Military spending can never keep up with the cost of baroque technology. But a spiraling relationship of this kind has, in logic, to reach some kind of limit. In this particular case, the limit is expressed in the unwillingness of the participants to continue to suffer the worsening consequences— a growing disaffection which is, perhaps, as yet unfocussed.

The Collapse of Consensus

Military failure in Vietnam was not just a matter of technological defeat. It resulted, in the first instance, from a breakdown in public consensus about America's world role. The cost, destructiveness, and ineffectiveness of modern military technology were all criticised. In contrast to World War II, the production of guns led neither to victory nor to the production of butter. Warfare and welfare were not compatible for America any more than for Vietnam. And there were, of course, wider issues to do with the development of the warfare state—bureaucracy, secrecy, and corruption for example—that were publicly exposed in the Watergate scandal. The breakdown in public consensus affected the armament sector itself. A central factor in America's defeat was the collapse of the structure of authority around which the weapons system is built.

In 1979, two former American Army officers, Richard Gabriel and Paul Savage, published a book entitled *Crisis in Command*. They argued that the "Army in Vietnam had literally destroyed itself under conditions of minimal combat stress,"[86] and that "by 1972, accommodation with the North Vietnamese was the only realistic alternative to risking an eventual military debacle in the field."[87] The symptoms of disintegration were desertion; "fragging"—a hand grenade thrown at officers; combat refusals; and widespread drug addiction. By 1971, when casualties were actually declining, the desertion rate reached 73.4 per thousand soldiers, higher than at any time in American history. Between 1969 and 1972, total admitted incidents of "fragging" reached 788. This does not include mutinous attempts by other means—rifles or mines, for example. A computer study of casualties in Vietnam included 89 deaths caused by "intentional" homicide, 534 deaths caused by "accidental" homicide and 1394 deaths caused by "other accidents." It has been suggested that the very high rate of helicopter crashes (which caused 17 percent of all officer losses) may have been partly due to sabotage. Combat refusals increased over the period "to the point of open disobedience."[88] In Vietnam, drugs were publicly available in places known to both officers and men. It is estimated that almost one-third of the Army in Vietnam had used a hard drug at some time. The trade was, in fact, organised by the Vietnamese government with American complicity, and both the CIA and America's diplomatic corps blocked investigation of the drug traffic by other branches of the federal government. And, in addition to these expressions of individual dissent in Vietnam, soldiers' resistance began to be organised in both Vietnam and the United States in the G.I. movement.

Gabriel and Savage view the crisis in command as the breakdown of "managerial" ethics. Operating a weapons system *is* different from running a factory. Managers, unlike leaders, are not

expected to die. No one was willing to face this fact. Gabriel
and Savage believe that the most important cause of the Army's
disintegration was the unwillingness of the individual officer

> to accept the ultimate sacrifice himself. This, above all, is what
> differentiates the military profession from others. Among the
> major findings that emerged from the research on the perform-
> ance of the military during Vietnam was the fact that officers
> often avoided the risks of combat by various means.[89]

In Vietnam, there were twice as many officers in relation to enlisted men as there were in the American Army in World War II.
Yet officer casualties per enlisted man were only one and a half
times as great as in World War II. Many of the officers were
technicians required to operate support systems in the rear. Because of the capital intensity of the weapons system, the ratio of
direct to indirect military manpower has dramatically fallen. In
Vietnam, the proportion of actual combat troops constituted 20
percent or less of any given operational base.

> While on an operation, they were exposed to the overwhelming
> share of the casualties, they returned to a base structure saturated
> with officers and NCOs who were largely insulated from the
> dangers that the combat troops faced.[90]

Managerial ethics, according to Gabriel and Savage, focussed
attention on trivial accomplishments which could contribute to
promotions. "Managers," i.e., officers, sought measures of accom-
plishment which might be equated with sales figures or profit
margins. Senior officers seemed to care only about "forms of
battle," about "body counts, status reports, reports of 'victories'
etc."[91] and this attitude went all the way up to the top. Brian
Jenkins pointed out that success in Vietnam was measured in
scores and statistics.

> On this basis, if twice as many bombs are dropped per month
> in 1969 as were dropped per month in 1967, we are doing bet-

ter . . . the same with leaflets, battalion days of operations, night patrols, and so on.[92]

General Westmoreland, the former commander of U.S. forces in Vietnam and later Chief of Staff of the Army, ordered a study of the state of military professionalism and leadership in the U.S. Army Corps. When it was completed in 1970, he had it suppressed. (It has since been made available to interested scholars.) The study reported that the "present climate" of the Army is

> conducive to self-deception because it fosters production of inaccurate information; it impacts on the long-term ability of the Army to fight and win because it frustrates young, idealistic, energetic officers who leave the service and are replaced by those who will tolerate if not condone ethical imperfection; it is corrosive of the Army's image because it falls short of the traditional idealistic code which is the key to the soldier's acceptance by a modern, free society; it lowers the credibility of our top military leaders because it often shields them from essential bad news; it stifles initiative, innovation, and humility because it demands perfection at every turn; it downgrades technical competence by rewarding instead trivial, measurable, quota-filling accomplishments; and it eventually squeezes much of the personal enjoyment and satisfaction out of being an officer.[93]

The study concluded that so long as senior officers receive promotion under the present system, this climate is not likely to change.

Since Vietnam, the All-Volunteer Force has been introduced and conscription has come to an end. Although disciplinary problems have improved, alcohol and drug abuses remain "continuous and endemic problems which could adversely impact upon individual and unit readiness and cohesiveness if not controlled . . ."[94] For Fiscal Year 1981, the Army requested $41 million for its Alcohol and Drug Abuse Control Program. There are similar programs in the Air Force and Navy.

There is also a very high rate of attrition among both officers and men. This is particularly serious in the Navy and the Marine Corps, where AWOL rates and desertion rates have soared. Vice Admiral James D. Watkins, Chief of Navy Personnel, has said:

> We believe the concept of [an] All-Volunteer Force "in" implies to an individual that he can possibly elect to volunteer "out" of the force as well, which isn't the case, as you know. They come in under a long-term contract and I don't believe that we can ready them adequately to accept the reality of sea duty. So they go AWOL or desert in too many instances.[95]

In all three services, retention or reenlistment rates are also falling.

Among the reasons cited are low rates of pay and other benefits compared with equivalent civilian jobs, dissatisfaction, particularly among officers, with shortages of ammunition, spares, and skilled personnel—in short, the consequences of the growing cost and complexity of weapons combined, presumably, with the unreality of anticipated military contingencies. There is growing pressure, among both officers and men, to form military unions—a trend which has been strongly supported by the American Federation of Government Employees (AFGE), which has grown enormously in recent years and has become much more militant. There are still a few GI groups left over from the organised resistance to Vietnam that focus increasingly on trade-union issues.

These developments are not peculiar to the United States. Pressure for unionization has spread throughout Western Europe. There have been armed-forces movements in France, Holland, and Sweden. Indeed, the Dutch conscript union adopted, in the early 1970s, a highly militant posture, with mass protests and demonstrations on such issues as censorship, the military penal code, overtime pay, mandatory hair length, saluting, and unnecessary formations, etc. After several important victories, the Dutch Army has become one of the most democratic and highly paid in the world.

In France, junior officers explicitly opposed the *force de frappe* on the grounds that the money could be better spent on more mundane conventional equipment. General Marcel Bigeard said: "There is afoot an enterprise of demoralization of armies on a French and European level which has been going on for five or six years . . . the matter is serious. . . ."[96]

Britain has experienced its own mini-Vietnam in Northern Ireland. The conflict has called into question the emphasis on expensive equipment designed for a war in Europe. There have been instances in which soldiers have fired on one another reminiscent of the "accidents" in Vietnam. Even the Cod War with Iceland, in which Royal Navy frigates were helpless against Icelandic tugs, caused a certain amount of self-questioning in the Navy. Problems of low pay, dissatisfaction with the state of "readiness," are perhaps even more widespread in the British armed forces than in the United States. For example, "moonlighting" is endemic in both the Army and the RAF.

> When the army was used to break the fireman's strike in the winter of 1977 resentment among soldiers that they were standing in for better paid firemen was widely noted; what was not publicly acknowledged was that a more serious frustration for soldiers, especially those stationed in London, was that their round-the-clock substitute firemen's duties cost them their nighttime jobs for security firms, night clubs and others.[97]

It is often argued that these problems would be solved by more money. But more money would be spent on more weapons systems, and as we have seen, more weapons systems or "bigger and better" weapons systems would reproduce the problems on a "bigger and better" scale. Further, the money solution, some would say, is part of the "managerial" ethics and would further undermine genuine military authority.

Practitioners like Gabriel and Savage advocate a return to "gladiatorial" ethics—the traditional values of the military profession. It is argued that a military career has become an "occupation," associated with monetary and career incentives, instead of

a "profession" or "calling," associated with self-sacrifice and dedi-
cation. The All-Volunteer Force and the growing use of civilian
contractors is adduced as evidence for this trend.[98] But this is not
an age of gladiators. The idea that the military, embedded as they
are in the products of modern industrial technology, could some-
how be insulated from modern society and inculcated with traditional respect for patriotism, loyalty, and similar values is difficult
to accept. In a democratic, "managerial" society, men cannot be
coerced to fight either through discipline or through the appeal
to outdated values. They will fight only for causes they believe in,
as was the case in World War II, or even in the Arab–Israeli wars.
A Dutch officer, talking to the newspapers after Dutch soldiers had
successfully saved hostages aboard a hijacked train, said:

> I am speaking personally, you understand, but the best kind of
> army we can have is where a soldier can say, "No I will not do
> that because I do not believe in it." Ideally, soldiers should have
> the right to elect—and dismiss their officers. . . . In a strike by
> a union, I cannot say that the army is fully prepared to fulfill
> its mission—and I am glad to say that.[99]

As war becomes more destructive and costly, and the possibility
of victory more remote, the occasions on which soliders are prepared to fight are likely to be fewer and fewer. A survey of four
combat battalions stationed in the southeastern United States
showed that only the elite Ranger battalions, which had the highest
porportion of college graduates, were largely (i.e., over 80 percent) prepared to fight regardless of the situation. Over 40 percent
of the infantry battalion, which had the highest proportion of
blacks, were *not* prepared to fight in any situation other than
foreign invasion of the United States.[100] Willingness to fight may
have increased since then. But nothing has occurred to make one
suppose that Army cohesion would be any greater in a future war
than it was in Vietnam.

It was not only the users of weapons systems that were disillu-
sioned by Vietnam; it was also the producers. The three main de-

fence trade unions in the United States are the United Automobile Workers (UAW), the International Association of Machinists and Aerospace Workers (IAM) and the United Electrical Workers (UEW). In 1969, the UAW proposed a conversion plan to cope with the winding down of the Vietnam War. The scheme was that each contractor would be required to set aside a portion of his profits as a conversion reserve to be held in a government fund and released only for conversion purposes. In proposing the plan to Congress, Walter Reuther, then president of the UAW, said:

> I think it is a terrible thing for a human being to feel that his security and the well-being of his family hinges upon a continuation of the insanity of the arms race. We have to give these people greater economic security and greater job opportunities in terms of the rewarding purposes of peace. . . .[101]

He recalled the end of World War II:

> I personally was privileged to participate in a ceremony at the Willow Run bomber plant where we turned out more bombers than any plant in the history of the free world.
>
> When we got to the end of that tremendous production achievement the Navy sent its brass and the Army sent its brass and we had a big ceremony and I represented, as the spokesman for the UAW, the 20,000-odd workers. The Navy brass and the Army brass thanked the workers for a tremendous production achievement and they gave them the "E" award for excellence.
>
> Then they told them: "The plant is expendable and you are all going to be laid off." That was the reward. If we are not careful, the major defense industries with no civilian production experience, the corporations operating those plants will walk away from them on the theory that they are expendable.[102]

There were, in fact, a few token schemes in response to the dramatic layoffs of the early 1970s. The Department of Housing and Urban Development undertook a $1.2 million pilot project to put unemployed aerospace professionals to work on urban problems.

The Technology Mobilization and Re-employment Program had
$25 million to retrain approximately 10,000 scientists and engi-
neers, plus $10 million for moving expenses, travel, and research.
But, in general, as we have seen, the corporations *did* operate on
the principle that workers are expendable. Although employment
picked up in the mid-1970s, the changing technology of the weapons system affected the composition of workers. There were more
jobs created in the electronic sector and fewer in aerospace. Further, the size and unevenness of contracts contributed to instability.

Those companies that won contracts were extremely overstretched, unable to keep to the terms of the original contract. In
response to charges about delays and cost overruns, management
often introduced measures that lowered standards of production
and soured labour relations. This, for instance, is what has largely
happened on the Trident programme. According to a labour leader
at Electric Boat's Quonset plant in Rhode Island:

> Since 1977, the shipyard has gotten far more deeply into pro-
> ductions problems such as they've never seen before. The man-
> agement has a theory that you can beat people into working.
> The enforced six-day work week is one example.
>
> We've got a lot of semi-skilled people. The skill mix has never
> been as low as it is now in semi-skilled versus skilled.[103]

Yet the only alternative to overwork is cancellation and massive
layoffs. When the B–1 bomber was cancelled, there were between
2,000 and 8,000 layoffs; the whole community of El Segundo was
more or less abandoned. Many people had to sell their homes at
ridiculously low prices because of the glut on the market. The
effect on the swelling ranks of engineers, who had never before
experienced mass layoffs and this kind of economic insecurity, was
devastating. A Lockheed engineer commented:

> Since I've been at Lockheed, I've been laid off a total of five
> times in nine years. Lay-offs are a real severe problem to people
> who are married, people who have house payments, families to

bring up. There's some fine people there. . . . I mean when you take the workforce at Lockheed, it's mostly salaried. There are something like 3,500 who are hourly, and the rest are salaried, close to 10,000 are really specialists, really brilliant in their areas. . . .[104]

Nor is it just the insecurity that has changed the attitudes of engineers in the defence industry. As technology becomes baroque, so the contribution of the individual engineer to a large-scale project becomes more specialised, more fragmented, and apparently less significant. A Rockwell engineer remembered that, during the 1950s:

there was literally an aerospace engineer's uniform. We all wore white shirts and black ties. Engineering was our entire lives. Many of us lived simply for the joy of solving complex technological problems presented to us. We believed that as long as we continued to perform high-quality work we would be taken care of.[105]

Now engineers have become migratory workers, flitting from job to job and from state to state. There are few second-generation engineers, and many of those that remain are deeply embittered.

Towards the end of the 1970s, the three defence unions renewed their efforts to propose conversion plans. All three unions have provided strong support for Senator McGovern's proposed Defense Economic Adjustment Act. As the numbers employed in defence diminish, the case for building up the civilian economy and creating new membership in the civilian sector has become increasingly attractive. The IAM commissioned a report on conversion, which was published in January 1979. The report concluded that a modest capital investment in railroads, mass-transit systems, resource-recovery systems (waste recycling), and solar energy could create approximately 700,000 jobs.[106] In other words, IAM workers would be much better off with civilian investment than military spending. The president of the IAM, in a speech to the

Coalition for a New Foreign and Military Policy, pointed out the
unfairness of the way workers were treated in the defence industry. The B–1 bomber contract indemnified Rockwell against
any loss, in the event of cancellation. He pointed out:

> We may call that socialism for the corporation and free enter-
> prise for the workers.
>   In any case, the injustice of the arrangement is readily appar-
> ent. Defense workers have a right to be idemnified against
> economic loss. In service to the national interest, they are called
> into defense production. It is worse than shabby to discard them
> like so much worthless surplus when the national interest no
> longer obtains. It is barbaric.[107]

The failure of the military business to guarantee stable employment has produced similar responses in Europe. This has proceeded
furthest in Britain, the country with the longest peacetime history
of an arms-intensive economy. Initiatives for conversion have come
from the shop-floor union representatives in factories all over
Britain. In the mid-1970s, Rolls Royce workers produced a pamphlet entitled *Buns Before the Gutter*. At BAC (Preston: now
Wharton), which makes MRCA, workers requested that management put 3 percent of the annual profits into a diversification
fund; in return, they were prepared to accept a lower rate of wage
increase. The plans prepared by workers at Vickers and Lucas
Aerospace for the manufacture of alternative socially useful products have become famous.[108] These plans have formed the basis
of mass campaigns to prevent redundancies and the closure of
factories. The Lucas Aerospace Workers have, in fact, achieved
a certain amount of success; they have, as a result of negotiations
which involved the Confederation of Shipbuilding and Engineering Union and the former Labour Government, succeeded in
persuading the management to open a new factory, in place of
one which is to be closed, and they themselves have developed
prototypes of some of their products, like their heat pump and
their road/rail bus. The ideas have been taken up by the Labour

Party and are contained in a report to the National Executive of the Party entitled *Sense About Defence*.[109] In the United States, the UAW presented an award to Mike Cooley, an aerospace engineer who played a key role in drawing up and publicising the plan, for the work done by him and his fellow shop stewards.

Similar, although much less developed, initiatives have been taken in other countries, particularly Sweden, Holland, Belgium, Finland, West Germany, and Italy. In West Germany, IG Metall, Europe's biggest union, has set up a special working party on armament technology and employment consisting of works council members from most of the important armament companies. In Italy, the metal-workers union, which accounts for most defence workers, has been extremely active in educating defence workers on these issues. The concern arose initially because the Italian arms industry was unable to guarantee "a high level of stable employment" owing to the "lack of a continuous flow of orders and uncertainty as to whether foreign contracts will be honoured."[110] The union has organised courses at factories in areas where defence work is concentrated, has set up national coordinating committees for workers in the defence sector, has helped to draft legislation which would impose political control over arms exports, has initiated various studies into the size of the problem and the possibilities for conversion, and has translated *Sense About Defence* into Italian and distributed it to workers in the defence industry. In a press release describing these activities, the union concludes:

> The FLM is convinced that these actions could, if tied to action by other unions and by international trade union organizations, make a significant contribution to building a lasting peace between all countries and all workers.[111]

In October 1979, the International Metal Workers (IMW) issued a report about arms production and employment which was drawn up on the basis of questionnaires to affiliated organisations.[112] IMW includes 14 million workers in 170 trade unions in seventy different countries. It is estimated that 2.8 million IMW

workers are directly or indirectly engaged in armaments production. On the basis of this report, the IMW unions jointly made
the following demands:

- Long-term capacity planning for research and development as
  well as production;
- Use of all kinds of public measures for maintaining and expanding the proportion of civilian production in establishments producing defence equipment;
- Avoidance of an expansion or shift of capacities through new
  armament orders which would increase the dependency on
  future arms orders;
- Right of union representatives at the various levels of defence
  production to both vigorously and regularly insist on policies
  for a continuous follow-up of efficient non-military production
  and timely action for the necessary development work.[113]

In explaining these proposals to the United Nations, the General
Secretary of IMW, Herman Rebhan, recalled the efforts of government to run economies during World War II. He asked:
"Why . . . cannot the government devote the same energy and
vision to utilising machinery and men in a planned expanding
program of production for peace?"[114]

To what extent could such initiatives offer a real opportunity
for breaking the military-industrial nexus which perpetuates the
weapons system? Or will the disgruntlement of soldiers and workers
which, after all, is not widely organized, be swept away in the new
wave of Cold War rhetoric and military spending? And when the
next generation of degenerate monstrosities enters military service
and vacates the factories, will dissent reemerge, in a different,
perhaps more sinister form? The conclusion speculates about these
questions.

Conclusion

The third postwar generation of weapons systems was, as we have seen, postponed by the Vietnam War. The rise in U.S. military spending which began in the mid-1970s was a direct consequence of the systems ordered hurriedly by the Nixon Administration at the depths of the post-Vietnam recession. Aircraft like the F–14, F–15, F–16, and AWACS; the new guided-missile destroyers and frigates; the new V/STOL aircraft carrier; the XM–1 tank; the Trident submarine, and all their associated munitions consume ever-increasing amounts of labour, plant, and equipment for their development and production. As these new weapons systems entered the factories, pressure on the defence budget began to mount. (Indeed, the cancellation of the B–1 bomber was welcomed by many in the defence industry and the armed services because it released funds to spread around on other contracts.) And as they enter operational service, they generate yet more pressures in their hunger for spares, fuel, and, above all, skilled personnel.

The situation was described in a recent Congressional report:

Following the Vietnam War, the Department of Defense began the most ambitious rebuilding program since World War II. Currently, this effort at increased weapon procurement is budgeted at $650 billion. If costs rise only 30 percent, which is much less than costs have risen over the last decade, this procurement outlay will require $725 billion over the next ten years. If that funding is based on efficient production rates, the Department of Defense will need twice the appropriations it received in fiscal year 1980 for procurement programs. . . .

Department of Defense budgets have been relatively fixed for many years. Unless a true national emergency occurred in the United States, it is very unlikely funds of the magnitude needed for the projected procurement could be provided.[1]

As was the case with previous generations of weapons systems in the early 1950s and the early 1960s, pressures for bigger defence budgets coincide with mounting international tensions, with growing fears about the Soviet Union, and with, perhaps, a wider sense of economic and social insecurity. These are the reasons for spending money on arms. But the content of military expenditure, the emphasis on ever more costly and complex weapons systems, can only be explained in the terms of the structure of the military industrial institutions—the competitive dynamic of the armourers combined with the conservatism of the armed forces.

Increases in military spending, however big, do not solve any problems. When the new systems move out of the factories, the corporations will have to find new markets or risk bankruptcy, as they did in the early 1970s. Foreign military sales, international collaboration, space or environmental products might fill the gaps for a while. But to stay in business, to occupy their best designers, to justify new purchases by the military, to win contracts in competition against each other, still newer systems, with even more cunning and extravagant characteristics, will have to be dreamed up. Already, some acorns, as they are often called, have been planted—the MX missile, the new family of air-, sea-, and ground-launched cruise missiles, follow-on fighter aircraft, the BX bomber, etc. The new systems will be even more expensive. They will demand, not only productive resources, but even more grotesque supply systems and communication systems, and, of course, more and more people. Unless the defence budget can continue to keep up with these demands—and it has never done so in the past—the problems of "unreadiness" and of "excess capacity" and the corresponding disaffection of soldiers and workers will recur in a more extreme form.

And these problems are merely an aspect of yet wider dilemmas. Weapons systems have been fed at the expense of the rest of American society. There was a time when military technology was not so very different from civil technology, when military spending could mobilise underemployed resources and stimulate research and development in ways that were useful to the civilian economy; this was probably the case immediately after the Second World War. It is no longer true today. The very degeneracy of modern military technology has dragged the American economy backwards, as it were, in a technological evolution that leads nowhere. The weapons system has not only frozen the industrial sectors that came to prominence in World War II; it has extended them, carried them along an autistic momentum whose only limit is the size of the defence budget. The continued survival of companies like Lockheed, Grumman, and Chrysler represents a kind of tumour, eating away at the cells of the American economy. They absorb expenditure that might otherwise be spent on investment or consumption in civilian industry. And they absorb skilled people—designers, scientists, engineers—who might otherwise be thinking up the innovations needed to better the future. The weapons system might stimulate civilian production within the arms-producing sectors, for instance, civil aircraft or merchant ships. However, precisely because these are sectors which reached their peak in the 1940s, expenditure in these activities results in less improvement—product or process innovation—than would expenditure in new, more dynamic sectors.

Insofar as the new sectors—like electronics and synthetic materials—are coopted into the armament sector as subcontractors to the established aerospace or automobile or shipbuilding companies, then ways of doing things, ideas about design and production, warped concepts of technical advance, trickle down and distort the application of the new technologies, further stunting their development. At present, the United States electronics companies, struggling to maintain their lead over Japanese companies, are only too conscious of the problems they face, not only in finding available technicians, but also in finding ones whose methods of work have not been shaped by the demands of the baroque weapons system. And these problems are compounded by patterns of civilian investment and consumption which are also caught in the era of the 1940s and which, therefore, limit the growth of potential markets for new electronic products in both industrial and consumer spheres. Further military spending can only exacerbate the tendency for low investment and low productivity growth, both in relation to the past and to other advanced industrial countries, that the United States has experienced since, at least, the mid-1960s.

Nor is economic decline offset by some definable addition to military power. The growing cost of the modern weapons system is matched by diminishing military effectiveness, even on the basis of criteria accepted by the practitioners of baroque military technology. As each new generation of weapons system yields an even smaller improvement in military effectiveness, so it gets easier for the Soviet Union to "catch up." And as the weapons system is exported all over the world, so the perceived gap between the superpowers and other nations, on the basis of their *own* criteria for measuring military power, narrows. And these criteria are, as I have argued, increasingly irrelevant to the military contingencies of the modern world. Events in Vietnam, Iran, and Ireland have called into question the efficacy in war of the modern weapons system. And they have also dented the more pervasive belief that these symbols of the American and Soviet victories in World War II are reminders that the two superpowers could, if necessary, replay their European experiences against each other—a belief which has shored up their postwar political position. This has been especially important for the United States.

The effects of military spending are not confined to America. The military-industrial institutions of the Soviet Union do not display the same autonomous dynamic as their capitalist counterparts. Rather, they are characterized by the conservatism and continuity that is typical of a centrally planned system. Every year, they expect and usually receive a constant share of the state budget. They experience none of the agonising troughs and heady peaks of Western armourers. Additional increments of military expenditure or new types of military projects, as I have shown, tend to be a response to developments in the United States. In a sense, the Soviet leaders have much greater influence over the military sector than do American military leaders. Although it is difficult to overcome the inexorable pressure for staying the same (something Khrushchev tried and failed), Soviet leaders, because of their control over the budget and the unusual degree of consumer sovereignty enjoyed by the military in the Soviet Union, are able to introduce new elements into the defence programme in response to what is happening in the United States. An increase in American military spending is likely to be followed by an increase in Soviet military spending.

Compared with American military spending, Soviet military spending plays an even more important role in the national economy. Because of the relative size and backwardness of the Soviet economy, the defence budget, although it is difficult to be precise, accounts for a much larger share of national income and manufacturing output than does the American defence budget. It thus competes directly, as is explicitly recognised by Soviet leaders, with resources for consumption and future growth. In the past, the absorption of resources may have been offset by the mobilising role of armaments. In the West, the armament sector introduces an element of planning into the capitalist system (as do other state sectors). The stability of the military-industrial institutions imparts a degree of stability to the economy as a whole, interrupting the normal process of capitalist change and conserving a part of the industrial structure. In the Soviet Union, the planning system imparts this kind of stability to the economy as a whole. In contrast, the Soviet armament sector, through the competition with the West, is able to introduce an element of capitalist dynamic, a boost to lagging technology. In the 1930s and 1940s, this was undoubtedly an important factor in raising the whole level of Soviet industrialisation. As military technology becomes baroque, this mobilising aspect of the armament sector could prove positively harmful. Furthermore, the growing Cold War that tends to accompany any spurt in the arms race is likely to reduce Soviet access to civilian Western technology—something which has, in recent years, become a central feature of the attempt to increase "intensive" (more productivity) as opposed to "extensive" (more people) forms of economic growth.

Low growth and high military spending may also be associated with repression. Frustration with low living standards, with waste and shortages, with hierarchical relations in the factories and other establishments tend to be manifested in such phenomena as absenteeism, sloppy work, and drunkenness, which are widespread in the Soviet Union. There is the occasional riot, reported by the CIA, and the occasional strike, as occurred recently in Togliatti-grad, where the Fiat cars are built under licence. Repression is the substitute for legal and political mechanisms which cope, for better or worse, with corresponding dissension in democracies. Further, repression is linked with militarisation because of a long-standing emphasis, by Soviet thinkers, on the connection between military weakness and internal disorder—the fear that military defeat could cause domestic revolt, as it has done before in Russian history.

Because Soviet weapons are, for the most part, more backward, their utility may be marginally greater than in the West. We know that, on the whole, Soviet weapons are simpler, more rugged and reliable than Western weapons. The problems of supplies, communications, and skilled personnel are likely to be less severe than in the West. However, as military spending increases, as the Soviet Union catches up with the West, Soviet weapons systems are likely to meet with similar shortcomings. To date, the Afghanistan War is at a very low level compared with the war in Vietnam. But there are already reports suggesting that the Soviet logistic system is stretched; and stories about Afghan guerrillas emerging from behind boulders after they have been supposedly smashed to smithereens by mighty Soviet rockets.[2] If the war is stepped up, it is not unreasonable to suppose that the effectiveness of the Soviet military machine would be sorely tested.

The ramifications of military spending, as it saps the economic and political weight of the superpowers, extend throughout the world. We have seen how the spread of the weapons system has accompanied the spread of industrialization and how this has entailed the combination of militarism and uneven development. These tendencies have been excerbated in the 1970s. The economic decline of America has reduced economic aid and increased the sale of arms and capital goods. The industrial poles of the Third World, like Brazil or India or Iran (before the revolution), have become, as it were, subimperial powers, while the rural periphery has been reduced to total and devastating destitution. The separate parts of the Third World have been pulled together through militarism and authoritarianism, or pulled apart by new forms of conflict—riots, revolution, or war—expressed in national, ethnic, or class terms. Yet the United States has become less capable of containing these conflicts; the defeat in Vietnam reduced the effectiveness of shows of force and the possibilities for military intervention. And so, in circular fashion, the turbulence that racks the international system has created the conditions for more military spending, for more of the same.

Could this lead to war? This survey, which is by its nature incomplete, of what is involved in the production and possession of the weapons system, reveals a series of interlocking and ever-widening vicious circles in which economic instability, conflict, and armament spur each other on towards some drastic outcome. A military solution is a sign of weakness—something which is tried when other solutions have failed. The vicious circle of military spending, low growth, and repression may have already propelled the Soviet Union towards a new adventurism, which may have been partly responsible for the invasion of Afghanistan. Could the combination of a tottering economy and a precarious military stature (which has also involved the growth of bureaucracy, authoritarianism, secrecy, and corruption, as was exposed in Watergate) have similar consequences in the United States? Or is there some alternative solution?

The apparent alternative to baroque military technology is cheap, simple, and effective weapons. In the previous chapter, I described the various alternative strategies proposed by analysts at the Rand Corporation and elsewhere, based on such weapons as precision guided munitions (PGMs)—small missiles, guided bombs and artillery, etc., together with small, cheap, reliable, single-purpose vehicles, ships, or aircraft. To what extent do such proposals represent *real* alternatives? It seems somewhat facile to suppose that a military "fix" of this kind could break the complicated and deep-rooted nexus which surrounds the baroque weapons system.

Technology cannot be treated in isolation. Perhaps the most important conclusion of this book is the proposition that technology is the product of a particular set of institutions nurtured in a given political and economic environment. Technical change is also social change. We have seen how nearly all attempts to create "austere alternatives" to the baroque weapons system have foundered. This was because such attempts did not deal with the underlying nature of the armament process. An effective alternative to baroque military technology would entail institutional change at every level: within the armed forces, within the wider geopolitical system, within the defence industry, and within the economy as a whole.

A PGM-type strategy, the newest form of defence in depth, involves the tactics of dispersal and concealment that are typical of guerrilla warfare, and are primarily suitable for the defence of territory against invasion. Such a strategy amounts to a repudiation of the present organisation of the armed forces; the highly centralised forms of authority which appear to be built around the technical division of labour required by the baroque weapons system. It would also shift the present world military order, by undermining present perceptions of military power based on the baroque weapons system and by removing the implicit threat of military intervention. With a PGM strategy, the present prime military contractors—the manufacturers of aircraft, ships, and automobiles—would be replaced by electronics companies, and this, in turn, would cause substantial economic dislocation.

Even supposing that all these institutional obstacles could be surmounted, would such a change in strategy amount to any more than a sinister twist in the arms race? So long as military competition persists, new "fixes" will be proposed. Already, some analysts advocate the use of massive area destruction weapons, like tactical nuclear weapons, chemical weapons, flame, or cluster munitions, in response to a PGM-based defence. And so long as military competition reflects and reinforces the competition among the armourers, a form of technological development will be set in motion which will transform the cheap, simple, effective weapons of the 1970s into the baroque military technology of the twenty-first century (assuming they survive that long) and which will entrench a new industrial culture, based primarily on electronics.

In this book I have hardly discussed the European nations, Japan, Australasia, and Canada. Some of these countries, like Britain and France, are junior partners in the arms-race enterprise. Others, like West Germany, Holland, the Scandinavian countries, and Japan, have spent relatively little on arms since the war and have relatively undeveloped arms industries. It may be partly for this reason that these countries have experienced a high degree of economic prosperity and political stability. At present, these countries enjoy an economic status that is not commensurate with their perceived military status and, therefore, have a vested interest in non-military solutions to international problems. However, there is a real danger that the present international economic and political situation might promote their militarisation. Already their military spending is increasing, particularly in West Germany and Japan. Already, there are pressures from important companies, hit by the world recession. In Japan, many companies with names familiar to students of prewar Japanese militarism—Mitsubishi Heavy Industries, Kawasaki Heavy Industries, Mitsui Engineering and Shipbuilding—are pressing for the relaxation of controls over domestic and foreign arms purchases.[3] For example, Sasebo Heavy Industries reportedly received priority recently in defence contracts because its survival was threatened.[4]

Is it possible that countries like Germany and Japan, which are not overloaded with institutional history and where electronics play a much more prominent role, might adopt a PGM-type strategy? And could the co-existence of different types of military technology encourage different perceptions about what constitutes military power and ultimately lead to the kind of miscalculation that may precipitate war?

If cheap, simple, and effective weapons are not a desirable alternative to baroque military technology, it is possible, however, that the circumstances which have led to proposals for PGM-type strategies could also provide an opportunity for more fundamental change. The present institutions of the arms race *are* beginning to break down. It is not just that the hardware costs too much and does not work. Military authority is already eroded, present perceptions of military power are already undermined, the viability of the arms manufacturers is increasingly threatened, and the economic base of the armament sector is weakening. The various vicious circles described above have thrown up protests in varied forms. In the previous chapter I described the alienation of soldiers and defence workers—sometimes organised and sometimes expressed in sporadic violence, absenteeism, drug addiction, etc. Elsewhere, I described the revolt, sometimes mute and sometimes explosive, of the rural poor and unemployed in the Third World. As well, large segments of the population in Western arms-intensive economies are beginning to recognise the connection between armaments and the different aspects—unemployment, inflation, cuts in welfare spending—of economic decline and are beginning to fear the consequences of the mystifying military theology that accompanies the weapons system. And, in the Soviet Union and Eastern Europe, widespread symptoms of social malaise must surely affect the armament sector itself; we know that the Soviet and East European leadership is not monolithic and that there are powerful factions which favour increased expenditure on raising standards of living and who favour increased ties with the West.

There is always the danger that some of these groups could be mollified by the exigencies of a militaristic posture. Afghanistan might be thought of as an escape from domestic Soviet problems. Or, in the West, increased military spending might increase employment and improve the conditions of soldiers; xenophobic fears of the Soviet Union might divert attention from the present concerns, and the memory of World War II, when warfare, welfare, and economic growth, all worked in harness, might reinstill satisfied fantasies about the system. But only so much employment can be created in the defence sector, the conditions of soldiers cannot be improved a lot, only so much xenophobia is credible, and only so much can be remembered from long ago. The alternative is to mobilise these groups in favour of a package of proposals which would unwind the armament process rather than modify it.

It would take another book to describe the content of such a package, for it would have to cover not only arms-limitation proposals but also alternative forms of military and industrial organisation, substitutes for warfare in international relations, and new ways of ordering the world economy which do not rely on armaments. But some brief conclusions can be drawn from the analysis in this book. First, the existence of baroque military technology implies the possibility of unilateral arms limitation. Precisely because modern weapons systems are so expensive and contribute so little to military effectiveness, it is possible to reduce national military spending without reducing, indeed possibly enhancing, the ability of a nation to defend itself from attack. There have already been a number of proposals in Britain and the United States aimed at eliminating baroque weapons systems from national arsenals; and thereby improving the cost effectiveness of military spending.[5] Second, new "revolutionary" military technologies which have not, as yet, been institutionalized imply the possibility of multilateral arms limitation. The practitioners of baroque military technology share a common interest with disarmers in preventing the spread of PGMs or of new weapons of mass destruction.

Finally, any attempt to limit armaments has to involve major institutional change. The role of the arms industry in the armament process has been an important theme of this book. A central element in the package of proposals would have to be industrial conversion, not in the *technical* sense of converting swords into ploughshares, but in the *social* sense of transforming the industrial basis of the armament sector. Baroque military technology is peculiarly a product of contemporary social systems, a mixture of capitalism and central planning, of the dynamic of one and the rigidity of the other. Industrial conversion might aim to create a new mixture which could overcome the rigidity of centrally planned economies and, at the same time, avoid the crises that are inextricably associated with the dynamic of capitalism.[6]

This is an ambitious agenda, but ultimately, we have to think ambitiously. If the armament process extends into every corner of society, then disarmament must eventually do the same. Practical aims, like getting rid of certain weapons or initiating experiments of industrial conversion, need to be located in a wider vision of the future to which we aspire. All modern armaments, whether baroque or not, are immensely destructive. They have to be abolished if human civilisation is to survive. And that means, however utopian it may sound, that we are going to have to create a society that does not need armaments.

Notes

Introduction

1 Joseph Schumpeter, *Business Cycles* (New York: McGraw-Hill, 1939); Nikolai Kondratieff, "The Major Economic Cycles," summarized in *Review of Economic Statistics*, Vol. 18 (1935).
2 *Race to Oblivion* (New York: Simon and Schuster, 1970), p. 44.
3 Alain C. Enthoven and Wayne K. Smith, *How Much Is Enough? Shaping the Defense Program* 1961–69 (New York: Harper, Colophon Books, 1972).

Chapter 1

1 New York: Free Press, 1960, p. 8.
2 *Ibid.*, p. 41.
3 Vernon Pizer (Lt. Colonel, U.S.A. Ret.), *The U.S. Army* (New York: Praeger, 1967), p. 39.
4 Quoted in Jonathan E. Medalia and A. A. Tinajero, "XM-1 Main Battle Tank Program," *Issue Brief Number IB* 75052, Washington, D.C.: Library of Congress, Congressional Research Service, July 1975, updated May 1978.
5 William D. White, *U.S. Tactical Air Power: Missions, Forces and Costs* (Washington, D.C.: The Brookings Institution, 1974), p. 5.
6 *Ibid.*
7 Janowitz, *op.cit.*, p. 230.
8 *U.S. Congressional Record*, 95th Cong., 1st Sess., CXXIII, Part 8, p. 9269, March 28, 1977.
9 Charles M. Tiebout, "The Regional Impact of Defense Expenditures: Its Measurement and Problems of Adjustment," in Roger E. Bolton, *Defense and Disarmament: The Economics of Transition* (Englewood Cliffs, N.J.: Prentice-Hall, 1966).

10   Quoted in J. R. Fox, *Arming America: How the U.S. Buys Weapons* (Cambridge, Mass.: Harvard University, 1974), pp. 100–1.

11   *Management in the Armed Forces: An Anatomy of the Military Profession* (London: McGraw-Hill, 1977), p. 195.

12   *Ibid.*, p. 198.

13   *Op.cit.*, pp. 27–28.

14   Seymour J. Deitchman, *New Technologies and Military Power: General Purpose Forces for the 1980s and Beyond* (Boulder, Colo.: Westview Press, 1979), p. 107.

15   Robert J. Art, *The TFX Decision: McNamara and the Military* (Boston: Little, Brown & Co., 1968), p. 15.

16   *Ibid.*, p. 25.

17   Ulrich Albrecht, *et al.*, "Das ender des MRCA?" in Studiengruppe Militärpolitik, *Ein Anti-Weisbuch Materialien für eine Alternative Militärpolitik* (Hamburg: Rowohlt, 1974), author's translation, p. 83.

18   J. W. Devanney in "The DX Competition," *U.S. Naval Institute Proceedings* (August 1975), pp. 25–26.

19   *Ibid.*

20   "The F–111," in *Commission on the Organization of the Government for the Conduct of Foreign Policy* (Murphy Commission) (Washington, D.C., June 1975), *Volume 4, Appendix K: Adequacy of Current Organization: Defense and Arms Control*, pp. 131–2.

21   Norman R. Augustine, "One Plane, One Tank, One Ship: Trend for the Future," *Defense Management Journal* (April 1975).

22   Aerospace Systems Analysis, McDonnell Douglas Astronautics Corp., *Cost of War Index* (Santa Monica, Calif.: September 1968).

23   "Two Views on Navy Fighters," *Armed Forces Journal* (November 1974).

24   Quoted in Jo. L. Husbands, "The Long Long Pipeline. Arms Sales and Technological Dependence," unpublished, Center for Defense Information, Washington, D.C., 1978.

25   Quoted in John Wicklein, "The Oldest Establishment Permanent Floating Anachronism in the Sea," *Washington Monthly* (February 1970).

CHAPTER 2

1   Quoted in David Dougan, *The Life of Lord Armstrong the Great Gunmaker* (Newcastle-upon-Tyne: Frank Graham, 1970), p. 59.

2 *The Unbound Prometheus: Technological Change and Industrial Development in Western Europe from 1750 to the Present* (Cambridge: Cambridge University Press, 1969), p. 235.

3 *Ibid.*, pp. 240–41.

4 Quoted in J. D. Scott, *Vickers—A History* (London: Weidenfeld and Nicholson, 1961), p. 42.

5 Quoted in Michael S. Moss and John R. Hume, *Workshop of the British Empire: Engineering and Shipbuilding in the West of Scotland* (London: Heineman, 1977), p. 119.

6 Quoted in Philip Noel-Baker, *The Private Manufacture of Arms* (London: Victor Gollancz Ltd., 1936), p. 58.

7 Clive Trebilcock, *The Vickers Brothers Armaments and Enterprise, 1854–1914* (London: Europa Publications Ltd., 1977), p. 76.

8 Quoted in Noel-Baker, *op.cit.*, p. 59.

9 Scott, *op.cit.*, p. 44.

10 *From Know-How to Nowhere: The Development of American Technology* (New York: Basic Books, 1974), pp. 156–7.

11 Quoted in Noel-Baker, *op.cit.*, pp. 411–12.

12 V. R. Berghahn, *Germany and the Approach of War in 1914* (London: Macmillan, 1973), p. 47.

13 Scott, *op.cit.*, p. 30.

14 Quoted in John Ellis, *The Social History of the Machine Gun* (New York: Pantheon Books, 1973), pp. 58–59.

15 *Ibid.*, p. 64.

16 *Ibid.*

17 Clive Trebilcock, "War and the Failure of Industrial Mobilisation 1899 and 1914," in J. M. Winter, ed., *War and Economic Development* (Cambridge: Cambridge University Press, 1975), p. 150.

18 *Ibid.*, p. 160.

19 Trebilcock, *The Vickers Brothers*.

20 *Ibid.*, p. 126.

21 *Ibid.*, p. 127.

22 "The Force Theory," in *Anti-Duhring* (first published in 1894) (London: Lawrence and Wishart, 1975), pp. 207–8.

23 Christopher Harrie, "Technological Change and Military Power in Historical Perspective," in *New Conventional Weapons and East-West Security*, Part I, *Adelphi Papers* No. 144, IISS (Spring 1978).

24 P. L. Payne, "The Emergence of the Large Scale Company in Britain, 1870–1914," *Economic History Review*, 20 (1967).

25   Moss and Hume, *op.cit.*, p. 129.
26   *Unbound Prometheus*, pp. 335–36.
27   See E. Hobsbawn, *Industry and Empire* (London: Weidenfeld and Nicholson, 1968).
28   Clive Trebilcock, " 'Spin-off' in British Economic History: Armaments and Industry 1760–1914," *Economic History Review*, 2nd series, Vol. XXII, No. 3 (December 1969).
29   Scott, *op.cit.*, p. 138.
30   M. M. Postan, *British War Production* (London: HMSO and Longmans, 1952), p. 8.
31   Ronald Miller and David Sawers, *The Technical Development of Modern Aviation* (London: Routledge Kegan and Paul, 1968), p. 51.
32   *Op.cit.*, p. 145.
33   *Ibid.*, p. 163.
34   Quoted in Noel-Baker, *op.cit.*, p. 64.
35   *Op.cit.*, p. 297.
36   *Ibid.*, p. 357.
37   Interview on Tyne-Tees Television, "Design Yourself Out of Trouble," June 13, 1977.
38   Moss and Hume, *op.cit.*, pp. 102 and 109.
39   *Ibid.*, p. 112.
40   Much of this section is based on the pamphlet: Vickers National Committee of Shop Stewards, *Building a Chieftain Tank and the Alternative Use of Resources* (Newcastle-upon-Tyne, 1977).
41   *The Making of the Tyne*, 1895, quoted in David Dougan, *The History of North East Shipbuilding* (London: George Allen and Unwin Ltd., 1968), p. 76.
42   For a description of the decline of West Newcastle, see Benwell Community Project, *West Newcastle: Its Growth and Decline* (July 1976) and *Social Change in Benwell* (October 1977).

Chapter 3

1   U.S. Congress, House of Representatives, *Historical Statistics of the United States, Colonial Times to 1970*, Bicentennial edition, 93rd Cong., 1st Sess., 1949, H.R. 93–78 (Part 2), p. 716.
2   Irving Brinton Holley, Jr., "Buying Aircraft Material. Procurement for the Army Air Forces," *U.S. Army in World War II, Special Studies*, Volume 7, (Washington, D.C.: Office of the Chief of Military History, Department of the Army, 1964), p. 22.

3   *The Car Culture* (Cambridge, Mass.: MIT Press, 1975), p. 33.

4   Miller and Sawers, *op.cit.*, p. 20.

5   Henry C. Thompson and Lida Mayo, *The Technical Services. The Ordnance Department: Procurement and Supply. U.S. Army in World War II* (Washington, D.C.: Office of the Chief of Military History, Department of the Army, 1960), p. 222.

6   "Wartime, Development of the Aircraft Industry," *United States Bureau of Labor Statistics, Bulletin No. 800*, reprinted from *Monthly Labor Review* (November 1944).

7   See U.S. Air Force, U.S.A.F. Historical Division, "Men and Planes," *The Army Air Forces in World War II*, Vol. 6, ed. by Wesley Frank Craven and James Lea Crate (University of Chicago Press, 1955), Chapter 9, "The Expansion of Aircraft Production."

8   J. B. Hutchins, "History and Development of the Shipbuilding Industry in the United States," in F. G. Fassett, Jr., ed., *The Shipbuilding Business in the United States*, Vol. 1 (New York: Society of Naval Architects and Marine Engineers, 1948), p. 59.

9   Thompson and Mayo, *op.cit.*, p. 204.

10 Roger A. Beaumont, "Quantum Increase: The MIC in the Second World War," Benjamin Franklin Cooling, ed., *War Business and American Society. Historical Perspectives on the Military-Industrial Complex* (New York: Kennikat Press, 1977), pp. 131–32.

11 National Planning Association, *National Policy for Aviation: A Special Committee Report*, Planning Pamphlets, Nos. 51–52, Washington, D.C. (1946).

12 Mundy I. Peale, "Industry Trends Since the End of World War II," in *Elements of American Air Power. Presentation of the Aircraft Industry before the President's Air Policy Commission*, Washington, D.C. (1947).

13 Boeing Company, *Boeing Annual Report*, 1948.

14 *Survival in the Air Age*, A Report by the President's Air Policy Commission, Washington, D.C., January 1, 1948 (Chairman Thomas K. Finletter), p. 21.

15 *Ibid.*, p. 45.

16 *Ibid.*, p. 49.

17 *Jane's All the World's Aircraft 1948* (London: Sampson, Low and Marston Company Ltd., 1948), p. i.

18 *Jane's Fighting Ships, 1948–49* (London: Sampson, Low and Marston Company Ltd., 1949).

19   *The United States in the World Arena* (New York: Harper, 1960).

20   "Why We Buy the Weapons We Do," *Foreign Policy*, No. 11 (1973).

21   Holley, *op.cit.*, p. 512.

22   *Arming America. How the U.S. Buys Weapons* (Cambridge, Mass.: Harvard University Press, 1974), p. 53.

23   *The High Priests of Waste* (New York: W. W. Norton, 1972), p. 7.

24   J. Fred Weston, ed., *Defense-Space Market Research* (Cambridge, Mass.: MIT Press, 1964), p. 28.

25   *Op.cit.*, p. 101.

26   See, U.S. Congress, House of Representatives, Committee on Government Operations, *Inaccuracy of Department of Defense Weapons Acquisition Cost Estimates*, 9th Report, 96th Cong., 1st Sess., No. 96–656, Washington, D.C., 1979.

27   See Office of the Under Secretary of Defense for Research and Engineering, *Report of the Acquisition Cycle Task Force*, Defense Science Board, 1977 Summer Study, Washington, D.C., March 15, 1978.

28   Michael H. Armacost, *The Politics of Weapons Innovation: The Thor-Jupiter Missile Controversy* (New York: Columbia University Press, 1969), p. 99.

29   *Ibid.*, p. 155.

30   *The Weapons Acquisition Process* (Cambridge, Mass.: Harvard University Press, 1962), Chapter 2.

31   A. W. Marshall and W. H. Meckling, "Predictability of the Costs, Time and Success of Development," in *The Rate and Direction of of Inventive Activity* (Washington, D.C.: National Bureau of Economic Research, 1962).

32   Robert Perry, *et al.*, *System Acquisition Strategies*, Rand Corporation, R–733–PR/ARPA (Santa Monica, Calif., 1971).

33   Weston, *op.cit.*, p. 14.

34   John R. Newell, "The Breakdown in Naval Shipbuilding," *Proceedings of the United States Naval Institute* (January 1978).

35   Deborah Shapley, "Addiction to Technology Is One Cause of the Navy's Shipbuilding Crisis," *Science* (May 19, 1978).

36   See Arthur Alexander, "The XM–1," in the appendix to the Murphy Commission, *op.cit.*

37   Jonathan E. Medalia and A. A. Tinajero, "XM–1 Main Battle

Tank Program," *Issue Brief Number IB75052*, Congressional Research Service, Washington, D.C., 1978.

38   Roger Bolton, evidence to U.S. Congress Joint Economic Committee, *Economic Impact of Vietnam War Spending*, 90th Cong., 1st Sess., Washington, D.C., 1967, pp. 154–56.

39   Norman Lyn, "Survival and Growth for Small, High Technology Aerospace Subcontractors," National Association of Aerospace Subcontractors, Palos Verdes Peninsula, Calif., July 28, 1972.

40   U.S. Congress, Joint Committee on Defense Production, Hearings, *Defense Industrial Base: Industrial Preparedness and Nuclear War Survival*, 94th Cong., Washington, D.C., November 17, 1976, p. 16.

41   "Let's Change the Way the Pentagon Does Business," *Harvard Business Review* (May–June 1977).

42   U.S. Congress, House of Representatives, Committee on Appropriations, Subcommittee on Department of Defense, Hearings, *Department of Defense Appropriations for FY 1981, Part 3, Research, Development and Acquisition*, 96th Cong., 2nd Sess., Weshington, D.C., 1980, p. 549.

43   Quoted in Emma Rothschild, *Paradise Lost: The Decline of the Auto Industrial Age* (New York: Random House, 1972), p. 44.

44   Chris Freeman, "The Kondratiev Long Waves, Technical Change and Unemployment," OECD Conference, *Structural Determinants of Employment and Unemployment* (Paris, March 7–11, 1979).

45   See OECD, *Patterns of Resources Devoted to Research and Development in the OECD Area*, 1963–71 (Paris, 1973).

46   *Op.cit.*, p. 245.

47   See U.S. Congress, Senate, Special Committee to Study Problems of American Small Business, *Economic Concentration in World War II*. Report of the Smaller War Plants Corporation, 79th Cong., 2nd Sess., Document No. 266, Washington, D.C., June 14, 1946.

48   Quoted in Holley, *op.cit.*, p. 29.

49   Quoted in Miller and Sawers, *op.cit.*, p. 155.

50   *Ibid.*, p. 271–72.

51   Daniel M. Mack-Forlist and Arthur Newman, *The Conversion of Shipbuilding from Military to Civilian Markets* (New York: Praeger, 1970), pp. 80 and 119.

52   Herschel Kanter, "The Effect of New Naval Procurement Prac-

238

tices on the Shipbuilding Industry," *Center for Naval Analysis,* University of Rochester, October 11, 1968.

53 Much of the information on the electronics industry was provided by Ed Sciberras of the Science Policy Research Unit, University of Sussex.

54 Anthony Golding, *The Semi Conductor in Britain and the United States. A Case Study in Innovation, Growth and Diffusion of Technology.* Unpublished D.Phil dissertation, University of Sussex, 1972.

55 Klieman, Herbert S., *The Integrated Circuit. A Case Study of Product Innovation in the Electronics Industry.* Unpublished Ph.D dissertation, George Washington University, 1966, p. 220.

56 John E. Tilton, *International Diffusion of Technology. The Case of Semi Conductors.* Brookings Institution, Washington, D.C. 1971.

57 Klieman, Herbert S., *Working Paper on the Microcomputer:* Technological Innovation and Transfer. Prepared for DoD ARPA, Battelle Memorial Institute, 16 December 1975.

58 *Electronics Times,* 14 December 1978.

59 "The Pentagon's Push for Super Fast ICs," *Business Week,* November 27, 1978.

60 Robert A. Solo, "Gearing Military R & D to Economic Growth," *Harvard Business Review,* Vol. XL (November–December 1962).

CHAPTER 4

1 Quoted in Arthur Alexander, "Decision-Making in Soviet Weapons Procurement," *Adelphi Papers,* Nos. 147 and 148, IISS (Winter 1978/79), p. 2.

2 Quoted in Ulrich Albrecht, *The Soviet Armaments Base: The Limits of Expansion,* paper presented to the Berlin Conference on Alarmism, Berghof Institut für Friedens und Konflikt Forschung, Berlin, October 1979.

3 Stockholm International Peace Research Institute, see *World Armaments and Disarmament, SIPRI Yearbook 1977* (Cambridge, Mass.: MIT Press, 1977).

4 R. P. Smith, *The Production of Security,* unpublished, Birkbeck College, London, 1978.

5 Edward L. Warner, *The Military in Contemporary Soviet Politics: An Institutional Analysis* (New York: Praeger, 1977), p. 134.

6   Quoted in Arthur Alexander, *Armor Development in the Soviet Union and the United States. A Report Prepared for the Director of Net Assessment, Office of the Secretary of Defense* (Santa Monica, Calif.: Rand R–1880–NA, September, 1976), p. 10.

7. Michael MccGwire, "Soviet Strategic Weapons Policy, 1955–70," in Michael MccGwire, Ken Booth, John McDonnell, eds., *Soviet Naval Policy: Objectives and Constraints* (New York: Praeger, 1975), p. 188.

8   See Kenneth Whiting, "The Peacetime Air Force at Home and Abroad, 1945–76," in Robin Higham and Jacob W. Kipp, eds., *Soviet Aviation and Air Power: An Historical View* (London: Brasseys, 1978).

9   David Holloway, "Military Technology," in R. Amann, J. M. Cooper, and R. W. Davies, eds., *The Technological Level of Soviet Industry* (London: Yale University Press, 1977), p. 455.

10 Alfred L. Monks, "The Soviet Strategic Air Force and Civil Defense," in Higham and Kipp, *op.cit.*

11 David Holloway, chapter in Amann and Cooper, eds., *Innovation in Soviet Industry*, forthcoming.

12 Quoted in Thomas W. Wolfe, *Soviet Naval Interaction with the United States and Its Influence on Soviet Naval Development* (Santa Monica, Calif.: Rand P–4913, October 1972).

13 Warner, *op.cit.*, p. 139.

14 Quoted in Jutta and Stephan Tiedke, "The Soviet Union's Internal Problems and the Development of the Warsaw Treaty Organization," in Egbert Jahn, ed., *Soviet Foreign Policy: Its Social and Economic Conditions* (London: Allison and Busby, 1978), p. 127.

15 Warner, *op.cit.*, p. 88.

16 Michael MccGwire, "The Rationale for the Development of Soviet Seapower," *United States Naval Institute Proceedings*, Vol. 106/5/927 (May 1980), p. 158.

17 Warner, *op.cit.*, p. 145.

18 *Khrushchev Remembers* (London: Andre Deutsch, 1971), p. 520.

19 Warner, *op.cit.*, p. 146.

20 See MccGwire, "Soviet Strategic Weapons Policy" and "The Evolution of Soviet Naval Policy 1960–74, in MccGwire, Booth, and McDonnell, *op.cit.*

21 General Lieutenant P. A. Zhilin, Chief of the Institute of Military History, quoted in Robert L. Arnett, "Soviet Military Doctrine— Views on Nuclear War," *Arms Control Today* (October 1978).

22   This argument is explored in Barry Blechman, *The Changing So-viet Navy* (Washington, D.C.: Brookings Institution, 1973).

23   See, for example, MccGwire, "The Rationale for the Development of Soviet Seapower" and Vernon V. Aspaturian, "Soviet Global Power and the Correlation of Forces," *Problems of Communism*, Vol. XXIX (May–June 1980).

24   Mikhail Agursky and Hannes Adomeit, "The Soviet Military-Industrial Complex," in *Survey: A Journal of East and West Studies*, Vol. 24, No. 2, 107 (Spring 1979), pp. 119–20.

25   Quoted in Holloway, "Military Technology."

26   U.S. Congress, Joint Economic Committee, prepared statement of Admiral Stansfield Turner, Director of CIA, in Subcommittee on Priorities and Economy in Government, Hearings, *Allocation of Resources in the Soviet Union and China—1977*, 95th Cong., 1st Sess., Washington, D.C., July 23 and 30, 1977, p. 41.

27   U.S. Congress, Joint Economic Committee, Subcommittee on Priorities and Economy in Government, Hearings, *Allocation of Resources in the Soviet Union and China—1979*, 96th Cong., 1st Sess., Washington, D.C., June 26 and July 9, 1979.

28   See Robert Perry, *Comparisons of Soviet and U.S. Technology* (Santa Monica, Calif.: Rand Corporation R–827–P7, June 1973).

29   Holloway, "Military Technology."

30   Arthur Alexander, *Weapon Acquisition in the Soviet Union, United States and France* (Santa Monica, Calif.: Rand P–49–89, March 1973), p. 8.

31   *Ibid.*, p. 8.

32   Quoted in Arthur J. Alexander, *R&D Soviet Aviation* (Santa Monica, Calif.: Rand R–589–PR, November 1970), p. 22.

33   Perry, *op.cit.*

34   Quoted in David Holloway, "Appendix on the Size of Soviet Military Effort," chapter in Amann and Cooper, *op.cit.*, p. 9.

35   "Soviet Military Doctrine: The Political Dimension," *Arms Control Today* (October 1978), p. 5.

36   *Essays in Capitalism and Socialism* (Oxford: Oxford University Press, 1970).

37   Chapter in Amann and Cooper, *op.cit.*

38   "Structural Causes of the Soviet Co-existence Policy," in Jahn, ed., *op.cit.*, p. 68.

39   Quoted in Alec Nove, *The Soviet Economic System* (London: George, Allen and Unwin, 1977), p. 141.

40   *Ibid.*, p. 107.

41 *Ibid.,* p. 167.
42 Amann, Cooper, Davies, *op.cit.,* Chapter 2, p. 52.
43 See Vernon Aspaturian, "The Soviet Military-Industrial Complex: Does it Exist?" in S. Rosen, ed., *Testing the Theory of the Military Industrial Complex* (Lexington, Mass.: Lexington Books, 1973).
44 Volchov, quoted in Warner, *op.cit.,* p. 91.
45 For a description of this, see John McDonell, "The Soviet Defence Industry as Pressure Group," in MccGwire, Booth, and McDonnell, *op.cit.*
46 Quoted in David Holloway, "War, Militarism and the Soviet State," in E. P. Thompson and Dan Smith, eds., *Protest and Survive* (London: Penguin Books, 1980), p. 145.
47 *Khrushchev Remembers,* p. 519.
48 "The Role of the Armaments Complex in Soviet Society," *Journal of Peace Research,* No. 4 (1974).
49 Jones, *op.cit.,* p. 4.
50 Perry, *op.cit.*
51 *Ibid.*
52 *Aim of a Lifetime,* trans. by V. Vezey (Moscow: Progress Publishers, 1972).
53 Holloway, chapter in Amann and Cooper, *op.cit.*
54 *Weapon Acquisition in the Soviet Union, United States and France,* p. 3.
55 Dr. Michael Checinski: "The Cost of Armament Production and the Profitability of Armament Exports in Comecon Countries," *Soviet and East European Research Centre,* Hebrew University of Jerusalem, Research Paper No. 10.
56 Holloway, chapter in Amann and Cooper, *op.cit.*
57 *Ibid.*
58 Quoted in Alexander, *Weapon Acquisition in the Soviet Union, United States and France,* p. 9.
59 Quoted in Alexander, *R&D in Soviet Aviation.*
60 Holloway, chapter in Amann and Cooper, *op.cit.*
61 Vickers Archives, 1933, quoted in Clive Trebilcock, *The Defence Sector and Technological Progress 1890–1945: An Historical Model.* Paper presented to the Royal Economic Society's Conference on Government and Innovation, Pembroke College, Cambridge, July 14–17, 1975.
62 The material on the 1930s comes from Julian Cooper, "Defence Production and the Soviet Economy, 1929–41," *CREES Discus-*

sion Paper, Centre for Russian and East European Studies, University of Birmingham, Soviet Industrialisation Project Series, SIPS No. 3, 1976.

63   *Ibid.*, p. 27.
64   *Ibid.*, p. 40.
65   R. T. Maddock, "Some Economic Constraints on Defence Spending in the Soviet Union," *RUSI Journal*, Royal United Services Institute for Defence Studies, Vol. 1244, No. 3 (September 1979).
66   Holloway, chapter in Amann and Cooper, *op.cit.*
67   Warner, *op.cit.*
68   *Op.cit.*
69   *Allocation of Resources in the Soviet Union and China*—1979.
70   *Allocation of Resources in the Soviet Union and China*—1977, p. 19.
71   Robin Campbell, "Management Spillovers from Soviet Space and Military Programmes," *Soviet Studies*, XXIII, 4 (April 1972), pp. 587–607.
72   Paul Cocks, "Rethinking the Organizational Weapon: The Soviet System in a Systems Age," *World Politics*, Vol. XXXII, No. 2 (1980).
73   Quoted in Holloway, "War, Militarism and the Soviet State," p. 146.
74   "Technological Progress in the Soviet Military Industry," unpublished, Jerusalem, 1977.

CHAPTER 5

1   *Militarism and Anti-Militarism* (first published Berlin, 1906) (Cambridge: Rivers Press, 1973).
2   *Technology Tradition and the State in Africa.* International African Institute (Oxford: Oxford University Press, 1971).
3   See C. M. Cipolla, *Guns and Sails in the Early Phase of European Expansion, 1400–1700* (London: Collins, 1965).
4   The phrase originated in Ralph E. Lapp, *The Weapons Culture* (W. W. Norton & Co. Inc., New York, 1968), but has been taken up by scholars in the Indian subcontinent; see studies by Rajni Kothari, Centre for the Study of Developing Societies, New Delhi, and Neelan Tirucheleem, Marga Institute, Sri Lanka.
5   *Composite Report of the President's Committee to Study the United States Military Assistance Program* (The Draper Report). Vol. 1, Washington, D.C., 1959, p. 141.
6   U.S. Department of State, Agency for International Development,

U.S. Overseas Loans and Grants and Assistance from International Organizations, Obligations and Loan Authorizations, July 1, 1945–September 30, 1977, Washington, D.C., 1978.

7 Known as the Petersen Report, this is quoted in Philip J. Farley, Stephen S. Kaplan, and William H. Lewis, *Arms Across the Sea* (Washington, D.C.: Brookings Institution, 1978), pp. 22–23.

8 U.S. Department of State, Arms Control and Disarmament Agency (ACDA), *World Military Expenditure and Arms Transfers 1968–77*, Washington, D.C., October 1979.

9 For a detailed description, see Stockholm International Peace Research Institute (SIPRI), *The Arms Trade with the Third World* (Stockholm: Almqvist and Wiksell, 1971).

10 This is calculated by comparing the statistics prepared by the Stockholm International Peace Research Institute (SIPRI) with official U.S. figures. *See SIPRI Arms Trade Registers. The Arms Trade with the Third World* (Stockholm: Almqvist and Wiksell, 1975).

11 Miles D. Wolpin, *Military Aid and Counter Revolution in the Third World* (Lexington, Mass.: Lexington Books, 1972).

12 Farley, *et al., op.cit.*

13 U.S. General Accounting Office, Staff Study, *Profiles of Military Assistance Advisory Groups in 15 Countries*, 1D–78–51, Washington, D.C., September 1978, p. 50.

14 *Ibid.*, pp. 6, 71, and 77.

15 Congressional Research Service, *United States Arms Transfers and Security Assistance Programs*, prepared for the U.S. Congress, House of Representatives, Committee on International Relations, Subcommittee on Europe and the Middle East, Washington, D.C., March 21, 1978.

16 General Fucqua in relation to training programs for trainees from Yemen, Afghanistan, and Syria. Quoted in Wolpin, *op.cit.*, p. 85.

17 U.S. Congress, House of Representatives, Committee on Foreign Affairs, Subcommittee on National Security Policy and Scientific Development, *Report of the Special Study Mission to Latin America on Military Assistance, Training and Developmental Television*, 91st Cong., 2nd Sess., Washington, D.C., May 7, 1970.

18 Wolpin, *op.cit.*, p. 41.

19 Quoted in *ibid.*, p. 40.

20 *Ibid.*, p. 100.

21 See ACDA, *op.cit.*

22 National Foreign Assessment Center, Central Intelligence Agency,

Communist Aid to Less Developed Countries of the Free World,
1977, ER–78–104780, November 1978.

23   ACDA, *op.cit.*

24   For a fuller description of defence production in Third World
countries, see SIPRI, *The Arms Trade with the Third World*
(1971), and Peter Lock and Herbert Wulf, *Register of Arms Pro-*
duction in Developing Countries (Hamburg: Study Group on
Armaments and Underdevelopment, March 1977).

25   Lock and Wulf, *op.cit.*, p. 87.

26   Fred Halliday, *Iran. Dictatorship and Development,* 2nd ed.
(London: Penguin, 1979), p. 72, emphasis in original.

27   For a detailed description, see Ulrich Albrecht, "Militarised Sub-
Imperialism: The Case of Iran," in M. Kaldor and A. Eide, eds.,
The World Military Order: The Impact of Military Technology
on the Third World (London: Macmillan, 1979).

28   U.S. Congress, Senate, Committee on Foreign Relations, Subcommittee on Foreign Assistance, *U.S. Military Sales to Iran,*
Staff Report, 94th Cong., 2nd Sess., Washington, D.C., July 1976.

29   Barry M. Blechman and Stephen S. Kaplan, *Force without War:*
U.S. Armed Forces as a Political Instrument (Washington, D.C.:
Brookings Institution, 1976), p. 6.

30   Quoted in Halliday, *op.cit.*, p. 273.

31   Robin Luckham, "Arms and Dependence in Africa," unpublished,
Sussex University, 1979.

32   Quoted in Maxime Rodinson, *Islam and Capitalism* (London:
Penguin, 1977), p. 127.

33   *Ibid.*, pp. 127–8.

34   Emile Benoit, *Defense and Economic Growth in Developing*
Countries (Lexington, Mass.: Lexington Books, 1973).

35   "Armies in the Process of Modernization," in J. Johnson, ed., *The*
Role of the Military in Underdeveloped Countries (Princeton:
Rand Corporation and Princeton University Press, 1962), p. 76.

36   Barton C. Hacker, "The Weapons of the West—Military Technology and Modernization in 19th Century China and Japan,"
Technology and Culture, 18(1) (January 1977), p. 52.

37   *Race and History* (Paris: UNESCO, 1968).

38   Quoted in Adeed Dawisha, "Saudi Arabia's Search for Security,"
Adelphi Papers, No. 158, IISS (Winter 1979–80).

39   Susan Helper, " 'Absorbing' Modern Weapons: Some Problems
in Iran," Center for Defense Information, unpublished, Washington, D.C., 1978.

40 K. V. Ahmad, *Break Up of Pakistan* (London: Social Sciences, 1972), p. 67.

41 David K. Whynes, *The Economics of Third World Military Expenditure* (London: Macmillan, 1979), p. 45.

42 A. Varas, C. Portales, and F. Aguero, "The National and International Dynamics of South American Armentism," unpublished, FLACSO, Santiago, Chile, 1979.

43 Lock and Wulf, *op.cit.*, p. 33.

44 Sunil K. Dawan and Nitish R. De, "Arms and Aid: An Exercise in Economy versus Development," *Human Futures* (Winter 1978).

45 Helper, *op.cit.*, p. 30.

46 Lock and Wulf., *op.cit.*

47 See Ajit Singh, "The 'Basic Needs' Approach to Development vs. the New International Economic Order: The Significance of Third World Industrialisation," *World Development*, Vol. 7, No. 6 (June 1979).

48 Lock and Wulf., *op.cit.*, pp. XXI–XXII.

49 *World Development Report*, 1980 (Washington, D.C.: The World Bank, August 1980).

50 *Arms and Dependence in Africa*, p. 15.

51 G. Chichilnisky and M. de Mello, "The Role of Armament Flows in the Market and in Development Strategies in a North-South Context," unpublished, Columbia University, New York and University of Essex, Colchester, U.K., June 1980.

52 See Michael T. Klare, *Supplying Repression: U.S. Support for Authoritarian Regimes Abroad* (Washington, D.C.: Institute for Policy Studies, 1977).

53 "Militarism: Force, Class and International Conflict," in Kaldor and Eide, eds., *op.cit.*

54 *Ibid.*, Table 9.1.

55 *Ibid.*, see also Robin Luckham, *The Nigerian Military: A Case Study in Authority and Revolt 1960–67*, African Studies Series 4 (Cambridge: Cambridge University Press, 1971).

56 See the survey article: Mary Kaldor, "The Military in Development," *World Development*, Vol. 4, No. 6 (June 1976).

57 Eric A. Nordlinger, "Soldiers in Mufti: The Impact of Military Rule upon the Economic and Social Change in the Non-Western States," *American Political Science Review*, Vol. LXIV, No. 4 (December 1970).

58 R. Neal Tannahill, "The Performance of Military and Civilian

Government in South America, 1948–67," *Journal of Political and Military Sociology*, Vol. 4, No. 2 (Fall 1976), p. 242.

59 *Egypt Military Society: The Army Regime, the Left and Social Change under Nasser* (New York: Vintage Books, 1968).

60. *Radical Military Regimes in Latin America: Revolution, Rhetoric and Reality in Peru and Ecuador*, paper presented to the Annual Meeting of the American Political Science Association, Washington, D.C., September 1977.

61 "Military Intervention, Political Competitiveness and Public Policy in Latin America: 1950–67," in Morris Janowitz and Jacques van Dorn, eds., *On Military Intervention* (Rotterdam: Rotterdam University Press, 1971).

62 Fitch, *op.cit.*, p. 14.

63 Whynes, *op.cit.*, p. 39.

64 A. Varas, *et al.*, *op.cit.*, p. 39.

65 Ulrich Albrecht, *et al.*, "Armaments and Underdevelopment," *Bulletin of Peace Proposals*, Vol. 5 (1974).

66 *The Stages of Economic Growth* (Cambridge: Cambridge University Press, 1960).

67 Quoted in G. Barraclough, "The Struggle for the Third World," *New York Review of Books* (November 9, 1978).

68 Calculated from ACDA, *op.cit.*

69 Pp. 19 and 39.

70 See Mary Kaldor, *The Disintegrating West* (London: Penguin, 1979).

71 See L. P. Bloomfield and A. C. Leiss, *The Control of Local Conflict*, ACDA/WEC-98, Vol. 3 (Cambridge, Mass.: Center for International Studies, MIT Press, 1967).

72 See Luigi R. Einaudi and Alfred C. Stepan III, *Latin American Institutional Development: Changing Military Perspective in Peru and Brazil* (Santa Monica, Calif.: Rand R–586–DOS, April 1971).

73 *The Military in Politics: Changing Patterns in Brazil* (Princeton: Rand Corporation and Princeton University Press, 1971).

74 "Liberation by Golpe. Restrospective Thoughts on the Demise of Authoritarian Rule in Portugal." *Armed Forces and Society*, Vol. 2, No. 1 (November 1975), p. 12.

75 Luckham, "Militarism: Force, Class and International Conflict," p. 239.

76 Helper, *op.cit.*, p. 16.

77 Halliday, *op.cit.*, p. 98.

78 *Op.cit.*, p. 317.

CHAPTER 6

1 *The Unchangeable War* (Santa Monica, Calif.: Rand Corporation RM–6278–2–ARPA, November 1970).
2 *Ibid.*, p. 2.
3 *Ibid.*, p. 6.
4 Seymour J. Deitchman, *New Technology and Military Power: General Purpose Military Forces for the 1980s and Beyond* (Boulder, Colo.: Westview Press, 1979), p. 7.
5 Cecil I. Hudson and Peter H. Haas, "New Technologies: The Prospects," in Johan J. Holst and Uwe Nerlich, eds., *Beyond Nuclear Deterrence: New Aims, New Arms* (New York: Russak and Company, 1977), p. 133.
6 *Boston Globe*, January 5–6, 1980.
7 Michael MccGwire, "Changing Naval Operations and Military Intervention," in Ellen P. Stern, ed., *The Limits of Military Intervention* (Beverly Hills/London: Sage Publications, 1977), p. 159.
8 Ori Even-Tov, "The NATO Conventional Defense Back to Reality," *Orbis* (Spring 1979).
9 James Digby, "Precision Weapons: Lowering the Risks with Aimed Shots and Aimed Targets," in Holst and Nerlich, eds., *op.cit.*, p. 173.
10 "The Alliance and Europe, Part IV: Military Doctrine and Technology," *Adelphi Papers* No. 109, London, IISS (Winter 1974–75).
11 Digby, *op.cit.*, p. 162.
12 See, for example, Ori Even-Tov, *op.cit.*; Richard Burt, "New Weapons Technologies: Debate and Direction," *Adelphi Papers* No. 126, IISS (Summer 1976); Daniel Gourier and Gordon McCormick, "Debate on Precision Guided Munitions," *Survival* (January/February 1980).
13 See Samuel J. Hall, "Weapon Choices and Advanced Technology: The RPV." *Cornell University Peace Studies Program*, Occasional Paper No. 10 (September 1978).
14 Graham T. Allison and Frederic A. Morris, "Precision Guidance for NATO: Justification and Constraints," in Holst and Nerlich, eds., *op.cit.*, p. 212.
15 See *Washington Star*, June 29, 1980.
16 *International Herald Tribune*, December 13, 1979.
17 *Chicago Sun Times*, May 18, 1980.

18 Jack N. Merritt and Pierre M. Sprey, "Negative Marginal Returns in Weapons Acquisition," in Richard G. Head and Ervin J. Rokke, ed., *American Defense Policy*, 3rd ed. (Baltimore and London: Johns Hopkins University Press, 1973), p. 489.
19 See Emma Rothschild, "Boom and Bust," *The New York Review of Books* (April 3, 1980).
20 See Bert H. Cooper, *Fighter Aircraft Engines: Air Force/Navy Development PROGRAMS*, Congressional Research Service, Report No. 80-46F, Washington, D.C., March 10, 1980.
21 See Dan Smith, *Defence of the Realm in the 1980s* (London: Croom Helm, 1980), p. 159.
22 William M. Carley, "Jinxed Jet?" *The Wall Street Journal*, February 20, 1978.
23 *Ibid.*
24 Reproduced in *Defense Attaché*, May/June 1979, p. 46.
25 *Guardian*, March 1, 1980.
26 *Defense Attaché, op.cit.*, p. 46.
27 *Ibid.*
28 "The XM-1 Tank's No-Win Future," *Business Week* (May 4, 1979), p. 113.
29 Cooper, *op.cit.*
30 See Chapter 3.
31 Robert Perry, "American Styles of Military R&D," in Franklin A. Long and Judith Reppy, *The Genesis of New Weapons Decision Making for Military R&D* (New York: Pergamon Press, 1980), p. 89.
32 John R. Pickett, "Aircraft and Military Intervention," in Stern, *op.cit.*, p. 147.
33 U.S. Congress, House of Representatives, Committee on Appropriations, Subcommittee on Department of Defense, Hearings, *Department of Defense Appropriations for 1981—Part 4: Military Readiness*, 96th Cong., 2nd Sess., Washington, D.C., 1980, p. 325.
34 Helper, *op.cit.*
35 *International Herald Tribune*, December 13, 1979.
36 Interview on *Piccadilly Radio*, August 1979.
37 See Richard Burt, *op.cit.*
38 International Institute of Strategic Studies, *Strategic Survey 1979* (London: 1980), p. 14.
39 Department of Defense, *Annual Report*, Fiscal Year 1980, Washington, D.C., January 25, 1979, p. 265.

40 U.S. General Accounting Office, Report to the Congress of the United States by the Comptroller General, *Impediments to Reducing the Costs of Weapon Systems*, PSAD–80–6, Washington, D.C., November 8, 1979.

41 Merritt and Sprey, *op.cit.*

42 Arthur Alexander, "XM–1," in the Murphy Commission, *op.cit.*, p. 206.

43 Desmond Ball, "The MX Basing Decision," *Survival* (March/April, 1980), pp. 59–60.

44 *Ibid.*, p. 60.

45 *Ibid.*

46 "Hiding MX," *The Economist*, May 31, 1980, p. 114.

47 "MX Basing Decisions Clear Way for Design Advances," *Aviation Week and Space Technology* (June 16, 1980).

48 Herbert Scoville, Jr., "America's Greatest Construction: Can it Work?" *The New York Review of Books* (March 20, 1980).

49 Ulrich Albrecht, *et al.*, "Das Ender des MRCA?", Studiengruppe Militärpolitik, *Ein Anti-Weisbuch: Materialen für eine Alternative Militärpolitik* (Hamburg: Rowohlt, 1974), p. 83.

50 Bill Gunston, "Tornado—The One Plane Airforce," in E. L. Cornwell, ed., *Aircraft Manual 1978* (London: Ian and Allan, Ltd., 1977), pp. 28–29.

51 See Chapter 2.

52 Evidence before the U.K. House of Commons Select Committee on Expenditure, Session 1976–7, HC–236v, Q505, London, 1977.

53 See William Walker, "The Multi Role Combat Aircraft," *Research Policy*, Vol. 2, No. 4 (1974).

54 See "Europe's New Fighter Projects: Is Collaboration Possible?", *Flight International* (April 29, 1978).

55 Office of the Assistant Secretary of Defense (Comptroller), *National Defense Budget Estimates for FY 1979*, Washington, D.C., 1978.

56 U.S. Department of Commerce, Bureau of Census, *Statistical Abstract of the United States, 1977*, Washington, D.C., 1978.

57 Jacques S. Gansler, *The Defense Industry* (Cambridge, Mass.: MIT Press, 1980).

58 See "Defense Production Gap. Why the U.S. Can't Rearm Fast," *Business Week* (February 4, 1980).

59 U.S. Department of Defense and Office of Management and Budget, *Aircraft Industry Capacity Study*, Washington, D.C., January 1977.

60 Gansler, *op.cit.*

61 Aerospace Industries Association of America, Inc., *Aerospace Facts and Figures 1980/81*, Washington, D.C., 1980, and *Aerospace Facts and Figures*, 1966, Washington, D.C., 1966.

62 Gansler, *op.cit.*, p. 62.

63 Dr. Aden Meinel, Professor of Optical Science, University of Arizona, quoted in Alan Bernstein, "Community Solar Development," *Ploughshare Press* (Fall, 1978), p. 8.

64 Emma Rothschild, "Transpo," *The New York Review of Books* (June 22, 1972).

65 See Mary Kaldor, "Economic Aspects of Arms Supply Policies to the Middle East," in Milton Leitenberg and Gabriel Scheffer, eds., *Great Power Intervention in the Middle East* (New York: Pergamon Press, 1979).

66 U.S. Congressional Budget Office, *Foreign Military Sales and U.S. Weapons Costs*, Staff Working Paper, Washington, D.C., May 5, 1976; U.S. Congressional Budget Office, *Budgetary Cost Savings to the Department of Defense Resulting from Foreign Military Sales*, Staff Working Paper, Washington, D.C., May 14, 1976.

67 U.S. Congress, House of Representatives, Committee on International Relations, Hearings, *International Security Assistance Act of 1976*, 94th Congress, November 11, 1975, p. 172.

68 U.S. Department of the Treasury, "Study of Economic Effects of Restraint in Arms Transfers," Annex 2, in U.S. Congress, Senate Committee on Foreign Relations, *Arms Transfer Policy*, 95th Cong., 1st Sess., Washington, D.C., July 1977, p. 50.

69 See SIPRI, *The Arms Trade with the Third World* (1971).

70 See Stern, *op.cit.*

71 See SIPRI, *The Arms Trade with the Third World* (1971), Chapter 5. The fall in exports was probably due to the entry of the Soviet Union and the United States into the arms market, providing free or subsidized military equipment.

72 *Financial Times*, February 5 and 8, 1979; *Aviation Week and Space Technology*, February 12, 1979.

73 See *Aviation Week and Space Technology*, January 14, 1980.

74 See Robert W. Dean, "The Future of Collaborative Weapons Acquisition," *Survival* (July/August 1979).

75 Dewey F. Bartlett, "Standardizing Military Excellence: The Key to NATO's Survival," *AEI Defense Review*, No. 6 (December 1977).

76 Dan Smith, *op.cit.*, p. 191.

77 Sir Clifford Cornford, "European Equipment Cooperation," *RUSI Journal*, Royal United Services Institute for Defense Studies, Vol. 124 (March, 1979), p. 47.

78 Deitchman, *op.cit.*

79 U.S. General Accounting Office, Report to the Congress of the United States by the Comptroller General, quoted in *The Multinational F–16 Aircraft Program: Its Progress and Concerns*, PSAD–79–63, Washington, D.C., June 25, 1979.

80 Quoted in *Flight International* (November 12, 1970).

81 See Mary Kaldor, *European Defence Industries—National and International Implications* (Brighton, ISIO Monograph, University of Sussex), 1972.

82 See Deitchman, *op.cit.*, p. 202.

83 James H. Polk, "Military Standardization within NATO. How Far Should We Go?", *AEI Defense Review*, No. 6 (December 1977), p. 24.

84 Quoted in Murphy Commission, *op.cit.*, p. 115.

85 U.S. General Accounting Office, *Impediments to Reducing the Cost of Weapon Systems*, p. 3.

86 New York: Hill and Wang, 1978, p. 7.

87 *Ibid.*, p. 9.

88 *Ibid.*, p. 45.

89 *Ibid.*, p. 171.

90 *Ibid.*, p. 71.

91 *Ibid.*, p. 81.

92 Jenkins, The Unchangeable War, *op.cit.*, p. 1.

93 U.S. Army War College, *Study on Professionalism*, Carlisle Barracks, Pa.: USAWC (June 30, 1970), pp. 28–29.

94 U.S. Congress, House of Representatives, Committee on Appropriations, Subcommittee on Department of Defense, Hearings, *Defense Appropriations for FY 1981—Part 5, Manpower and Training Programs*, 96th Cong., 2nd Sess., Washington, D.C., 1980.

95 Quoted in Sam Nunn, "National Security with the All-Volunteer Force: AVF—A Verified Fact of a Visible Fiction," *AEI Defense Review*, No. 5 (October 1977).

96 Strom Thurmond, "Military Unions: No," *AEI Defense Review*, No. 1 (February 1977).

97 Dan Smith, *op.cit.*, p. 147.

98   See Sam C. Sarkesian, "Professional Problems and Adaptations,"
      in Stern, *op.cit.*
99   Thurmond, *op.cit.*
100   Charles W. Brown and Charles C. Moskos, Jr., "The Volunteer
      Soldier—Will He Fight?", *Military Review* (June 1976).
101   *Swords into Plowshares,* Statement to the Senate Committee on
      Labor and Public Welfare, December 1, 1969.
102   *Ibid.*
103   Peter Lord and Dan Stets, "EB Readies Big Bill for Trident
      Overrun," *Providence Journal,* December 7, 1980.
104   Quoted in *Ploughshare Press* (Spring 1976).
105   Quoted in *Ploughshare Press* (Summer 1978).
106   Marion Anderson, *The Impact of Military Spending on the Ma-
      chinists Union* (Washington, D.C., IAM, January 1979).
107   William W. Winpisinger, Speech to the Coalition for a New
      Foreign and Military Policy, April 6, 1978.
108   See Lucas Aerospace Combine Committee, *Corporate Plan* 1976;
      Vickers National Combine Committee of Shop Stewards, *Build-
      ing a Chieftain Tank and the Alternative Use of Resources* and
      *The ASW Cruiser—Alternative Work for Naval Shipbuilding
      Workers,* Newcastle-upon-Tyne, 1977.
109   The Report of the Labour Party Study Group, (London: Quartet
      Books, 1977); see also Mary Kaldor, Dan Smith, and Steve
      Vines, eds., *Democratic Socialism and the Cost of Defence* (Lon-
      don: Croom Helm, 1979). (This reprints *Sense About Defence*
      as well as the Lucas Aerospace and Vickers Plans.)
110   Press release, "Initiatives by FLM—Federazione Lavoratori
      Metal Meccanici," Rome, March 1979.
111   *Ibid.*
112   *Metal Workers and the Armament Industry: An Enquiry of the
      Impact of Armament Production on Employment.* (Vienna:
      IMW Central Committee, October 18–19, 1979).
113   *Ibid.,* p. 16.
114   Herman Rebham, General Secretary of IMW, Speech to the UN
      Group of Experts on the Relationship between Disarmament and
      Development, September 16, 1980.

CONCLUSION

1   U.S. Congress, House of Representatives, Committee on Govern-
     ment Operations, *Inaccuracy of Department of Defense Weapons*

Acquisition Cost Estimates, Ninth Report, 96th Cong., 1st Sess., Washington, D.C., November 16, 1979, p. 22, emphasis author's.

2 See, for example, the reports by Philip Jacobson in the London *Sunday Times.*

3 Lawrence Minard, "Guns Instead of TV Sets?" *Forbes* (March 20, 1978).

4 "In Self-Defence of Jobs," *Economist* (April 22, 1978).

5 See Boston Study Group, *The Price of Defense* (New York: Times Books, 1979); Labour Party Study Group, *Sense About Defence* (London: Quartet Books, 1977).

6 This is explored at greater length in Mary Kaldor, "Disarmament: The Armament Process in Reverse," in Thompson and Smith, *op.cit.*

Bibliography

Historical Studies

BEAN, David. *Armstrong's Men: The Story of the Shop Stewards Movement in the Tyneside Works.* Newcastle-upon-Tyne: Vickers Ltd., North East Works, 1967.

Benwell Community Project, Final Report Series No. 6. *The Making of a Ruling Class: Two Centuries of Capitalist Development on Tyneside.* Newcastle-upon-Tyne: 1978.

BERGHAHN, V. R. *Germany and the Approach of War in 1914.* London: Macmillan, 1973.

BEST, Geoffrey, and Wheatcroft, Andrew, eds. *War, Economy and the Military Mind.* London: Croom Helm, Rownan and Littlefield, 1976.

BRODIE, Bernard. "Technical Change, Strategic Doctrine, and Political Outcomes," in Klaus Knorr, ed., *Historical Dimensions of National Security Problems.* Kansas: University of Kansas Press, 1976.

CIPOLLA, C. M. *Guns and Sails in the Early Phase of European Expansion, 1400–1700.* London: Collins, 1965.

COOLING, Benjamin Franklin, ed. *War, Business and American Society: Historical Perspectives on the Military-Industrial Complex.* New York: Kennikat Press, 1977.

DOUGAN, David. *The History of North East Shipbuilding.* London: George Allen and Unwin, 1968.

——. *The History of Lord Armstrong: The Great Gunmaker.* Newcastle-upon-Tyne: Frank Graham, 1970.

ELLIS, John. *The Social History of the Machine Gun.* New York: Pantheon Books, 1973.

ENGELS, Friedrich. "The Force Theory," in *Anti-Duhring* (first published, 1894). London: Lawrence and Wishart, 1975.

FASSET, F. G. Jr., ed. *The Shipbuilding Business in the United States.* Vol. 1. New York: Society of Naval Architects and Marine Engineers, 1948.

GOODY, Jack. *Technology Tradition and the State in Africa*. International African Institute. Oxford: Oxford University Press, 1971.

HACKER, Barton C. "The Weapons of the West: Military Technology and Modernization in 19th Century China and Japan." *Technology and Culture*, 18 (1) (January 1977).

HARRIE, Christopher. "Technological Change and Military Power in Historical Perspective," in "New Conventional Weapons and East-West Security, Part I," *Adelphi Papers No. 144*, IISS, London (Spring 1978).

HOBSBAWM, E. *Industry and Empire*. London: Weidenfeld and Nicholson, 1968.

KOSTINEN, Paul A. C. *The Military-Industrial Complex: A Historical Perspective*. New York: Praeger, 1980.

LANDES, David S. *The Unbound Prometheus: Technological Change and Industrial Development in Western Europe from 1750 to the Present*. Cambridge: Cambridge University Press, 1969.

LIEBKNECHT, Karl. *Militarism and Anti-Militarism* (first published, Berlin, 1906). Cambridge: Rivers Press, 1973.

MORISON, Elting. *From Know-How to Nowhere: The Development of American Technology*. New York: Basic Books, 1974.

MOSS, Michael S., and Hume, John R. *Workshop of the British Empire: Engineering and Shipbuilding in the West of Scotland*. London: Heineman, 1977.

National Planning Association. *National Policy for Aviation*, A Special Committee Report, Planning Pamphlets, Nos 51/2. Washington, D.C. (1946).

NEF, John. *War and Human Progress*. London: Routledge, 1950.

NOEL-BAKER, Philip. *The Private Manufacture of Arms*. London: Victor Gollancz, 1936.

ROSENBERG, Nathan. "Technical Change in the Machine Tool Industry, 1840–1910," *Perspectives in Technology*. Cambridge: Cambridge University Press, 1977.

SCOTT, J. D. *Vickers: A History*. London: Weidenfeld and Nicholson, 1961.

TREBILCOCK, Clive. "Spin-off in British Economic History: Armaments and Industry 1760–1914." *Economic History Review*, XXII (December 1969).

——. *The Vickers Brothers Armaments and Enterprise 1854–1914*. London: Europa Publications, 1977.

WAGTS, Alfred. *A History of Militarism: Civil and Military*. Rev. ed. New York: Free Press, 1959.

WINTER, J. M., ed. *War and Economic Development*. Cambridge: Cambridge University Press, 1975.

The Soviet Weapons Acquisition Process

AGURSKY, Michael, and Adomeit Hannes. "The Soviet Military Industrial Complex," in *Survey: A Journal of East and West Studies*, Vol. 24, No. 2, 107 (Spring 1979).

ALBRECHT, Ulrich. *The Soviet Armaments Base—the Limits of Expansion*. Paper presented to the Berlin Conference on Alarmism, Berghof Institut für Friedens Und Konflikt Forschung, Berlin, October 1979.

ALEXANDER, Arthur. *Armor Development in the Soviet Union and the United States: A Report Prepared for the Director of Net Assessment. Office of the Secretary of Defense*. Santa Monica, Calif.: Rand R–1880–NA, September 1976.

——. "Decision-Making in Soviet Weapons Procurement." London: *Adelphi Papers No. 147 and 148*, IISS (Winter 1978/79).

ALEXANDER, Arthur J. *The Process of Soviet Weapons Design*. Santa Monica, Calif.: Rand Corporation P–6137, March 1978.

——. *R&D in Soviet Aviation*. Santa Monica, Calif.: Rand Corporation R–589–PR, November 1970.

ARNETT, Robert L. "Soviet Military Doctrine—Views on Nuclear War," *Arms Control Today* (October 1978).

ASPATURIAN, V. "Soviet Global Power and the Correlation of Forces," *Problems of Communism*, Vol. XXIX (May/June 1980).

BLECHMAN, Barry. *The Changing Soviet Navy*. Washington, D.C.: Brookings Institution, 1973.

CAMPBELL, Robin. "Management Spillovers from Soviet Space and Military Programmes," *Soviet Studies*, XXIII 4 (April 1972).

CHECINSKI, Michael. "The Cost of Armament Production and the Profitability of Armament Exports in Comecon Countries," Jerusalem: Soviet and East European Research Centre, Research Paper No 10, Hebrew University of Jerusalem, November 1974.

COCKS, Paul. "Rethinking the Organizational Weapon: The Soviet System in a Systems Age," *World Politics*, Vol. XXXII, No. 2 (1980).

COOPER, Julian. "Defence Production and the Soviet Economy, 1929–41," Birmingham SIPS No. 3: *CREES Discussion Paper*, Soviet Industrialisation Project Series, 1976.

HIGHAM, Robin, and Kipp, Jacob W., ed. *Soviet Aviation and Air Power: An Historical View.* London: Brasseys, 1978.

HOLLOWAY, David. "Military Technology," in Amann R., Cooper, J. M., and Davies, R. W., eds. *The Technological Level of Soviet Industry.* London: Yale University Press, 1977.

JAHN, Egbert, ed. *Soviet Foreign Policy: Its Social and Economic Conditions.* London: Allison and Busby, 1978.

——. "The Role of the Armaments Complex in Soviet Society," *Journal of Peace Research*, No. 4 (1974).

JONES, Christopher D. "Soviet Military Doctrine. The Political Dimension," *Arms Control Today* (October 1978).

Khrushchev Remembers. London: Andre Deutsch, 1971.

LANGE, Oscar. *Essays in Capitalism and Socialism.* Oxford: Oxford University Press, 1970.

MADDOCK, R. T. "Some Economic Constraints on Defence Spending in the Soviet Union," *Royal United Services Institute Journal*, Vol. 124, No. 3 (September 1979).

MCCGWIRE, Michael. "The Rationale for the Development of Soviet Seapower," *United States Naval Institute Proceedings*, Vol. 1061/5/927 (May 1980).

——. *Soviet Naval Developments: Capability and Context.* New York: Praeger, 1973.

——, Booth, Ken, and McDonnell, John, eds. *Soviet Naval Policy: Objectives and Constraints.* New York: Praeger, 1975.

——, and McDonnell, John. *Soviet Naval Influence: Domestic and Foreign Dimensions.* New York: Praeger, 1977.

NOVE, Alec. *The Soviet Economic System.* London: George Allen and Unwin, 1977.

PERRY, Robert. *Comparisons of Soviet and U.S. Technology.* Santa Monica, Calif.: Rand Corporation R–827PR, June 1973.

SMITH, R. P. "The Production of Security," unpublished. Birkbeck College, 1978.

WOLFE, Thomas W. *Soviet Naval Interaction with the United States and Its Influence on Soviet Naval Development.* Santa Monica, Calif.: Rand Corporation P–4913, October 1972.

WARNER, Edward L. *The Military in Contemporary Soviet Politics: An Institutional Analysis.* New York: Praeger, 1977.

YAKOVLEV, A. S. *The Aim of a Lifetime.* Translated by V. Vezey. Moscow: Progress Publishers, 1972.

Arms Trade, Military Assistance, Militarism, and the Third World

AHMAD, K. V. *Break-Up of Pakistan*. London: Social Sciences, 1972.

ALBRECHT, Ulrich. *Der Handel mit Waffen*. Munich: Carl Hanser Verlag, 1971.

——, and Sommer, Bergit A. *Deutsche Waffen für die Dritte Welt*. Hamburg: Rowohlt, 1972.

——, *et al.* "Armaments and Underdevelopment," *Bulletin of Peace Proposals*, Vol. 5 (1974).

——, *et al. Rüstung und Unterentwicklung*. Hamburg: Rowohlt, 1976.

BARRACLOUGH, G. "The Struggle for the Third World," *New York Review of Books* (November 9, 1978).

BENOIT, Emile. *Defense and Economic Growth in Developing Countries*. Lexington, Mass.: Lexington Books, 1973.

BLECHMAN, Barry M., and Kaplan, Stephen S. *Force without War: U.S. Armed Forces as a Political Instrument*. Washington, D.C.: Brookings Institution, 1978.

BLOOMFIELD, L. P., and Leiss, A. C. *The Control of Local Conflict*, ACDA/WEC–98, Vol. 3. Cambridge, Mass.: Center for International Studies, MIT Press, 1967.

BRZOSKA, Michael, and Wulf, Herbert. "*Rejoinder to Benoit's 'Growth and Defense in Developing Countries'—Misleading Results and Questionable Methods*," Unpublished Study Group on Armaments and Underdevelopment. Hamburg: Institute for Peace Research and Security Policy, 1978.

CAHN, Anne Hessing, *et al. Controlling Future Arms Trade*. The 1980s Project/Council on Foreign Relations. New York: McGraw-Hill, 1977.

CANNIZZO, Cindy, ed. *The Gun Merchants: Politics and Policies of the Major Arms Suppliers*. Oxford and New York: Pergamon Press, 1980.

CHICHILNISKY, G., and Mello, M. de. *The Role of Armament Flows in the International Market and in Development Strategies in a North–South Context*. New York: Columbia University and University of Essex, June 1980.

DAWAN, Sunil K., and De, Nitish R. "Arms and Aid: An Exercise in the Economy versus Development," *Human Futures* (Winter 1978).

DAWISHA, Adeed. "Saudi Arabia's Search for Security," *Adelphi Papers* No. 158, IISS, London (Winter 1979–80).

EINAUDI, Luigi R., and Stepan, Alfred C. III. *Latin American Institu-*

tional Development: Changing Military Perspectives in Peru and Brazil. Santa Monica, Calif.: Rand Corporation R–586–DOS, April 1971.

EINAUDI, Luigi, *et al. Arms Transfers to Latin America: Toward a Policy of Mutual Respect.* Santa Monica, Calif.: Rand Corporation R–1173–DOS, June 1973.

FARLEY, Philip J., Kaplan, Stephen S., and Lewis, William H. *Arms across the Sea.* Washington: Brookings Institution, 1978.

FIDEL, Kenneth, ed. *Militarism in Developing Countries.* Brunswick, N.J.: Transaction Books, 1975.

FIELDS, Rona M. *The Portuguese Revolution and the Armed Forces Movement.* New York: Praeger, 1976.

FIRST, Ruth. *The Barrel of a Gun: Political Power in Africa and the Coup d'Etat.* London: Penguin, 1970.

FISH, H. M. "Foreign Military Sales," *Commander Digest*, No. 17 (May 29, 1975).

FRANK, L. A. *The Arms Trade.* New York: Praeger, 1968.

GELB, Leslie. "Arms Sales," *Foreign Policy*, No. 25 (Winter 1976–77).

HALLIDAY, Fred. *Iran, Dictatorship and Development*, 2nd ed. London: Penguin, 1979.

HARKAVY, R. E. *The Arms Trade.* Cambridge, Mass.: Ballinger, 1973.

HOROWITZ, Irving Louis, and Trimberger, Ellen Kay. "State Power and Military Nationalism in Latin America," *Comparative Politics*, Vol. 8, No. 2 (January 1976).

HOVEY, H. *United States Military Assistance.* New York: Praeger, 1965.

HUSBANDS, J. L. *The Long Long Pipeline: Arms Sales and Technological Dependence.* Unpublished. Washington, D.C.: Center for Defense Information, 1978.

Institute of International Education. *Military Assistance Training Programs.* New York, 1964.

JANOWITZ, Morris, and van Doorn, Jacques, eds. *On Military Intervention.* Rotterdam: Rotterdam University Press, 1971.

JOHNSON, J., ed. *The Role of the Military in Underdeveloped Countries.* Rand Corporation. Princeton: Princeton University Press, 1962.

JOLLY, Richard, ed. *Disarmament and World Development.* Oxford: Pergamon Press, 1978.

JOSHUA, W., and Gilbert, S. *Arms for the Third World: Soviet Military Aid Diplomacy.* Baltimore: Johns Hopkins University Press, 1969.

KALDOR, Mary, and Eide, A., eds. *The World Military Order: The Im-*

pact of Military Technology on the Third World. London: Macmillan, 1979.

———. "The Military in Development," *World Development* (June 1976).

KLARE, Michael T. *Supplying Repression: U.S. Support for Authoritarian Regimes Abroad.* Washington, D.C.: Institute for Policy Studies, 1977.

KODZIC, P. *Military Effect and Aims of Developing Countries: A Select Annotated Bibliography.* Ljubljana, Yugoslavia: Co-operation with Developing Countries Research Center, 1971.

LEFEVER, Ernest W. "The Military Assistance Training Program," *Annals of the American Political and Social Sciences*, No. 424 (1976).

LEISS, A. C., *et al. Arms Transfers to Less Developed Countries.* Cambridge, Mass.: Center for International Studies, MIT Press, 1970.

LEITENBERG, Milton, and Schaffer, Gabriel, eds. *Great Power Intervention in the Middle East.* Oxford: Pergamon Press, 1979.

LÉVI-STRAUSS, Claude. *Race and History.* Paris: UNESCO, 1968.

LOCK, Peter, and Wulf, Herbert. *Register of Arms Production in Developing Countries.* Hamburg: Study Group on Armament and Underdevelopment, March 1977.

———. "New Trends and Actors in the Arms Transfer Process to Peripheral Countries: A Preliminary Assessment of Peace Research, Some Hypotheses and Research Proposals," *Instant Research on Peace and Violence*, Vol. V, Tampere, Finland: 1975.

LUCKHAM, Robin. *The Nigerian Military: A Case Study in Authority and Revolt 1960–67.* African Studies Series 4. Cambridge: Cambridge University Press, 1971.

McKINLAY, R. D., and Cohan, A. S. "A Comparative Analysis of the Political and Economic Performance of Military and Civilian Regimes. A Cross-national Aggregate Study," *Comparative Politics* (October 1975).

MALEK, Anouar Abdel. *Egypt Military Society, the Army Regime, the Left and Social Change under Nasser.* New York: Vintage Books, 1968.

NEWMAN, Stephanie G., and Harkavy, Robert E. *Arms Transfers in the Modern World.* New York: Praeger, 1979.

NORDLINGER, Eric A. "Soldiers in Mufti: The Impact of Military Rule upon the Economic and Social Change in the non-Western States," *American Political Science Review*, Vol. LXIV, No. 4 (December 1970).

PAUKER, Guy J., et al. In Search of Self-Reliant U.S. Security Assistance to the Third World under the Nixon Doctrine. Santa Monica, Calif.: Rand Corporation R–1092–ARPA, June 1973.

PEARTON, M., and Stanley, J. The International Trade in Arms. London: Chatto and Windus, 1972.

RAANAN, U. The U.S.S.R. Arms the Third World. Cambridge, Mass.: MIT Press, 1969.

RODINSON, Maxime. Islam and Capitalism. London: Penguin Books, 1977.

ROSTOW, W. W. The Stages of Economic Growth. Cambridge: Cambridge University Press, 1960.

SAMPSON, Anthony. The Arms Bazaar: The Companies, the Dealers, the Bribes: From Vickers to Lockheed. London: Hodder and Stoughton, 1977.

SAUNDERS, John. "Impact and Consequences of the Military Transfer of Technology to Developing Countries," Australia and New Zealand Journal of Sociology, 12, 3 (October 1976).

SCHMITTER, Phillipe C. "Liberation by Golpe: Retrospective Thoughts on the Demise of Authoritarian Rule in Portugal," Armed Forces and Society, Vol. 2, No. 1 (November 1975).

SINGH, Ajit. "The 'Basic Needs' Approach to Development versus the New International Economic Order: The Significance of Third World Industrialisation," World Development, Vol. 7 (1979).

STEPAN, Alfred. The Military in Politics: Changing Patterns in Brazil. Rand Corporation. Princeton: Princeton University Press, 1971.

STERN, Ellen P., ed. The Limits of Military Intervention. Beverly Hills/London: Sage Publications, 1977.

Stockholm International Peace Research Institute. The Arms Trade with the Third World. Stockholm: Almqvist and Wicksell, 1971.

——. SIPRI Arms Trade Registers: The Arms Trade with the Third World. Stockholm: Almqvist and Wicksell, 1975.

SUTTON, J. L., and Kemp, G. "Arms to Developing Countries, 1945–65." Adelphi Paper No. 28. London: International Institute for Strategic Studies, 1966.

TANNAHILL, R. Neal. "The Performance of Military and Civilian Government in South America, 1948–67," Journal of Political and Military Sociology, Vol. 4, No. 2 (Fall 1976).

THAYER, G. The War Business: The International Trade in Armaments. London: Weidenfeld & Nicholson, 1969.

VARYNYNEN, Raimo. Arms Trade, Military Aid and Arms Production. Basel: Herder Verlag, 1973.

Whynes, David K. *The Economics of Third World Military Expenditure*. London: Macmillan, 1979.

Wolf, Charles Jr. *United States Policy and the Third World*. Boston, Mass.: Little, Brown & Co., 1976.

Wolpin, Miles D. *Military Aid and Counter Revolution in the Third World*. Lexington, Mass.: Lexington Books, 1972.

World Development Report 1979. Washington, D.C.: The World Bank, August 1979.

World Development Report 1980. Washington, D.C.: The World Bank, August 1980.

Weapons Acquisition, the Arms Industry, and the Economy in Western Countries

Aerospace Industries Association of America Inc., *Aerospace and the U.S. Economy: Its Role, Contributions and Critical Problems*. Washington, D.C.: Aerospace Research Center, November 1971.

Aerospace Systems Analysis. *Cost of War Index*. Santa Monica, Calif.: McDonnell Douglas Astronautics Corporation, September 1968.

Albrecht, Ulrich, *et al.* "Das Ende des MRCA?" in Studiengruppe Militärpolitik *Ein Anti-Weissbuch: Materialien für eine Alternative Militärpolitik*. Hamburg: Rowohlt, 1974.

Albrecht, Ulrich, Lock, Peter, and Wulf, Herbert. *Arbeitsplätze durch Rüstung? Warnung vor falschen Hoffnungen*. Hamburg: Rowohlt, 1978.

Alexander, Arthur J., and Nelson, J. R. *Measuring Technological Change: Aircraft Turbine Engines*. Santa Monica, Calif.: Rand Corporation R–1017–ARPA/PR, May 1972.

Anderson, James R. *Bankrupting America: The Military Budget for the Next Five Years*. A Report of Employment Research Associates. Lansing, Mich., 1980.

Anderson, Marian. *The Empty Pork Barrel: Unemployment and the Pentagon Budget*. Mich.: Public Interest Research Group (PIRGIM), April 1975.

——. *The Impact of Military Spending on the Machinists Union*. Washington, D.C.: International Association of Machinists, January 1979.

Angus, Rae. "Collaborative Weapons Acquisition. The MRCA (Tornado) Panavia Project," *Aberdeen Studies in Defence Economics*, No. 12 (October 1979).

——. "The Organisation of Defence Procurement and Production in the United Kingdom," *Aberdeen Studies in Defence Economics, No. 13* (December 1979).

——, and Greenwood, David. "The Organisation of Defence Procurement and Production in the Federal Republic of Germany," *Aberdeen Studies in Defence Economics, No. 15* (Spring 1980).

ANNERSTEDT, Jan. *Maktn Över Forskningen: om Statlig Forsknings-organisation och Forsknings Planering i Dagens Sverige.* Lund: Bo Cavefors Bokförlag, 1972.

ARMACOST, Michael H. *The Politics of Weapons Innovation: The Thor-Jupiter Missile Controversy.* New York: Columbia University Press, 1969.

ART, Robert J. *The TFX Decision: McNamara and the Military.* Boston, Mass.: Little, Brown & Co., 1968.

AUGUSTINE, Norman R. "One Plane, One Tank, One Ship. Trend for the Future," *Defence Management Journal* (April 1975).

BALDWIN, William Lee. *The Structure of the Defense Market.* Durham, N.C.: Duke University Press, 1967.

BALL, Desmond. "The MX Basing Decision," *Survival* (March/April 1980).

BARAN, Paul, and Sweezy, Paul. *Monopoly Capital.* London: Penguin, 1966.

BARNET, Richard J. *The Economy of Death: A Hard Look at the Defense Budget, the Military Industrial Complex, and What You Can Do about Them.* New York: Atheneum, 1970.

BARTLETT, Dewey F. "Standardizing Military Excellence: The Key to NATO's Survival," *AEI Defense Review,* No. 6 (December 1977).

BENOIT, Emile, and Boulding, Kenneth E. *Disarmament and the Economy.* New York: Harper and Row, 1963.

BEYNON, Huw, and Wainwright, Hilary. *The Workers Report on Vickers.* London: Pluto Press, 1979.

BINKIN, Martin, and Record, Jeffrey. *Where Does the Marine Corps Go from Here?* Washington, D.C.: Brookings Institution, 1976.

BOBROW, D. B., ed. *Weapons System Decisions.* London: Praeger, 1969.

BOLTON, Roger E., ed. *Defense and Disarmament: The Economics of Transition,* Englewood Cliffs, N.J.: Prentice Hall, 1966.

Boston Study Group. *The Price of Defense.* New York: Times Books, 1979.

Bristol Aircraft Workers. *A New Approach to Public Ownership.* IWC Pamphlet No. 43. Nottingham, 1974.

COOK, Fred J. *The Warfare State*. New York & London: Macmillan, 1962.

COOPER, Richard V. L., and Roll, Charles Robert Jr. *The Allocation of Military Resources: Implications for Capital-Labor Substitution*. Santa Monica, Calif.: Rand Corporation P–5036–1, May 1974.

DEAN, Robert W. "The Future of Collaborative Weapons Acquisition," *Survival* (July/August 1979).

DEVANNEY, J. W. "The DX Competition," *U.S. Naval Institute Proceedings* (August 1975).

EBERHARD, Hans L. "European and Transatlantic Armaments Cooperation from the German View Point," *National Defense* (April 1980).

EVANS, Harold. *Vickers Against the Odds 1956–77*. London: Hodder and Stoughton, 1978.

FIORELLO, Marco R. *Problems in Avionics Life-Cycle Analysis*. Santa Monica, Calif.: Rand Corporation P–5136, December 1973.

——. *Getting "Real" Data for Life-Cycle Costing*. Santa Monica, Calif.: Rand Corporation P–5345, January 1975.

——. *Estimating Life-Cycle Costs: A Case Study of the A–7D*. Santa Monica, Calif.: Rand Corporation R–1518–PR, February 1975.

FITZGERALD, A. Ernest. *The High Priests of Waste*. New York: W. W. Norton, 1972.

FLINK, James J. *The Car Culture*. Cambridge, Mass.: MIT Press, 1975.

FOX, J. R. *Arming America: How the U.S. Buys Weapons*. Cambridge, Mass.: Harvard University Press, 1974.

FREEDMAN, L. *Arms Production in the United Kingdom: Problems and Prospects*. London: Royal Institute for International Affairs, 1978.

GABRIEL, Richard A., and Savage, Paul L. *Crisis in Command*. New York: Hill and Wang, 1978.

GALBRAITH, J. K. *How to Control the Military*. New York: Doubleday, 1969.

GANSLER, Jacques S. *The Defense Industry*. Cambridge, Mass.: MIT Press, 1980.

——. "Let's Change the Way the Pentagon Does Business," *Harvard Business Review* (May–June 1977).

General Research Corporation, *NATO Standardization and Licensing Policy Exploratory Phase*, Vols. 1–3, OAD–CR–167. Virginia; MclLean, 1976.

GERVASI, Tom. *Arsenal of Democracy: American Weapons Available for Export. What They Cost. What They Do. Who Makes Them. Who Has Them.* New York: Grove Press, 1977.

GOLDING, Anthony. *The Semi-Conductor Industry in Britain and the United States: A Case Study in Innovation, Growth and Diffusion of Technology,* unpublished D.phil. dissertation, University of Sussex.

GREENWOOD, David. "The Employment Consequences of Reduced Defence Spending," *Aberdeen Studies in Defence Economics,* No. 8 (May 1976).

———. "The Organisation of Defence Procurement and Production in France," *Aberdeen Studies in Defence Economics,* No. 14 (February 1980).

———, and Short, John. "Military Installations and Local Economics: A Case Study: The Moray Ait Stations," *Aberdeen Studies in Defence Economics,* No. 4 (December 1973).

HARMAN, Alvin J. *A Methodology For Cost Factor Comparison and Prediction.* Santa Monica, Calif.: Rand Corporation RM6269–ARPA, August 1970.

———. *Acquisition Cost Experience and Predictability.* Santa Monica, Calif.: Rand Corporation P–4505, January 1971.

———. *Analysis of Aircraft Development.* Santa Monica, Calif.: Rand Corporation P–4976, March 1973.

HARTLEY, Keith. "Development Time Scales for British and American Military Aircraft," *Scottish Journal of Political Economy,* Vol. XIX, No. 2 (June 1972).

HITCH, Charles J., and McKEAN, R. N. *The Economics of Defense in the Nuclear Age.* Cambridge, Mass.: Harvard University Press, 1970.

Metal Workers and the Armament Industry: An Inquiry into the Impact of Armament Production on Employment. Vienna: International Metalworkers Federation Central Committee, October 18–19, 1979.

KALDOR, Mary. "Technical Change in the Defence Industry," in Keith Pavitt, ed. *Technical Innovation and British Economic Performance.* London: Macmillan, 1979.

———. *European Defence Industries—National and International Implications.* ISIO Monograph. University of Sussex, 1972.

KALDOR, Mary, Smith, Dan, and Vines, Steve, eds. *Democratic Socialism and the Cost of Defence.* London: Croom Helm, 1979.

KANTER, Herschel. *The Effect of New Naval Procurement Practises on the Shipbuilding Industry.* Center for Naval Analyses. University of Rochester, October 11, 1968.

KAUFMAN, Richard F. *The War Profiteers*. New York: Anchor Books, 1970.

KENNEDY, Gavin. *The Economics of Defence*. London: Faber and Faber, 1975.

KIDRON, Michael. *Western Capitalism Since the War*. London: Penguin, 1970.

KLIEMAN, Herbert S. *Working Paper on the Microcomputer: Technical Innovation and Transfer*. Prepared for DOD ARPA, Battelle Memorial Institute, December 16, 1975.

——. "The Integrated Circuit: A Case Study of Product Innovation in the Electronics Industry," unpublished Ph.D. dissertation. George Washington University, 1966.

KURTH, James. "Why We Buy the Weapons We Do," *Foreign Policy*, No. 11 (1973).

Labour Party Study Group. *Sense About Defence*. London: Quartet Books, 1977.

LAPP, Ralph E. *The Weapons Culture*. New York: W. W. Norton, 1968.

LARGE, Joseph P. *Bias in Initial Cost Estimates: How Low Estimates Can Increase the Cost of Acquiring Weapon Systems*. Santa Monica, Calif.: Rand Corporation R–1467–PA & E, July 1964.

——, Hoffmayor, Karl, and Kontrovich, Frank. *Production Rate and Production Cost*. Santa Monica, Calif.: Rand Corporation R–1609–PA & E, December 1974.

LENS, Sidney. *The Military-Industrial Complex*. London: Stanmore Press, 1971.

LEON, Peter de. *The Laser-Guided Bomb: Case History of a Development*. Santa Monica, Calif.: Rand Corporation R–1312–1–PR, June 1976.

LONG, Franklin A. "Science and the Military," *Peace Studies Program Occasional Papers Number 1*. Ithaca, N.Y.: Cornell University, June 1971.

——, and Reppy, Judith. *The Genesis of New Weapons: Decision Making for R&D*. Oxford: Pergamon Press, 1980.

Lucas Aerospace Combine Committee of Shop Stewards. *Corporate Plan*. April 1976.

LYNN, Norman. "Survival and Growth for Small, High Technology Aerospace Subcontractors." *National Association of Aerospace Subcontractors*. Palos Verdes Peninsula, Calif., July 28, 1972.

MACK-FORLIST, Daniel M., and Newman, Arthur. *The Conversion of Shipbuilding from Military to Civilian Markets*. New York: Praeger, 1970.

MARSHALL, A. W., and Meckling, W. H. "Predictability of the Costs, Time and Success of Development," in *The Rate and Direction of Inventive Activity*. Washington, D.C.: National Bureau of Economic Research, 1962.

MEEKER, T. A. *The Military-Industrial Complex: A Source Guide*. Los Angeles: Center for the Study of Armament and Disarmament, 1973.

MELMAN, Seymour. *The Permanent War Economy: American Capitalism in Decline*. New York: Simon and Schuster, 1974.

——, ed. *The War Economy of the United States: Readings in Military Industry and Economy*. New York: St. Martin's Press, 1971.

——. *The Defense Economy. Conversion of Industries and Occupations to Civilian Needs*. New York: Praeger, 1970.

——. *Pentagon Capitalism: The Political Economy of War*. New York: McGraw-Hill, 1970.

——. *Barriers to Conversion from Military to Civilian Industry in Market, Planned and Developing Countries*. Report to the U.N. Group of Government Experts on the Relationship between Disarmament and Development. New York: April 1980.

MERRITT, Jack N., and Sprey, Pierre M. "Negative Marginal Returns in Weapons Acquisition," in Richard G. Head and Ervin J. Rokke, eds. *American Defense Policy*, 3rd ed. Baltimore: Johns Hopkins University Press, 1973.

MEYERS, William, ed. *Conversion from War to Peace: Social, Economic and Political Problems*. New York: Gordon and Breach, 1972.

MILLER, Glen H. Jr. and Able, Stephen L. "Defense Spending and Economic Activity," *Economic Review* (July-August 1980).

MILLER, Ronald, and Sawers, David. *The Technical Development of Modern Aviation*. London: Routledge, Kegan and Paul, 1968.

"Defense for a Small Planet. An Interview with Philip Morrison," *Technology Review* (November 1979).

NELKIN, Dorothy. *The University and Military Research, Moral Politics at MIT*. Ithaca and London: Science Technology and Society Series, Cornell University Press, 1972.

NEWELL, John R. "The Breakdown in Naval Shipbuilding," *Proceedings of the United States Naval Institute*. January 1978.

NUNN, Sam. "National Security with the All-Volunteer Force. AVF— a Verified Fact of a Visible Fiction," *AEI Defense Review*, No. 5 (October 1977).

OECD. *Patterns of Resources Devoted to Research and Development in the OECD Area, 1963–71*. Paris, November 1974.

PECK, Merton J., and Scherer, W. *The Weapons Acquisition Process.* Cambridge, Mass.: Harvard University Press, 1962.

PERRY, Robert, *et al. System Acquisition Strategies.* Santa Monica, Calif.: Rand Corporation R–733–PR/ARPA, 1971.

——. *European and U.S. Aircraft Development Strategies.* Santa Monica, Calif.: Rand Corporation P–4748, December 1971.

——. *A Prototype Strategy for Aircraft Development.* Santa Monica, Calif.: Rand Corporation RM–5597–1–PR, July 1972.

——. *A Dassault Dossier: Aircraft Acquisition in France.* Santa Monica, Calif.: Rand Corporation R–1148–PR, September 1973.

PHILLIPS, Almarin. *Technology and Market Structure: A Study of the Aircraft Industry.* Lexington, Mass.: Heath Lexington Books, 1971.

POLK, James H. "A Military Standardization within NATO: How Far Should We Go?" *AEI Defense Review,* No. 6 (December 1977).

PORTELLA, John L. "United States Military Research and Development," in Peter Whitten, ed. *Science and Society.* New York: Franklin Watts, 1980.

PROXMIRE, William. *Report from the Wasteland.* New York: Praeger, 1973.

PUTNAM, W. D. *The Evolution of Air Force System Acquisition Management.* Santa Monica, Calif.: Rand Corporation R–868–PR, August 1972.

REED, Arthur. *Britain's Aircraft Industry: What Went Right? What Went Wrong?* London: J. M. Dent & Sons, 1973.

REPPY, Judith V. "The R&D Program of the Department of Defense," *Cornell University Peace Studies Program Occasional Papers No. 6,* March 1976.

ROSEN, S., ed. *Testing the Theory of the Military Industrial Complex.* Lexington, Mass.: Lexington Books, 1973.

ROTHSCHILD, Emma. "Boom and Bust," *The New York Review of Books* (April 3, 1980).

——. *Paradise Lost: The Decline of the Auto-Industrial Age.* New York: Random House, 1972.

RUSSETT, Bruce. *What Price Vigilance? The Burdens of National Defense.* New Haven, Conn.: Yale University Press, 1970.

SAPOLSKY, Harvey M. *The Polaris System Development Bureaucratic and Programmatic Success in Government.* Cambridge, Mass.: Harvard University Press, 1972.

SARKESIAN, S. C., ed. *The Military-Industrial Complex: A Reassessment.* Beverly Hills: Sage Publications, 1971.

SCOVILLE, Herbert Jr. "America's Greatest Construction, Can It Work?" *The New York Review of Books* (March 20, 1980).

SCHERER, Frederic M. *The Weapons Acquisition Process: Economic Incentives.* Cambridge, Mass.: Harvard University Press, 1964.

SCHILLER, Herbert I., and Phillips, Joseph D., eds. *Super State Readings in the Military Industrial Complex.* Chicago: University of Illinois Press, 1972.

SHAPLEY, Deborah. "Addiction to Technology Is One Cause of the Navy's Shipbuilding Crisis," *Science* (May 19, 1978).

SHORT, John, Stone, Timothy, and Greenwood, David. "Military Installations and Local Economies: A Case Study: The Clyde Submarine Base," *Aberdeen Studies in Defence Economics,* No. 5 (August 1974).

SMITH, Dan. *Defence of the Realm in the 1980s.* London: Croom Helm, 1980.

Society of British Aerospace Companies. *A Future Plan for Britain's Aerospace Companies.* London: January 1972.

SOLO, Robert A. "Gearing Military R&D to Economic Growth," *Harvard Business Review,* Vol. XL (November/December 1962).

STEKLER, Herman O. *The Structure and Performance of the Aerospace Industry.* Berkeley, Calif.: University of California Press, 1965.

Stockholm International Peace Research Institute, *Resources Devoted to Military Research and Development,* Stockholm: Almqvist and Wicksell, 1972.

SUAREZ, James M. "Profits and Performance of Aerospace Defense Contractors," *Journal of Economic Issues,* Vol. X, No. 2 (June 1976).

TILTON, John E. *International Diffusion of Technology: The Case of Semi-Conductors.* Washington, D.C.: Brookings Institution, 1971.

TUCKER, Samuel A., ed. *A Modern Design for Defense Decision. A McNamara—Hitch Enthoven Anthology.* Washington, D.C.: Industrial College of the Armed Forces, 1966.

TUOMI, Helen, and Vayryren, Raimo. "Transnational Corporations, Armament and Development: A Study of Transnational Military Production, International Transfer of Military Technology and Their Impact on Development," *Tampere Peace Research Institute Research Report* No. 22. Tampere, Finland: 1980.

UDIS, Bernard, ed. *The Economic Consequences of Reduced Military Spending.* Lexington, Mass.: Lexington Books, 1973.

ULSAMER, Edgar. "A Solid Case for MX," *Air Force* (April 1980).

United Nations, Report of the Secretary General. *Economic and Social Consequences of Disarmament*. New York: 1961.

——. *Economic and Social Consequences of the Arms Race and Military Expenditure*. New York: 1972.

——. *Disarmament and Development Report of the Group of Experts on the Economic and Social Consequences of Disarmament*. New York: 1972.

——. *Economic and Social Consequences of the Armaments Race and Its Extremely Harmful Effects on World Peace and Security*. Report of the Secretary General A/32/88, New York: 1977.

Vickers National Combine Committee of Shop Stewards. *The ASW Cruiser—Alternative Work for Naval Shipbuilding Workers*. Newcastle-upon-Tyne: 1977.

Vickers National Combine Committee of Shop Stewards. *Building a Chieftain Tank and the Alternative Use of Resources*. Newcastle-upon-Tyne: 1977.

WALKER, William. "The Multi-Role Combat Aircraft," *Research Policy*, Vol. 2, No. 4 (1974).

WESTON, J. Fred, ed. *Defense-Space Market Research*. Cambridge, Mass.: MIT Press, 1964.

WHITE, William D. *U.S. Tactical Air Power*. Washington, D.C.: Brookings Institution, 1974.

WIEDENBAUM, Murray L. *The Economics of Peacetime Defense*. New York: Praeger, 1974.

WILLIAMS, Geoffrey, Gregory, Frank, and Simpson, John. *Crisis in Procurement: A Case Study of the TSR–2*. London: Royal United Service Institution, 1969.

WOLF, Charles Jr. *Military-Industrial Simplicities, Complexities and Realities*. Santa Monica, Calif.: Rand Corporation P–4747, December 1971.

YARMOLINSKY, A. *The Military Establishment: Its Impact on American Society*. New York: Harper and Row, 1971.

Related Matters

BROWN, Charles W., and Moskos, Charles C. Jr. "The Volunteer Soldier—Will He Fight?", *Military Review* (June 1976).

BURT, Richard. "New Weapons Technologies: Debate and Direction." *Adelphi Papers No. 126*, IISS (Summer 1976).

CANBY, Steven L. *NATO Military Policy: The Constraints Imposed by an Inappropriate Military Structure*. Santa Monica, Calif.: Rand Corporation P–4783, February 1972.

——. *NATO Military Policy: Obtaining Conventional Comparability with the Warsaw Pact*. Santa Monica, Calif.: Rand Corporation R–1088–ARPA, June 1973.

——. "The Alliance and Europe, Part IV, Military Doctrine and Technology," *Adelphi Papers No. 109*, IISS (1974).

CORTWRIGHT, David. *Soldiers in Revolt: The American Military Today*. New York: Anchor Press, 1975.

DEITCHMAN, Seymour J. *New Technologies and Military Power: General Purpose Forces for the 1980s and Beyond*. Boulder, Colo.: Westview Press, 1979.

DONOVAN, James A. *Militarism U.S.A.* New York: Scribner's, 1970.

DOWNEY, John. *Management in the Armed Forces: An Anatomy of the Military Profession*. London: McGraw-Hill, 1977.

ENTHOVEN, Alain C., and Smith, K. Wayne. *How Much Is Enough? Shaping the Defense Program 1961–69*. New York: Harper Colophon Books, 1972.

EVEN-TOV, Ori. "The NATO Conventional Defense Back to Reality," *Orbis* (Spring 1979).

GOURIER, Daniel, and McCormick, Gordon. "Debate on Precision-Guided Munitions," *Survival* (January/February 1980).

HALL, Samuel J. "Weapons Choices and Advanced Technology, the RPV," *Cornell University Peace Studies Program*, Occasional Paper No. 10. (September 1978).

HOLST, John J., and Nerlich, Uwe, eds. *Beyond Nuclear Deterrence: New Aims, New Arms*. New York: Crane, Russak, 1977.

JANOWITZ, Morris. *The Professional Soldier*. New York: Free Press, 1960.

——, with Little, Roger. *Sociology and the Military Establishment*. New York: Russell Sage Foundation, 1965.

JENKINS, Brian M. *The Unchangeable War*. Santa Monica, Calif.: Rand Corporation RM–6278–2–ARPA, November 1970.

JUST, Ward. *Military Men*. New York: Knopf, 1970.

KOMER, R. W. *Treating NATO's Self-Inflicted Wound*. Santa Monica, Calif.: Rand Corporation P–5092, October 1973.

MARGIOTTA, Franklin D., ed. *The Changing World of the American Military*. Boulder, Colo.: Westview Press, 1978.

PIZER, Vernon. *The U.S. Army*. New York: Praeger, 1967.

TAYLOR, William J. Jr., Arango, Roger J., and Lockwood, Robert S., eds. *Military Unions: U.S. Trends and Issues.* Beverly Hills: Sage Publications, 1977.

THOMPSON, E. P., and Smith, Dan, eds. *Protest and Survive.* London: Penguin, 1980.

THURMOND, Strom. "Military Unions: No," *AEI Defense Review,* No. 1. (February 1977).

YORK, Herbert. *Race to Oblivion.* New York: Simon and Schuster, 1970.

United States Government Publications*

U.S. Army War College. *Study on Professionalism.* Carlisle Barracks, Pennsylvania, June 30, 1970.

Central Intelligence Agency, National Foreign Assessment Center. *Communist Aid to Less Developed Countries of the Free World,* 1977, ER–78–104780, November 1978.

Commission on Government Procurement Report, Vols. 1–4, plus index—Bibliography—Acronyms, December 1972.

Commission on the Organization of the Government for the Conduct of Foreign Policy (Murphy Commission), "Appendix K: Adequacy of Current Organization: Defense and Arms Control," Volume 4, June 1975.

U.S. CONGRESS, CONGRESSIONAL BUDGET OFFICE. *Foreign Military Sales and U.S. Weapons Costs.* Staff Working Paper, May 5, 1976.

——. *Budgetary Cost Savings to the Department of Defense Resulting from Foreign Military Sales.* Staff Working Paper, May 14, 1976.

——. *Planning U.S. General Purpose Forces: Army Procurement Issues.* December 1976.

——. *U.S. Strategic Nuclear Forces: Deterrence Policies and Procurement Issues.* April 1977.

——. *The MX Missile and Multiple Protective Structure Basing: Long-Term Budgetary Implications.* June 1979.

——. *SALT II and the Costs of Modernizing U.S. Strategic Forces.* September 1979.

U.S. CONGRESS, JOINT COMMITTEE ON DEFENSE PRODUCTION. *Defense Production Act, Progress Report—No. 49.* Hearings, 90th Congress, 1st Session, 1967.

* For U.S. government documents, place of publication is Washington, D.C., unless otherwise noted.

———. *Conflict of Interest and the Condor Missile Program*. Report by the Subcommitte on Investigations, 94th Congress, September 1976.

———. *Defense Industrial Base: Industrial Preparedness and Nuclear War Survival*. Hearings, 94th Congress, November 17, 1976.

U.S. CONGRESS, JOINT ECONOMIC COMMITTEE. *Dimensions of Soviet Economic Power*. Hearings (together with study papers), 87th Congress, 1962.

———. *Economic Impact of Vietnam War Spending*. 90th Congress, 1st Session, 1967.

———. *Economics of Military Procurement*. Hearings, Subcommittee on Economy in Government, Parts 1 and 2, 90th and 91st Congress, 1968 and 1969.

———. *Economics of Military Procurement*. Report of the Subcommittee on Economy in Government, 90th Congress, May 1969.

———. *The Dismissal of A. Ernest Fitzgerald by the Department of Defense*. Hearings, Subcommittee on Economy in Government, 91st Congress, 1st Session, 1969.

———. *The Military Budget and National Priorities*. Hearings, Subcommittee on Economy in Government, 91st Congress, 1969.

———. *The Military Budget and National Economic Priorities*. Report of the Subcommittee on Economy in Government, 91st Congress, 1969.

———. *The Acquisition of Weapons Systems*. Hearings, Subcommittee on Economy in Government, Parts 1–2, 91st Congress, 1969.

———. *Economic Performance and Military Burden in the Soviet Union*. A Compendium of Papers Submitted to the Subcommittee on Foreign Economic Policy, 91st Congress, 1970.

———. *Economic Issues in Military Assistance*. Hearings, Subcommittee on Economy in Government, 92nd Congress, 1971.

———. *The Acquisition of Weapons Systems*, Hearings, Subcommittee on Priorities and Economy in Government, Parts 3 & 4, 92nd Congress, 1971 and 1972.

———. *The Acquisition of Weapons Systems*. Hearings, Subcommittee on Priorities and Economy in Government, Part 6, 92nd Congress, 1972 and 1973.

———. *The Acquisition of Weapons Systems*. Hearings, Subcommittee on Priorities and Economy in Government, Part 7, 93rd Congress, 1973.

———. *Soviet Economic Outlook*. Hearings, 93rd Congress, 1973.

———. *Soviet Economic Prospects for the Seventies*. A Compendium of

Papers Submitted to the Joint Economic Committee, 93rd Congress, 1973.

——. *Allocation of Resources in the Soviet Union and China.* Hearings, Subcommittee on Priorities and Economy in Government, 93rd Congress, 1974.

——. *Allocation of Resources in the Soviet Union and China—1975.* Part 1. Hearings, Subcommittee on Economy and Priorities in Government, 94th Congress, 1975.

——. *Defense Procurement in Relationship Between Government and Its Contractors.* Subcommittee on Priorities and Economy in Government, 94th Congress, 1975.

——. *Allocation of Resources in the Soviet Union and China—1976,* Part 2. Hearings, Subcommittee on Priorities and Economy in Government, 94th Congress, 1976.

——. *Economics of Defense Procurement: Shipbuilding Claims.* Subcommittee on Priorities and Economy in Government, 94th and 95th Congress, 1976 and 1977.

——. *Allocation of Resources in Soviet Union and China—1977.* Parts 1, 2, and 3. Subcommittee on Priorities and Economy in Government, 95th Congress, 1977.

——. *Soviet Economic Problems and Prospects.* A Study Prepared for the Subcommittee on Priorities and Economy in Government, 95th Congress, 1977.

——. *Allocation of Resources in the Soviet Union and China—1979.* Hearings, Subcommittee on Priorities and Economy in Government, 96th Congress, 1st Session, June 26 and July 9, 1979.

U.S. CONGRESS, HOUSE OF REPRESENTATIVES. *Historical Statistics of the United States, Colonial Times to 1970.* Bicentennial ed. 93rd Congress, House Document No. 93–78 (Part 2), 1975.

U.S. CONGRESS, HOUSE OF REPRESENTATIVES, COMMITTEE ON APPROPRIATIONS. *Department of Defense Appropriations for 19—,* Hearings, Subcommittee on Department of Defense Annual.

U.S. CONGRESS, HOUSE OF REPRESENTATIVES, COMMITTEE ON ARMED SERVICES. *Hearings on Military Posture . . . to Authorize Appropriations during the Fiscal Year 19—,* Hearings, annual.

U.S. CONGRESS, HOUSE OF REPRESENTATIVES, COMMITTEE ON FOREIGN AFFAIRS. *The Foreign Military Sales Act.* Hearings, 90th Congress, June 26–27, 1968.

——. *Background Material. Foreign Assistance Act, Fiscal Year 1970.* 91st Congress, 1969.

——. *Foreign Assistance Act of 1969.* Hearings, 91st Congress, June–August, 1969.

——. *Report of the Special Study Mission to Latin America on Military Assistance, Training and Developmental Television.* Subcommittee on National Security Policy and Scientific Development, 91st Congress, May 7, 1970.

——. *Military Assistance Training.* 91st Congress, 1970.

——. *Military Assistance Training.* 92nd Congress, 1971.

——. *Foreign Assistance Act of 1971.* 92nd Congress, April–June 1971.

U.S. CONGRESS, HOUSE OF REPRESENTATIVES, COMMITTEE ON GOVERNMENT OPERATIONS. *Government Procurement and Contracting.* Hearings, Subcommittee, Parts 1–6, 91st Congress, 1969.

——. *Inaccuracy of Department of Defense Weapons Acquisition Cost Estimates.* Hearings, Subcommittee, 96th Congress, June 25 and 26, 1979.

——. *Inaccuracy of Department of Defense Weapons Acquisition Cost Estimates.* Ninth Report by the Committee on Government Operations. 96th Congress, House Report No. 96–656, 1979.

U.S. CONGRESS, HOUSE OF REPRESENTATIVES, COMMITTEE OF INTERNATIONAL RELATIONS. *U.S. Defense Contractors. Training of Foreign Military Forces.* Hearings, Subcommittee on International Political and Military Affairs, 94th Congress, March 20, 1975.

——. *The Activities of American Multinational Corporations Abroad.* Hearings, Subcommittee on International Economic Policy, Committee on International Relations, 94th Congress, 1975.

——. *International Security Assistance Act of 1976.* Hearings, 94th Congress, November, December 1975, and January, February, 1976.

——. *International Security Assistance Act of 1976,* House Report No. 94–818, 94th Congress, February 24, 1976.

——. *International Security Assistance and Arms Export Control Act of 1976.* 94th Congress, November, December 1975 and March, April 1976.

——. *NATO Standardization: Political, Economic and Military Issues for Congress.* Report prepared by Foreign Affairs and National Defense Division, Congressional Research Division, Congressional Research Service, Library of Congress, March 29, 1977.

——. *Human Rights Practices in Countries Receiving U.S. Security Assistance.* Hearings, 95th Congress, April 25, 1977.

——. *The Soviet Union and the Third World: A Watershed in Great Power Policy.* Report by Senior Specialists Division, Congressional

Research Service, Library of Congress, 95th Congress, May 8, 1977.

———. *Conventional Arms Transfer Policy, Background Information*, Subcommittee on International Security and Scientific Affairs, 95th Congress, 1978.

———. *Review of the President's Conventional Arms Transfer Policy*. Subcommittee on International Security and Scientific Affairs, 95th Congress, February 1–2, 1978.

———. *United States Arms Transfer and Security Assistance Programs*. Subcommittee on Europe and the Middle East, prepared by the Foreign Affairs and National Defense Division, Congressional Research Service, March 21, 1978.

———. *Foreign Assistance Legislation for Fiscal Year 1979 (Part 2)*. Hearings, Subcommittee on International Security and Scientific Affairs, 95th Congress, March–April 1978.

U.S. CONGRESS, HOUSE OF REPRESENTATIVES, COMMITTEE ON SMALL BUSINESS. *The Position and Problems of Small Business in Government Procurement*. Subcommittee on Government Procurement, 92nd Congress, 1972.

U.S. CONGRESS, SENATE, COMMITTEE ON APPROPRIATIONS. *Department of Defense, Appropriations for Fiscal Year 19—*. Defense Subcommittee, annual.

U.S. CONGRESS, SENATE, COMMITTEE ON ARMED FORCES. *Fiscal Year 19—. Authorizations for Military Procurement*. Hearings, annual.

U.S. CONGRESS, SENATE, COMMITTEE ON FOREIGN RELATIONS. *Mutual Security Act of 1951*. Hearings, 82nd Congress, July and August 1951.

———. *Mutual Security Act of 1959*. Hearings, 86th Congress, June 22, 1959.

———. *Foreign Assistance Act of 19—*. Hearings available for 1965, 1967, 1968, 1969, and 1973.

———. *Arms Sales and Foreign Policy*. Staff Study, 90th Congress, January 25, 1967.

———. *International Security Assistance and Arms Export Control Act of 1976*. Hearings, 94th Congress, 1976.

———. *International Security Assistance*. Subcommittee on Foreign Assistance, 94th Congress, March, April 1976.

———. *Multinational Corporations and United States Foreign Policy*. Hearings, Subcommittee on Multinational Corporations, on Lockheed Aircraft Corporation, Part 14, 94th Congress, February 4 and 6 and May 4, 1976.

——. *Multinational Corporations and United States Foreign Policy.* Hearings, Subcommittee on Multinational Corporations, on Grumman Sale of F–14's to Iran, Part 17, 94th Congress, 1976.

——. *U.S. Military Sales to Iran.* Staff Report, Subcommittee on Foreign Assistance, 94th Congress, July 1976.

——. *Arms Transfer Policy.* Report to Congress, Committee on Foreign Relations, U.S. Senate, 95th Congress, July 1977.

——. *Implications of President Carter's Conventional Arms Transfer Policy.* Report to the Committee on Foreign Relations, by Subcommittee on Foreign Assistance, prepared by the Foreign Affairs and National Defense Division, Congressional Research Service, Library of Congress, December 1977.

U.S. CONGRESS, SENATE, COMMITTEE ON LABOR AND PUBLIC WELFARE. *Swords into Plowshares.* Walter P. Reuther, president of UAW, Statement to the Senate Committee on Labor and Public Welfare, December 1, 1969.

U.S. CONGRESS, SENATE, SPECIAL COMMITTEE TO STUDY PROBLEMS OF AMERICAN SMALL BUSINESS. *Economic Concentration in World War II. Report of the Smaller War Plants Corporation.* 79th Congress, Document No. 266, June 14, 1946.

U.S. DEPARTMENT OF THE ARMY. Henry C. Thompson and Lida Mayo. *The Technical Services. The Ordnance Department: Procurement and Supply. U.S. Army in World War II.* Office of the Chief of Military History, Department of the Army, 1960.

——. Irving Brinton Holley, Jr., *Buying Aircraft Matériel. Procurement for the Army Air Forces. U.S. Army in World War II, Special Studies,* Office of the Chief of Military History, Department of the Army, Vol. 7, 1964.

U.S. DEPARTMENT OF THE AIR FORCE. U.S.A.F. Historical Division. *The Army Air Forces in World War II,* Volume 6, *Men and Planes,* edited by Wesley Frank Craven and James Lea Crate, Chicago: University of Chicago Press, 1955.

U.S. DEPARTMENT OF COMMERCE, BUREAU OF THE CENSUS. *Shipments of Defense Oriented Industries 19——.* Current Industrial Reports Series MA–175, annual.

——. *Statistical Abstract of the United States, 19——.* Annual.

U.S. DEPARTMENT OF COMMERCE, BUREAU OF ECONOMIC ANALYSIS. *Defense Indicators,* Series ES 4, monthly.

U.S. DEPARTMENT OF DEFENSE. *The Economics of Defense Spending: A Look at the Realities.* Office of the Assistant Secretary of Defense (Comptroller), July 1972.

——. *Aircraft Industry Capacity Study*, with Office of Management and Budget, January 1977.

——. *Report of the Acquisition Cycle Task Force, Defense Science Board, Summer 1977 Study*, Office of the Undersecretary of Defense for Research and Engineering, March 15, 1978.

——. *Program Acquisition Costs by Weapons System, Department of Defense Budget for FY 19—.* Annual.

——. *Military Assistance and Sales Facts*. Defense Security Assistance Agency, annual.

——. *Security Assistance Program*. Defense Security Assistance Agency, Congressional Presentation, annual.

——. *100 Companies Receiving the Largest Dollar Volume of Military Prime Contract Awards*. Office of Assistant Secretary of Defense (Comptroller), Directorate for Information, Operations and Reports, PO1, annual.

——. *500 Contractors Receiving the Largest Dollar Volume of Military Prime Contract Awards for Research, Development, Test and Evaluation*. Office of Assistant Secretary of Defense (Comptroller), Directorate for Information, Operations and Reports, PO2, annual.

——. *Military Prime Contract Awards*. Office of Assistant Secretary of Defense (Comptroller), Directorate for Information, Operations and Reports, PO3, semiannual.

——. *Companies Participating in the DoD Subcontracting Programs*. Office of Assistant Secretary of Defense (Comptroller), Directorate for Information, Operations and Reports, SO1, quarterly.

——. *Geographical Distribution of Subcontracting Awards*. Office of Assistant Secretary of Defense (Comptroller), Directorate for Information, Operations and Reports, SO2, annual.

——. *National Defense Budget Estimates for FY 19—.* Office of the Secretary of Defense (Comptroller), annual.

——. *Selected Acquisition Reports*. Office of Assistant Secretary of Defense (Comptroller), quarterly.

U.S. DEPARTMENT OF LABOR, BUREAU OF LABOR STATISTICS. "Wartime, Development of the Aircraft Industry." *United States Bureau of Labor Statistics, Bulletin No. 800*. Reprinted from *Monthly Labor Review* (November 1944).

——. Richard P Oliver, "Employment Effects of Reduced Defense Spending," *Monthly Labor Review* (December 1971).

——. *Projections of the Post-Vietnam Economy, 1975*. Bulletin 1733, 1972.

——. *Foreign Defense Sales and Grants, Fiscal Years 1973–1975*. Prepared for Office of the Assistant Secretary of Defense (International Security Affairs), Defense Security Assistance Agency, and Arms Control and Disarmament Agency, July 1971.

U.S. DEPARTMENT OF STATE, ARMS CONTROL AND DISARMAMENT AGENCY. *A Case Study of the Effects of the Dyna-Soar Contract Cancellation upon Employees of the Boeing Company in Seattle.* 1965.

———. *The Implications of Reduced Defense Demand for the Electronics Industry.* September 1965.

———. *Defense Industry Diversification: An Analysis with 12 Case Studies.* January 1966.

———. *Final Report on Industrial Conversion Potential in the Ship-Building Industry.* Contract No. ACDA/E–66, MRI Project 2833–D, March 18, 1966.

———. *Defense Systems: Resources in the Civil Sector.* Contract ACDA/E–103, July 1967.

———. *The Defense Dependency of the Metal Working and Equipment Industry and Disarmament Implications.* ACDA E–130, May 1969.

———. *The Economic Impact of Reductions in Defense Spending. Summary of Research Prepared for the United States Arms Control and Disarmament Agency.* Washington, D.C., July 1, 1972.

———. *The International Transfer of Conventional Arms.* A Report to the Congress, 93rd Congress, April 12, 1974.

———. *World Military Expenditures and Arms Transfers.* Annual.

U.S. DEPARTMENT OF STATE, AGENCY FOR INTERNATIONAL DEVELOPMENT. *U.S. Overseas Loans and Grants and Assistance from International Organizations, Obligations and Loan Authorizations.* Annual.

U.S. GENERAL ACCOUNTING OFFICE. *Application of "Should Cost" Concepts in Reviews of Contractors' Operations.* B–159896, February 26, 1971.

———. *Defense Industry Profit Study.* B–159896, March 17, 1971.

———. *Acquisition of Major Weapons Systems.* B–163058, July 17, 1972.

———. *Use of Excess Defense Articles and Other Resources to Supplement the Military Assistance Program.* B–163742, March 21, 1973.

———. *Issues Related to U.S. Military Sales and Assistance to Iran.* B–133258, October 21, 1974.

———. *How to Improve the Selected Acquisition Reporting System.* PSAD–75–63, March 27, 1975.

——. *Inefficient Management of F–14 Spare Parts.* PSAD–75–70, May 2, 1975.

——. *Coproduction Programs and Licensing Arrangements in Foreign Countries.* ID–76–23, December 2, 1975.

——. *27 Years Experience with Defense Industrial Funds.* FGMSD–76–51, October 5, 1976.

——. *Foreign Military Sales—a Potential Drain on U.S. Defense Posture.* LCD–77–440, September 2, 1977.

——. *Status of the Trident Submarine and Missile Programs.* PSAD–77–34, March 8, 1977.

——. *Perspectives on Military Sales to Saudi Arabia.* ID–77–19, October 26, 1977.

——. *Profiles of Military Assistance Advisory Groups in 15 Countries.* ID–78–51, September 1978.

——. *The Multinational F–16 Aircraft Program: Its Progress and Concerns.* PSAD–79–63, June 25, 1979.

——. *Impediments to Reducing the Costs of Weapons Systems.* PSAD, November 8, 1979.

——. *The MX Weapon System—a Program with Cost And Schedule Uncertainties.* PSAD–80–29, February 29, 1980.

——. *"SARs"—Defense Department Reports That Should Provide More Information to the Congress.* PSAD–80–37, May 9, 1980.

U.S. LIBRARY OF CONGRESS, CONGRESSIONAL RESEARCH SERVICE. Edward Knight, *Economic Aspects of Reduced Defense Spending 1960–71: A Selected Bibliography.* Arranged chronologically. July 1, 1971.

——. Charles V. Ciccone. *The Economic Impact on the U.S. of U.S. Government and Commercial Military Sales and Assistance Programs.* August 27, 1975.

——. Alva M. Bowen, *Comparison of U.S. and U.S.S.R. Naval Shipbuilding,* VM gen. 76–91F, March 5, 1976.

——. Bert H. Cooper. *The Navy F–14/Phoenix Weapon System: A Background Report on Major Program Developments in 1973–6.* UC 400 U.S.B. 76–180F, September 30, 1976.

——. Alva M. Bowen. *Navy Shipbuilding.* Issue Brief No. 1B 77013, 1977.

——. *United States Arms Transfers and Security Assistance Programs.* Prepared for the Subcommittee on Europe and the Middle East, Committee on International Relations, U.S. House of Representatives, March 21, 1978.

——. Jonathan E. Medalia and A.A. Tinajero. *XM–1 Main Battle*

Tank Program, Issue Brief Number IB 75052, July 1975, updated May 1978.

——. Jonathan E. Medalia and A. A. Tinajero. *Trident Program,* Issue Brief No. 1B 73001, 1978.

——. A. A. Tinajero. *M–X Intercontinental Ballistic Missile Program,* Issue Brief No. 1B 77080, 1978.

——. Bert H. Cooper, *Fighter Aircraft Program: F–14,* Issue Brief No. 1B 76056, May 25, 1978.

——. Bert H. Cooper, *V/S T81 Aircraft Development.* Issue Brief No. 1B 78020, July 5, 1978.

——. Bert Cooper, *Fighter Aircraft Programs (lightweight) F–16 and F–18.* Issue Brief No. 1B 75063, July 7, 1978.

——. Bert H. Cooper. *Fighter Aircraft Engines: Air Force/Navy Engine Development Programs,* Congressional Research Service Report No. 80–46F, March 10, 1980.

OFFICE OF THE PRESIDENT. *Survival in the Air Age.* A Report by the President's Air Policy Commission, January 1, 1948.

——. *Composite Report of the President's Committee to Study the United States Military Assistance Program* (The Draper Report). Vol. 1, 1959.

——. *Report of the Committee on the Economic Impact of Defense and Disarmament.* July 1965.

——. *U.S. Foreign Assistance in the 1970s: A New Approach.* Report from Task Force on International Development, 1970.

——. *Report to the President and the Secretary of Defense on the Department of Defense.* Blue Ribbon Defense Panel, July 1, 1970.

Other Government Publications

BRITISH GOVERNMENT PUBLICATIONS. M. M. Postan. *British War Production.* London: HMSO and Longmans, 1952.

——. *Report of the Committee of Inquiry of Aviation under the Chairmanship of Lord Plowden, 1964–65.* London: HMSO, December 1965.

——. *Shipbuilding Inquiry Committee 1965–66.* (Geddes Report). London: HMSO, March 1966.

——. *Productivity of the National Aircraft Effort.* Report of a Committee Appointed by the Minister of Technology and the President of the Society of British Aerospace Companies under the Chairmanship of Mr. St. John Elstub. London: HMSO, 1969.

——. *Defence Research: Report, Minutes of Evidence, Appendices and Index.* Second Report from the Select Committee on Science and Technology, Session 1968–69, HC Papers 213, London: HMSO, March 1969.

——. *Government Organisation for Defence Procurement and Civil Aerospace.* Cmnd 4641, London, HMSO, 1971.

——. *Report of the Committee on Government Industrial Establishments* (the Mallabar Committee). Cmnd 4713, London: HMSO, 1971.

——. Department of Trade and Industry, *British Shipbuilding 1972*, Report to the Department of Trade and Industry, Booz-Allen and Hamilton, International BU, London: HMSO, 1973.

——. U.K. Ministry of Defence (Defence Sales Organisation), *British Defence Equipment Catalogue*, London: annual.

——. *Statement on the Defence Estimates 19——.* Command Paper No. — London: HMSO, annual.

——. *Defence Accounts 19——.* HC Papers, Session —, London: HMSO, annual.

FEDERAL REPUBLIC OF GERMANY. Press and Information Office of the German Federal Government, *White Paper 19— on the Security of the Federal Republic of Germany and on the State of German Federal Armed Forces.* Bonn, irregular.

Reference Books and Journals

AEI Defense Review. American Enterprise Institute for Public Policy Research, Washington, D.C., bimonthly.

Aerospace Industries Association. *Aerospace.* Washington, D.C., quarterly.

Aerospace Industries Association of America, Inc., *Aerospace Facts and Figures.* Washington, D.C., annual.

Ulrich Albrecht, *et al. A Short Research Guide on Arms and Armed Forces.* London: Croom Helm, 1978.

Armed Forces and Society. Chicago, Ill.: Inter University Seminar on Armed Forces and Society, quarterly.

Annuaire de L'Afrique et du Moyen Orient 19——. Less Armée et La Défense, Paris: Jeune Afrique, annual.

Aviation Week and Space Technology. New York: McGraw-Hill, weekly.

Aviation Advisory Services. *International Air Forces and Military*

Aircraft Directory. Essex, England: Stapleford Airfield, updated monthly.

Aviation Advisory Services. *Milavnews.* Essex, England: Stapleford Airfield, monthly.

Aviation Studies (International) Ltd. *Official Price List,* Sussex House, Parkside, London, periodically updated.

Aviation Studies (International) Ltd. *Military Aircraft and Missile Data Sheets.* Sussex House, Parkside London, periodically updated.

Aviation Studies (International) Ltd. *Armament Data Sheets.* Sussex House, Parkside, London, periodically updated.

Business Week. New York, weekly.

British Defence Equipment Guide. Whitton Press Ltd., Eton, Berkshire, annual.

Center for Defense Information. *Defense Monitor,* Washington, D.C., usually bimonthly.

Defence, Eton, Berks: Whitton Press Ltd., monthly.

Defense Management Journal. Washington, D.C., quarterly.

Defense et Diplomatie, Paris, weekly.

DMS Market Intelligence Report. Seattle, periodically updated.

Electronics Times. London, weekly.

Flight International. London, weekly.

Interavia. Geneva, monthly.

International Defence Review. Geneva: Interavia, monthly.

International Institute of Strategic Studies. *Survival.* London, bimonthly.

——. *The Military Balance.* London, annual.

Jane's Armour and Artillery. London: Jane's Yearbooks, annual

Jane's Infantry Weapons. London: Jane's Yearbooks, annual.

Jane's Fighting Ships. London: Jane's Yearbooks, annual.

Jane's Weapon Systems. London: Jane's Yearbooks, annual.

Jane's All the World's Aircraft. London: Jane's Yearbooks, annual.

National Science Foundation. *National Patterns of R & D Resources, Funds & Manpower in the United States.* Washington, D.C., annual.

RUSI Journal. Royal United Services Institute, London, quarterly.

Sivard, Ruth L. *World Military and Social Expenditures.* Annual.

Stockholm International Peace Research Institute. *World Armaments and Disarmament, SIPRI Yearbook.* London: Taylor and Francis, annual.

United Nations. *U.N. Statistical Yearbook.* New York, annual.

U.S. Naval Institute Proceedings. Annapolis, Md., monthly.

Index